THE **BIG**

NINJA FOODI DIGITAL

AIR FRYER OVEN COOKBOOK

Simpler & Crispier Air Crisp, Air Roast, Air Broil, Bake, Dehydrate,
Toast and More Recipes for Anyone

Yvette Shepard

Table of Contents

Chapter 6 Red Meat Recipes..................91

Chapter 7 Dessert Recipes 110

Conclusion 125

Appendix 1 Measurement Conversion Chart
.. 126

Appendix 2 Air Fryer Cooking Chart 127

Appendix 3 Recipes Index..................... 128

Introduction

Known for several of its advanced features, the Ninja Digital Air Fry Oven is the ultimate Kitchen companion. Unlike conventional oven or Air fryers, the Ninja Foodi Air Fry oven comes with an adjustable space feature, which means that you can place the oven both horizontally and vertically over the kitchen shelf. For cooking, the oven can be placed in its horizontal position. And when not in use, the cleaned oven can be flipped to stand vertically on the shelf. This creates an extra space over the shelf without doing much. Just make sure to flip the oven only when it is completely cooled and clean. This Air Fry oven comes with 8 functions in one. A user can Air fry, Air roast, bake, toast bread, and bagel, dehydrate and broil food just with a press of a button. You can also switch from one mode to another during the cooking if needed. The toast and bagel function give you options to select the darkness of the bread as desired. If you are wondering about how to use all its advanced cooking features, then try all the recipes from this cookbook! Here you will number of flavorsome ideas to put your Air fryer oven to best use.

Ninja Foodi is known for its energy-efficient technology. The device works on 1800 watts per hour, and it preheats quickly to reach the desired temperature. It only takes few seconds to Air Fry and bakes your favorite meal. The device also manages to keep the food warm until it is being attended to. One of the best features of the Ninja Air Fry oven is to also have a perfect toaster. This oven gives two different options to Toast bread and Bagel. The Toast button is pressed to toast the bread, and the Bagel mode is used to toast the bagel. The bars of darkness indicate the intensity of darkness of the toast you desire. In this way, you can enjoy lightly soft brown toasts to dark brown crispy toasts. The Ninja Foodi Air Fryer oven has this extremely user-friendly control panel. It has a different button for its functions and a dial to switch between modes and increase or decrease the Time and Temperature.

If you want to feed your family healthy and delicious food in less time, the Ninja Foodi Digital Air Fry Oven is the perfect kitchen appliance.

BE FOODIE!

What is Ninja Foodi Digital Air Fry Oven?

The Ninja Foodi Digital Air Fry Oven offers eight different cooking modes. This oven has a powerful heating system that runs on 1800 watts and it cooks food in less time. Before using this appliance, read all instructions about it. This oven has fantastic speed and creating delicious food. The control panel has easy-to-understand operating buttons. You can make your favorite food with different methods. After selecting desired cooking function, you can adjust temperature and cooking time by rotating the dial. The oven automatically preheats once given instructions.

Different functions are following:
The main function of the Ninja Foodi Digital Air Fry Oven is Air Fry. In addition, it can also perform various cooking functions such as air broil, air roast, bake, toast, dehydrate, keep warm, and bagel. The display helps to track the temperature and cooking time setting. The display also shows the slice and darkness setting while using bagel and toast mode.

Air Fry
Air fry is one of the healthiest cooking methods because it fried food in less oil or fat. You need only 1 tablespoon of oil for making French fries, crispy beans, chicken wings, and chicken nuggets using air fry cooking mode. It gives you crispy, tender, and juicy food. Re-create your favorite fried food using the air fry cooking function.

Air Roast
Ninja Foodi Digital Air Fry Oven allows you to cook all sheet pan meals such as sheet pan fajita. It gives you tender and light brown texture food. Using the air roast cooking function, you can roast your favorite food like veggies, beef, chicken, seafood, and lamb. No doubt, Ninja Foodi Digital Air Fry Oven is a master in air roasting.

Air Broil
Air broil cooking mode takes less time for cooking. In only approximately twenty minutes on average, you will get crispy and perfect texture of food with the air broil function. You can broil your favorite food like chicken, veggies, fruits, and seafood, etc.

Bake
Using bake cooking mode, you can also bake muffins, pizza, bread, cakes, cupcakes, brownies, and veggies. Bake is one of the favorite cooking functions of everyone. You can use this option for special occasions.

Toast
The Ninja Foodi Digital Air Fry Oven allows you to toast nine slices of bread at a time. You can adjust the darkness of bread on the control panel. Now, you don't need a separate appliance for toasting the bread.

Bagel
This function is similar with the toast function. Now, you can prepare bagel halves using this function. You will get crispy, golden, and delicious bagels using Ninja Foodi Digital Air Fry oven. The display shows the darkness option how you want to dark or light the bagel.

Dehydrate
You can dehydrate fruit, jerky, dried fruit, veggies, and other your favorite food. The average time taken by this cooking function is approximately 10 to 11 hours. It gives you perfect, delicious, and healthy food. The more time you give, the more dehydrated your food will be.

Keep Warm
With this function, you can keep your food warm for up to 2 hours. Now, you don't need to reheat the food. If there is time to serve the food, you can keep your food warm using this cooking mode. The food is perfectly preserved and perfectly warm with the function of Ninja Foodi Digital Air Fry Oven.

The following accessories are:
- Main unit
- Crumb tray
- Wire rack
- Sheet pan
- Air fry basket

Benefits of the Ninja Foodi Digital Air Fry Oven

The Ninja Foodi Digital Air Fry Oven is one of the modern and unique cooking appliances that come with many benefits. Ninja Foodi Digital Air Fry Oven offers a wide array of advantages. Some of the advantages of the Ninja Foodi Digital Air Fry Oven are stated below:

● **Multipurpose Cooking Appliance**
The Ninja Foodi Digital Air Fry Oven is loaded with different functions such as Air Fry, Air Broil, Air Roast, Dehydrate, Bake, Bagel, Keep Warm, and Toast. You will get different functions only in one oven. This oven handles all tasks by touching the appropriate function button.

● **Fast and Healthy Cooking with XL Capacity**
Ninja Foodi Digital Air Fry Oven cooks your food 60% faster than other appliances. This oven takes 1 minute to preheat. It has an extra-large capacity. You can cook food for a large family. It consumes 75 to 85% less fat or oil. It is the healthiest choice for your kitchen.

● **Easy to Clean**
You can remove all accessories from the Ninja Foodi Digital Air Fry Oven and clean it easily. Such as air fry basket, crumb tray, and sheet pan, etc. When all parts get completely dry, you can use it again.

User Guide of Ninja Foodi Digital Air Fry Oven

The control panel is where you choose how to cook the food, set the temperature and time, and specify the darkness of bagels and toast. There are 5 operating buttons and a dial on the Ninja Foodi Digital Air Fry Oven.

START/PAUSE button:
Press to start or pause the cooking.

TIME/SLICE button:
If you want to adjust the cooking time, press the TIME button and use the dial to adjust the cooking time. If you are using the Bagel or Toast function, this button will allow you to select the number of slices instead of time.

TEMP/DARKNESS button:
If you want to adjust the temperature, press the TEMP button and then use the dial to adjust the cooking temperature. But, if you are using the Bagel or Toast function, this button will allow you to adjust the darkness level of slices instead of temperature.

LIGHT button:
Press the light button to turn the oven's interior light ON and OFF.

POWER button:
Press the power button to turn the oven NO or OFF.

Function/Time/Temperature dial:
It is used to select the cooking time, cooking temperature according to recipe instructions. Or you can adjust the number of slices and darkness level when you are using bagel or toast functions. When you press the start/pause button for three seconds, it will return to the function selection.

The Ninja Foodi Digital Air Fry Oven is easy to clean and easy to maintain. You need to follow these simple steps:

• Firstly, unplug the appliance before start cleaning. Let it cool if it is hot. Then, start the cleaning process. If the oven is hot, then allow it to cool down thoroughly.
• Remove all accessories such as air fry basket, sheet pan, wire rack, and crumb tray from the unit.
• Clean all accessories with soapy water, or you can clean them in the dishwasher.
• Flip up the oven into the storage position and press the push button to remove the back cover of the unit.
• Take a soft cloth and clean the interior part of the unit. But, do not use chemicals because they can damage the surface of the unit.
• Do not immerse the main unit into the water or any other liquid.
• When all parts of the unit get dry, return to the unit. But, first, place the back cover of the unit at its original position. Then, place all accessories into the unit.

4 Weeks Meal Plan

Week 1

Day 1:
Breakfast: Raisin Bran Muffins
Lunch: Broccoli with Cauliflower
Snack: Tortilla Chips
Dinner: Citrus Pork Chops
Dessert: Roasted Bananas

Day 2:
Breakfast: Egg in Hole
Lunch: Sweet Potato Casserole
Snack: Tofu Nuggets
Dinner: Air Fryer Nashville Hot Chicken
Dessert: Caramel Apple Pie

Day 3:
Breakfast: Broiled Bacon
Lunch: Air Fryer Pumpkin Fries
Snack: Fiesta Chicken Fingers
Dinner: Spicy Bay Scallops
Dessert: Cranberry-Apple Pie

Day 4:
Breakfast: Air Fryer Candied Bacon
Lunch: Roast Cauliflower and Broccoli
Snack: Air Fryer Blueberry Bread

Dinner: Crispy Chicken Drumsticks
Dessert: Blueberry Hand Pies

Day 5:
Breakfast: Air Fryer Bacon Crescent Rolls
Lunch: Soy Sauce Green Beans
Snack: Cauliflower Poppers
Dinner: Air Fryer Beef Taquitos
Dessert: Strawberry Cupcakes

Day 6:
Breakfast: Blueberry-Lemon Scones
Lunch: Parmesan Broccoli
Snack: Vegan Dehydrated Cookies
Dinner: Spiced Chicken Breasts
Dessert: Air Fryer Roasted Bananas

Day 7:
Breakfast: Cinnamon Sugar Donuts
Lunch: Eggplant Parmesan
Snack: Eggplant Fries
Dinner: Seafood Medley Mix
Dessert: Nutella Banana Muffins

Day 1:
Breakfast: Breakfast Potatoes
Lunch: Vinegar Green Beans
Snack: Zucchini Fries
Dinner: Tangy Sea Bass
Dessert: Cherry Jam tarts

Day 2:
Breakfast: Puffed Egg Tarts
Lunch: Vegetable Casserole
Snack: Chicken & Parmesan Nuggets
Dinner: Crispy Sirloin Steaks
Dessert: Brownie Bars

Day 3:
Breakfast: Zucchini Fritters
Lunch: Fried Tortellini
Snack: French Toast Bites
Dinner: Tender Italian Baked Chicken
Dessert: Honeyed Banana

Day 4:
Breakfast: Breakfast Casserole
Lunch: Roasted Green Beans

Snack: Potato Chips
Dinner: Garlic Braised Ribs
Dessert: Air Fryer Churros

Day 5:
Breakfast: Banana & Walnut Bread
Lunch: Brussels Sprouts Gratin
Snack: Air Fryer Pop-Tarts
Dinner: Buttered Trout
Dessert: Shortbread Fingers

Day 6:
Breakfast: Pumpkin Muffins
Lunch: Roasted Vegetables
Snack: Persimmon Chips
Dinner: Chinese Chicken Drumsticks
Dessert: Butter Cake

Day 7:
Breakfast: Hard Boiled Eggs
Lunch: Broccoli Cheese Casserole
Snack: Baked Potatoes
Dinner: Crispy Chicken Thighs
Dessert: Apple Pastries

Day 1:
Breakfast: Savory Sausage & Beans Muffins
Lunch: Vegetable Nachos
Snack: Spicy Spinach Chips
Dinner: Crispy Roasted Chicken
Dessert: Chocolate Bites

Day 2:
Breakfast: Air Fryer Breakfast Cookies
Lunch: Tofu with Broccoli
Snack: Avocado Fries
Dinner: Air Fryer Chicken Taco Pockets
Dessert: Air Fried Churros

Day 3:
Breakfast: Mushrooms Frittata
Lunch: Creamy Roast Mushrooms
Snack: Bacon-Wrapped Filled Jalapeno
Dinner: Air Fryer Low-Carb Taco Casserole
Dessert: Raisin Bread Pudding

Day 4:
Breakfast: Eggs, Tofu & Mushroom Omelet
Lunch: Cauliflower Au Gratin
Snack: Air Fryer Sweet Potato Tots

Dinner: Garlic Shrimp with Lemon
Dessert: Peanut Brittle Bars

Day 5:
Breakfast: Parmesan Eggs in Avocado Cups
Lunch: Beans & Veggie Burgers
Snack: Loaded Potatoes
Dinner: BBQ Pork Chops
Dessert: Chocolate Oatmeal Cookies

Day 6:
Breakfast: Pancetta & Spinach Frittata
Lunch: Quinoa Burgers
Snack: Dehydrated Strawberries
Dinner: Herbed Chuck Roast
Dessert: Vanilla Soufflé

Day 7:
Breakfast: Ham and Cheese Scones
Lunch: Tofu in Sweet & Sour Sauce
Snack: Cod Nuggets
Dinner: Spiced Shrimp
Dessert: Mini Crumb Cake Bites

Week 4

Day 1:
Breakfast: Potato & Corned Beef Casserole
Lunch: Cauliflower in Buffalo Sauce
Snack: Corn on the Cob
Dinner: Roast Beef and Yorkshire Pudding
Dessert: Cherry Clafoutis

Day 2:
Breakfast: Air Fryer Cheesy Baked Eggs
Lunch: Wine Braised Mushrooms
Snack: Air Fryer Ravioli
Dinner: Lemony Whole Chicken
Dessert: Chocolate Chip Cookie

Day 3:
Breakfast: Ricotta Toasts with Salmon
Lunch: Air Fryer Sweet and Roasted Carrots
Snack: Sweet Potato Fries
Dinner: Fish in Yogurt Marinade
Dessert: Walnut Brownies

Day 4:
Breakfast: Mushroom Frittata
Lunch: Parmesan Carrot

Snack: Baked Eggplant Sticks
Dinner: Rosemary Lamb Chops
Dessert: Banana Pancakes Dippers

Day 5:
Breakfast: Bacon, Spinach & Egg Cups
Lunch: Stuffed Eggplants
Snack: Air Fried Buffalo Cauliflower Bites
Dinner: Roasted Duck
Dessert: Chocolate Chip Cookies

Day 6:
Breakfast: Cheddar & Cream Omelet
Lunch: Broccoli Casserole
Snack: Baked Mozzarella Sticks
Dinner: Spicy Chicken Legs
Dessert: Air Fried Doughnuts

Day 7:
Breakfast: Sausage Patties
Lunch: Air Fryer Roasted Cauliflower
Snack: Potato Croquettes
Dinner: Lamb Chops with Rosemary Sauce
Dessert: Air Fried Butter Cake

Savory French Toast

Preparation Time: 10 minutes
Cooking Time: 5 minutes
Servings: 2
Ingredients:
- ¼ cup chickpea flour
- 3 tablespoons onion, finely chopped
- 2 teaspoons green chili, seeded and finely chopped
- ½ teaspoon red chili powder
- ¼ teaspoon ground turmeric
- ¼ teaspoon ground cumin
- Salt, to taste
- Water, as needed
- 4 bread slices

Preparation:
1. Add all the ingredients except bread slices in a large bowl and mix until a thick mixture form.
2. With a spoon, spread the mixture over both sides of each bread slice.
3. Arrange the bread slices into the lightly greased sheet pan.
4. Press "Power" button of Ninja Foodi Digital Air Fry Oven and turn the dial to select "Air Fry" mode.
5. Press TIME/SLICE button and again turn the dial to set the cooking time to 5 minutes.
6. Now push TEMP/DARKNESS button and rotate the dial to set the temperature at 390 degrees F.
7. Press "Start/Pause" button to start.
8. When the unit beeps to show that it is preheated, open the oven door and insert the sheet pan in oven.
9. Flip the bread slices once halfway through.
10. When cooking time is completed, open the oven door and serve warm.

Serving Suggestions: Serve with the topping of butter.
Variation Tip: You can add herbs of your choice in flour batter.
Nutritional Information per Serving:
Calories: 151 | Fat: 2.3g | Sat Fat: 0.3g | Carbohydrates: 26.7g | Fiber: 5.4g | Sugar: 4.3g | Protein: 6.5g

Ham & Egg Cups

Preparation Time: 10 minutes
Cooking Time: 18 minutes
Servings: 6
Ingredients:
- 6 ham slices
- 6 eggs
- 6 tablespoons cream
- 3 tablespoons mozzarella cheese, shredded
- ¼ teaspoon dried basil, crushed

Preparation:
1. Lightly grease 6 cups of a silicone muffin tin.
2. Line each prepared muffin cup with 1 ham slice.
3. Crack 1 egg into each muffin cup and top with cream.
4. Sprinkle with cheese and basil.
5. Press "Power" button of Ninja Foodi Digital Air Fry Oven and turn the dial to select "Air Fry" mode.
6. Press TIME/SLICE button and again turn the dial to set the cooking time to 18 minutes.
7. Now push TEMP/DARKNESS button and rotate the dial to set the temperature at 350 degrees F.
8. Press "Start/Pause" button to start.
9. When the unit beeps to show that it is preheated, open the oven door.
10. Arrange the muffin tin over the wire rack and insert in the oven.
11. When cooking time is completed, open the oven door and place the muffin tin onto a wire rack to cool for about 5 minutes.
12. Carefully invert the muffins onto the platter and serve warm.

Serving Suggestions: Serve alongside the buttered bread slices.
Variation Tip: Use room temperature eggs.
Nutritional Information per Serving:
Calories: 156 | Fat: 10g | Sat Fat: 4.1g | Carbohydrates: 2.3g | Fiber: 0.4g | Sugar: 0.6g | Protein: 14.3g

Zucchini Fritters

Preparation Time: 15 minutes
Cooking Time: 7 minutes
Servings: 4
Ingredients:
- 10½ ounces zucchini, grated and squeezed
- 7 ounces Halloumi cheese
- ¼ cup all-purpose flour
- 2 eggs
- 1 teaspoon fresh dill, minced
- Salt and ground black pepper, as required

Preparation:
1. In a large bowl and mix all the ingredients together.
2. Make small-sized fritters from the mixture.
3. Press "Power" button of Ninja Foodi Digital Air Fry Oven and turn the dial to select "Air Fry" mode.
4. Press TIME/SLICE button and again turn the dial to set the cooking time to 7 minutes.
5. Now push TEMP/DARKNESS button and rotate the dial to set the temperature at 355 degrees F.
6. Press "Start/Pause" button to start.
7. When the unit beeps to show that it is preheated, open the oven door.
8. Arrange fritters into the greased sheet pan and insert in the oven.
9. When cooking time is completed, open the oven door and serve warm.

Serving Suggestions: Serve with the topping of sour cream.
Variation Tip: Make sure to squeeze the zucchini completely.
Nutritional Information per Serving:
Calories: 253 | Fat: 17.2g | Sat Fat: 1.4g | Carbohydrates: 10g | Fiber: 1.1g | Sugar: 2.7g | Protein: 15.2g

Cinnamon Sugar Donuts

Preparation Time: 10 minutes
Cooking Time: 5 minutes
Servings: 8
Ingredients:
- 450g refrigerated flaky jumbo biscuits
- ½ cup granulated white sugar
- 2 teaspoons ground cinnamon
- 4 tablespoons butter, melted
- Olive oil spray

Preparation:
1. Combine the sugar and cinnamon in a bowl; leave aside.
2. Take the biscuits out of the can, divide them, and lay them out on a flat surface. Make holes in each biscuit with a 1-inch-round biscuit cutter.
3. Using an olive or coconut oil spray, lightly coat the baking tray.
4. In the sheet pan, arrange 4 doughnuts in a single layer. Make certain they aren't in contact.
5. Turn on your Ninja Foodi Digital Air Fry Oven and rotate the knob to select "Bake".
6. Select the timer for 5 minutes and the temperature for 360 degrees F.
7. Serve and enjoy!

Serving Suggestions: Serve with chocolate sauce.
Variation Tip: Sprinkle sugar on top.
Nutritional Information per Serving:
Calories: 316 | Fat: 15g | Sat Fat: 5g | Carbohydrates: 42g | Fiber: 1g | Sugar: 16g | Protein: 3g

Banana & Walnut Bread

Preparation Time: 15 minutes
Cooking Time: 25 minutes
Servings: 10
Ingredients:
- 1½ cups self-rising flour
- ¼ teaspoon bicarbonate of soda
- 5 tablespoons plus 1 teaspoon butter
- ⅔ cup plus ½ tablespoon caster sugar
- 2 medium eggs
- 3½ ounces walnuts, chopped
- 2 cups bananas, peeled and mashed

Preparation:
1. In a bowl, mix the flour and bicarbonate of soda together.
2. In another bowl, add the butter and sugar and beat until pale and fluffy.
3. Add the eggs, one at a time, along with a little flour and mix well.
4. Stir in the remaining flour and walnuts.
5. Add the bananas and mix until well combined.
6. Grease a loaf pan.
7. Place the mixture into the prepared pan.
8. Press "Power" button of Ninja Foodi Digital Air Fry Oven and turn the dial to select the "Air Fry" mode.
9. Press TIME/SLICE button and again turn the dial to set the cooking time to 10 minutes.
10. Now push TEMP/DARKNESS button and rotate the dial to set the temperature at 355 degrees F.
11. Press "Start/Pause" button to start.
12. When the unit beeps to show that it is preheated, open the oven door.
13. Arrange the pan into the air fry basket and insert in the oven.
14. After 10 minutes of cooking, set the temperature at 340 degrees F for 15 minutes.
15. When cooking time is completed, open the oven door and place the pan onto a wire rack to cool for about 10 minutes.
16. Carefully invert the bread onto the wire rack to cool completely before slicing.
17. Cut the bread into desired sized slices and serve.

Serving Suggestions: Serve with strawberry jam.
Variation Tip: Walnuts can be replaced with pecans.
Nutritional Information per Serving:
Calories: 270 | Fat: 12.8g | Sat Fat: 4.3g | Carbohydrates: 35.5g | Fiber: 2g | Sugar: 17.2g | Protein: 5.8g

Eggs, Tofu & Mushroom Omelet

Preparation Time: 15 minutes
Cooking Time: 35 minutes
Servings: 2
Ingredients:
- 2 teaspoons canola oil
- ¼ of onion, chopped
- 1 garlic clove, minced
- 3½ ounces fresh mushrooms, sliced
- 8 ounces silken tofu, pressed, drained, and crumbled
- Salt and ground black pepper, as needed
- 3 eggs, beaten

Preparation:
1. In a skillet, heat the oil over medium heat and sauté the onion, and garlic for about 4-5 minutes.
2. Add the mushrooms and cook for about 4-5 minutes.
3. Remove from the heat and stir in the tofu, salt and black pepper.
4. Place the tofu mixture into a sheet pan and top with the beaten eggs.
5. Press "Power" button of Ninja Foodi Digital Air Fry Oven and turn the dial to select "Air Fry" mode.
6. Press TIME/SLICE button and again turn the dial to set the cooking time to 25 minutes.
7. Now push TEMP/DARKNESS button and rotate the dial to set the temperature at 355 degrees F.
8. Press "Start/Pause" button to start.
9. When the unit beeps to show that it is preheated, open the oven door.
10. Arrange pan over the wire rack and insert in the oven.
11. When cooking time is completed, open the oven door and remove the sheet pan.
12. Cut into equal-sized wedges and serve hot.

Serving Suggestions: Serve alongside the greens.
Variation Tip: Make sure to drain the tofu completely.
Nutritional Information per Serving:
Calories: 224 | Fat: 14.5g | Sat Fat: 2.9g | Carbohydrates: 6.6g | Fiber: 0.9g | Sugar: 3.4g | Protein: 17.9g

Ricotta Toasts with Salmon

Preparation Time: 10 minutes
Cooking Time: 4 minutes
Servings: 2
Ingredients:
- 4 bread slices
- 1 garlic clove, minced
- 8 ounces ricotta cheese
- 1 teaspoon lemon zest
- Freshly ground black pepper, to taste
- 4 ounces smoked salmon

Preparation:
1. In a food processor, add the garlic, ricotta, lemon zest and black pepper and pulse until smooth.
2. Spread ricotta mixture over each bread slices evenly.
3. Press "Power" button of Ninja Foodi Digital Air Fry Oven and turn the dial to select "Air Fry" mode.
4. Press TIME/SLICE button and again turn the dial to set the cooking time to 4 minutes.
5. Now push TEMP/DARKNESS button and rotate the dial to set the temperature at 355 degrees F.
6. Press "Start/Pause" button to start.
7. When the unit beeps to show that it is preheated, open the oven door and insert the sheet pan in oven.
8. When cooking time is completed, open the oven door and transfer the slices onto serving plates.
9. Top with salmon and serve.
Serving Suggestions: Serve with the garnishing of fresh herbs.
Variation Tip: Ricotta cheese can be replaced with feta.
Nutritional Information per Serving:
Calories: 274 | Fat: 12g | Sat Fat: 6.3g | Carbohydrates: 15.7g | Fiber: 0.5g | Sugar: 1.2g | Protein: 24.8g

Cheddar & Cream Omelet

Preparation Time: 10 minutes
Cooking Time: 8 minutes
Servings: 2
Ingredients:
- 4 eggs
- ¼ cup cream
- 1 teaspoon fresh parsley, minced
- Salt and ground black pepper, as required
- ¼ cup Cheddar cheese, grated

Preparation:
1. In a bowl, add the eggs, cream, parsley, salt, and black pepper and beat well.
2. Place the egg mixture into a small baking pan.
3. Press "Power" button of Ninja Foodi Digital Air Fry Oven and turn the dial to select "Air Fry" mode.
4. Press TIME/SLICE button and again turn the dial to set the cooking time to 8 minutes.
5. Now push TEMP/DARKNESS button and rotate the dial to set the temperature at 350 degrees F.
6. Press "Start/Pause" button to start.
7. When the unit beeps to show that it is preheated, open the oven door.

8. Arrange a sheet pan over the wire rack and insert in the oven.
9. After 4 minutes, sprinkle the omelet with cheese evenly.
10. When cooking time is completed, open the oven door and remove the sheet pan.
11. Cut the omelet into 2 portions and serve hot.
Serving Suggestions: Serve alongside the toasted bread slices.
Variation Tip: You can add the seasoning of your choice.
Nutritional Information per Serving:
Calories: 202 | Fat: 15.1g | Sat Fat: 6.8g | Carbohydrates: 1.8g | Fiber: 0g | Sugar: 1.4g | Protein: 14.8g

Simple Bread

Preparation Time: 15 minutes
Cooking Time: 18 minutes
Servings: 4
Ingredients:
- ⅞ cup whole-wheat flour
- ⅞ cup plain flour
- 1¾ ounces pumpkin seeds
- 1 teaspoon salt
- ½ of sachet instant yeast
- ½-1 cup lukewarm water

Preparation:
1. In a bowl, mix the flours, pumpkin seeds, salt and yeast and mix well together.
2. Slowly, add the desired amount of water and mix until a soft dough ball forms.
3. With your hands, knead the dough until smooth and elastic.
4. Place the dough ball into a bowl.
5. With a plastic wrap, cover the bowl and set aside in a warm place for 30 minutes or until doubled in size.
6. Press "Power" button of Ninja Foodi Digital Air Fry Oven and turn the dial to select "Air Fry" mode.
7. Press TIME/SLICE button and again turn the dial to set the cooking time to 18 minutes.
8. Now push TEMP/DARKNESS button and rotate the dial to set the temperature at 350 degrees F.
9. Press "Start/Pause" button to start.
10. Place the dough ball in a greased sheet pan and brush the top of the dough with water.
11. When the unit beeps to show that it is preheated, open the oven door.
12. Place the sheet pan into the air fry basket and insert in the oven.
13. When cooking time is completed, open the oven door and place the pan onto a wire rack for about 10-15 minutes.
14. Carefully, invert the bread onto the wire rack to cool completely cool before slicing.
15. Cut the bread into desired sized slices and serve.
Serving Suggestions: Serve with your favorite jam.
Variation Tip: Don't use hot water.
Nutritional Information per Serving:
Calories: 268 | Fat: 6g | Sat Fat: 1.1g | Carbohydrates: 43.9g | Fiber: 2.5g | Sugar: 1.1g | Protein: 9.2g

French Toast

Preparation Time: 5 minutes
Cooking Time: 6 minutes
Servings: 4
Ingredients:
- 1 cup heavy cream
- 1 egg, beaten
- ¼ powdered sugar
- 1 teaspoon cinnamon
- 8 slices of bread

Preparation:
1. Place your bread on the wire rack.
2. Turn on your Ninja Foodi Digital Air Fry Oven and rotate the knob to select "Air Roast".
3. Select the timer for 4 minutes and the temperature for 390 degrees.
4. While the bread is toasting, combine the remaining ingredients in a mixing bowl.
5. Dip bread in batches into the mixture, making sure both sides are covered.
6. Place them on the air fry basket.
7. Now again, turn on your Ninja Foodi Digital Air Fry Oven and rotate the knob to select "Air Fry".
8. Select the timer for 4 minutes and the temperature for 390 degrees F.
9. Serve with butter.

Serving Suggestions: Top with maple syrup.
Variation Tip: You can also use low-carb bread.
Nutritional Information per Serving:
Calories: 342 | Fat: 29g | Sat Fat: 15g | Carbohydrates: 16g | Fiber: 8g | Sugar: 2g | Protein: 13g

Mushroom Frittata

Preparation Time: 15 minutes
Cooking Time: 36 minutes
Servings: 4
Ingredients:
- 2 tablespoons olive oil
- 1 shallot, sliced thinly
- 2 garlic cloves, minced
- 4 cups white mushrooms, chopped
- 6 large eggs
- ¼ teaspoon red pepper flakes, crushed
- Salt and ground black pepper, as required
- ½ teaspoon fresh dill, minced
- ½ cup cream cheese, softened

Preparation:
1. In a skillet, heat the oil over medium heat and cook the shallot, mushrooms, and garlic for about 5-6 minutes, stirring frequently.
2. Remove from the heat and transfer the mushroom mixture into a bowl.
3. In another bowl, add the eggs, red pepper flakes, salt and black peppers and beat well.
4. Add the mushroom mixture and stir to combine.
5. Place the egg mixture into a greased sheet pan and sprinkle with the dill.
6. Spread cream cheese over egg mixture evenly.
7. Press "Power" button of Ninja Foodi Digital Air Fry Oven and turn the dial to select "Air Fry" mode.
8. Press TIME/SLICE button and again turn the dial to set the cooking time to 30 minutes.
9. Now push TEMP/DARKNESS button and rotate the dial to set the temperature at 330 degrees F.
10. Press "Start/Pause" button to start.
11. When the unit beeps to show that it is preheated, open the oven door.
12. Arrange the pan over the wire rack and insert in the oven.
13. When cooking time is completed, open the oven door and place the sheet pan onto a wire rack for about 5 minutes
14. Cut into equal-sized wedges and serve.

Serving Suggestions: Serve with green salad.
Variation Tip: For better taste, let the frittata sit at room temperature for a few minutes to set before cutting.
Nutritional Information per Serving:
Calories: 290 | Fat: 24.8g | Sat Fat: 9.7g | Carbohydrates: 5g | Fiber: 0.8g | Sugar: 1.9g | Protein: 14.1g

Parmesan Eggs in Avocado Cups

Preparation Time: 10 minutes
Cooking Time: 22 minutes
Servings: 2
Ingredients:
- 1 large ripe avocado, halved and pitted
- 2 eggs
- Salt and ground black pepper, as required
- 2 tablespoons Parmesan cheese, grated
- Pinch of cayenne pepper
- 1 teaspoon fresh chives, minced

Preparation:
1. With a spoon, scoop out some of the flesh from the avocado halves to make a hole.
2. Arrange the avocado halves onto a baking pan.
3. Crack 1 egg into each avocado half and sprinkle with salt and black pepper.
4. Press "Power" button of Ninja Foodi Digital Air Fry Oven and turn the dial to select "Air Fry" mode.
5. Press TIME/SLICE button and again turn the dial to set the cooking time to 22 minutes.
6. Now push TEMP/DARKNESS button and rotate the dial to set the temperature at 350 degrees F.
7. Press "Start/Pause" button to start.
8. When the unit beeps to show that it is preheated, open the oven door and grease the air fry basket.
9. Arrange the avocado halves into the air fry basket and insert in the oven.
10. After 12 minutes of cooking, sprinkle the top of avocado halves with Parmesan cheese.
11. When cooking time is completed, open the oven door and transfer the avocado halves onto a platter.
12. Sprinkle with cayenne pepper and serve hot with the garnishing of chives.

Serving Suggestions: Serve alongside baby greens.
Variation Tip: Use ripe but firm avocado.
Nutritional Information per Serving:
Calories: 286 | Fat: 25.2g | Sat Fat: 6.1g | Carbohydrates: 9g | Fiber: 0.9g | Sugar: 0.9g | Protein: 9.5g

Savory Sausage & Beans Muffins

Preparation Time: 15 minutes
Cooking Time: 20 minutes
Servings: 6
Ingredients:
- 4 eggs
- ½ cup cheddar cheese, shredded
- 3 tablespoons heavy cream
- 1 tablespoon tomato paste
- ¼ teaspoon salt
- Pinch of freshly ground black pepper
- Cooking spray
- 4 cooked breakfast sausage links, chopped
- 3 tablespoons baked beans

Preparation:
1. Grease a 6-cup muffin pan.
2. In a bowl, add the eggs, cheddar cheese, heavy cream, tomato paste, salt and black pepper and beat until well combined.
3. Stir in the sausage pieces and beans.
4. Divide the mixture into prepared muffin cups evenly.
5. Press "Power" button of Ninja Foodi Digital Air Fry Oven and turn the dial to select "Bake" mode.
6. Press TIME/SLICE button and again turn the dial to set the cooking time to 20 minutes.
7. Now push TEMP/DARKNESS button and rotate the dial to set the temperature at 350 degrees F.
8. Press "Start/Pause" button to start.
9. When the unit beeps to show that it is preheated, open the oven door.
10. Arrange the muffin pan over the wire rack and insert in the oven.
11. When cooking time is completed, open the oven door and place the muffin pan onto a wire rack to cool for 5 minutes before serving.

Serving Suggestions: Serve with drizzling of melted butter.
Variation Tip: You can use cooked beans of your choice.
Nutritional Information per Serving:
Calories: 258 | Fat: 20.4g | Sat Fat: 9.3g | Carbohydrates: 4.2g | Fiber: 0.8g | Sugar: 0.9g | Protein: 14.6g

Cloud Eggs

Preparation Time: 10 minutes
Cooking Time: 7 minutes
Servings: 2
Ingredients:
- 2 eggs, whites and yolks separated
- Pinch of salt
- Pinch of freshly ground black pepper

Preparation:
1. In a bowl, add the egg white, salt, and black pepper and beat until stiff peaks form.
2. Line a baking pan with parchment paper.
3. Carefully, make a pocket in the center of each egg white circle.
4. Press "Power" button of Ninja Foodi Digital Air Fry Oven and turn the dial to select the "Air Broil" mode.
5. Press TIME/SLICE button and again turn the dial to set the cooking time to 7 minutes.
6. Press TEMP/DARKNESS button and again turn the dial to set LO. To set the temperature, press the TEMP/DARKNESS button again.
7. When the unit beeps to show that it is preheated, open the oven door and insert the sheet pan in the oven.
8. Place 1 egg yolk into each egg white pocket after 5 minutes of cooking.
9. Press "Start/Pause" button to start.
10. When cooking time is completed, open the oven door and serve.

Serving Suggestions: Serve alongside toasted bread slices.
Variation Tip: Make sure to use a cleaned bowl for whipping the egg whites.
Nutritional Information per Serving:
Calories: 63 | Fat: 4.4g | Sat Fat: 1.4g | Carbohydrates: 0.3g | Fiber: 0g | Sugar: 0.3g | Protein: 5.5g

Bacon, Spinach & Egg Cups

Preparation Time: 15 minutes
Cooking Time: 16 minutes
Servings: 3
Ingredients:
- 3 eggs
- 6 cooked bacon slices, chopped
- 2 cups fresh baby spinach
- ⅓ cup heavy cream
- 3 tablespoons Parmesan cheese, grated
- Salt and ground black pepper, as required

Preparation:
1. Heat a nonstick skillet over medium-high heat and cook the bacon for about 5 minutes.
2. Add the spinach and cook for about 2-3 minutes.
3. Stir in the heavy cream and Parmesan cheese and cook for about 2-3 minutes.
4. Remove from the heat and set aside to cool slightly.
5. Grease 3 (3-inch) ramekins.
6. Crack 1 egg in each prepared ramekin and top with bacon mixture.
7. Press "Power" button of Ninja Foodi Digital Air Fry Oven and turn the dial to select "Air Fry" mode.
8. Press TIME/SLICE button and again turn the dial to set the cooking time to 5 minutes.
9. Now push TEMP/DARKNESS button and rotate the dial to set the temperature at 350 degrees F.
10. Press "Start/Pause" button to start.
11. When the unit beeps to show that it is preheated, open the oven door and grease the air fry basket.
12. Arrange the ramekins into the air fry basket and insert in the oven.
13. When cooking time is completed, open the oven door and sprinkle each ramekin with salt and black pepper.
14. Serve hot.

Serving Suggestions: Serve alongside the English muffins.
Variation Tip: Use freshly grated cheese.
Nutritional Information per Serving:
Calories: 442 | Fat: 34.5g | Sat Fat: 12.9g | Carbohydrates: 2.3g | Fiber: 0.5g | Sugar: 0.4g | Protein: 29.6g

Pancetta & Spinach Frittata

Preparation Time: 15 minutes
Cooking Time: 16 minutes
Servings: 2
Ingredients:
- ¼ cup pancetta
- ½ of tomato, cubed
- ¼ cup fresh baby spinach
- 3 eggs
- Salt and ground black pepper, as required
- ¼ cup Parmesan cheese, grated

Preparation:
1. Heat a nonstick skillet over medium heat and cook the pancetta for about 5 minutes.
2. Add the tomato and spinach cook for about 2-3 minutes.
3. Remove from the heat and drain the grease from skillet.
4. Set aside to cool slightly.
5. Meanwhile, in a small bowl, add the eggs, salt and black pepper and beat well.
6. In the bottom of a greased sheet pan, place the pancetta mixture and top with the eggs, followed by the cheese.
7. Press "Power" button of Ninja Foodi Digital Air Fry Oven and turn the dial to select "Air Fry" mode.
8. Press TIME/SLICE button and again turn the dial to set the cooking time to 8 minutes.
9. Now push TEMP/DARKNESS button and rotate the dial to set the temperature at 355 degrees F.
10. Press "Start/Pause" button to start.
11. When the unit beeps to show that it is preheated, open the oven door.
12. Arrange the pan over the wire rack and insert in the oven.
13. When cooking time is completed, open the oven door and remove the baking dish.
14. Cut into equal-sized wedges and serve.
Serving Suggestions: Serve alongside the green salad.
Variation Tip: You can use bacon instead of pancetta.
Nutritional Information per Serving:
Calories: 287 | Fat: 20.8g | Sat Fat: 7.2g | Carbohydrates: 1.7g | Fiber: 0.3g | Sugar: 0.9g | Protein: 23.1g

Sweet & Spiced Toasts

Preparation Time: 10 minutes
Cooking Time: 4 minutes
Servings: 3
Ingredients:
- ¼ cup sugar
- ½ teaspoon ground cinnamon
- ⅛ teaspoon ground cloves
- ⅛ teaspoon ground ginger
- ½ teaspoons vanilla extract
- ¼ cup salted butter, softened
- 6 bread slices
- Pepper, as you need

Preparation:
1. In a bowl, add the sugar, vanilla, cinnamon, pepper, and butter. Mix until smooth.
2. Spread the butter mixture evenly over each bread slice.

3. Press "Power" button of Ninja Foodi Digital Air Fry Oven and turn the dial to select "Air Fry" mode.
4. Press TIME/SLICE button and again turn the dial to set the cooking time to 4 minutes.
5. Now push TEMP/DARKNESS button and rotate the dial to set the temperature at 400 degrees F.
6. Press "Start/Pause" button to start.
7. When the unit beeps to show that it is preheated, open the oven door and grease the air fry basket.
8. Place the bread slices into the prepared air fry basket, buttered-side up. and insert in the oven.
9. Flip the slices once halfway through.
10. When cooking time is completed, open the oven door and transfer the French toasts onto a platter.
11. Serve warm.
Serving Suggestions: Serve with the drizzling of maple syrup.
Variation Tip: Adjust the ratio of spices according to your taste.
Nutritional Information per Serving:
Calories: 261 | Fat: 12g | Sat Fat: 3.6g | Carbohydrates: 30.6g | Fiber: 0.3g | Sugar: 22.3g | Protein: 9.1g

Breakfast Potatoes

Preparation Time: 10 minutes
Cooking Time: 25 minutes
Servings: 7
Ingredients:
- 3 pounds red potatoes, diced
- ½ cup sweet onion, diced
- 2 green bell peppers, sliced
- 2 red bell peppers, sliced
- ½ teaspoon garlic powder
- ½ teaspoon seasoned salt
- ½ teaspoon fennel seed
- Cooking spray

Preparation:
1. Begin by prepping the veggies and, if necessary, chopping them.
2. Apply a light application of cooking oil spray to the air fry basket.
3. Fill the air fry basket with all of the vegetables.
4. Top evenly with seasonings.
5. Apply a generous application of cooking oil spray.
6. Turn on your Ninja Foodi Digital Air Fry Oven and rotate the knob to select "Air Fry".
7. Select the timer for 20 minutes and the temperature for 360 degrees F.
8. It's a good idea to check on the basket after around 10-15 minutes to mix or toss it up.
9. Serve once everything is ready.
Serving Suggestions: Top with sesame seeds before serving.
Variation Tip: You can also add olives.
Nutritional Information per Serving:
Calories: 187 | Fat: 2g | Sat Fat: 0g | Carbohydrates: 38g | Fiber: 4g | Sugar: 8g | Protein: 5g

Raisin Bran Muffins

Preparation Time: 15 minutes.
Cooking Time: 18 minutes.
Servings: 6
Ingredients:
- 1 cup wheat bran
- 1 cup boiling water
- 4 ounces plain, non-fat Greek yogurt
- 2 large eggs
- 1 ½ cups whole wheat flour
- 5 ½ ounces all-purpose flour
- ¾ cup sugar
- ½ ounce ground cinnamon
- 2 teaspoons baking powder
- ¾ teaspoon kosher salt or sea salt
- ¼ teaspoon baking soda
- ⅛ teaspoon grated nutmeg
- 6 ounces butter
- 1 cup golden raisins
- ¾ ounce flaxseed

Preparation:
1. Mix wheat bran with boiling water in a bowl and leave it for 5 minutes.
2. Add eggs, wheat flour, sugar, Greek yogurt, cinnamon, salt, baking soda, baking powder, butter, and nutmeg into the wheat bran, then mix well in a mixer.
3. Stir in raisins and mix the batter gently.
4. Divide this bran muffin batter into 12 greased muffin cups.
5. Transfer the muffin cups to the Ninja Foodi Digital Air Fry Oven and close the door.
6. Select "Bake" mode by rotating the dial.
7. Press the TIME/SLICE button and change the value to 18 minutes.
8. Press the TEMP/DARKNESS button and change the value to 400 degrees F.
9. Press Start/Pause to begin cooking.
10. Serve fresh.
Serving Suggestion: Serve these muffins with caramel sauce.
Variation Tip: Inject apple sauce into the muffins.
Nutritional Information Per Serving:
Calories 204 | Fat 32g | Sodium 890mg | Carbs 4.3g | Fiber 4g | Sugar 8g | Protein 5g

Mushrooms Frittata

Preparation Time: 15 minutes.
Cooking Time: 15 minutes.
Servings: 2
Ingredients:
- 1 cup egg whites
- 2 tablespoons skim milk
- ¼ cup tomato, sliced
- ¼ cup mushrooms, sliced
- 2 tablespoons fresh chives, chopped
- Black pepper, to taste

Preparation:
1. Beat egg whites with mushrooms and the rest of the ingredients in a bowl.
2. Spread this egg white mixture in a suitable casserole dish.
3. Transfer the dish to the Ninja Foodi Digital Air Fry Oven and close the door.
4. Select "Air Fry" mode by rotating the dial.
5. Press the TIME/SLICE button and change the value to 15 minutes.
6. Press the TEMP/DARKNESS button and change the value to 320 degrees F.
7. Press Start/Pause to begin cooking.
8. Slice and serve warm.
Serving Suggestion: Serve the mushrooms frittata with crispy bacon on the side.
Variation Tip: Add chopped bell pepper to the frittata.
Nutritional Information Per Serving:
Calories 354 | Fat 7.9g | Sodium 704mg | Carbs 6g | Fiber 3.6g | Sugar 6g | Protein 18g

Banana Bread

Preparation Time: 15 minutes.
Cooking Time: 25 minutes.
Servings: 6
Ingredients:
- 4 medium bananas, peeled and sliced
- ¼ cup plain Greek yogurt
- 2 large eggs
- ½ ounce vanilla extract
- 10 ounces all-purpose flour
- ¾ cup sugar
- 3 ounces oat flour
- 1 teaspoon baking powder
- 1 teaspoon baking soda
- ¾ teaspoon kosher salt
- ¾ teaspoon ground cinnamon
- ½ teaspoon ground cloves
- ¼ teaspoon ground nutmeg
- ¾ cup coconut oil
- 1 cup toasted pecan

Preparation:
1. Layer a 10.5-inch-by-5.5-inch loaf pan with a parchment sheet and keep it aside.
2. Mash the banana in a suitable bowl and add eggs, vanilla, and Greek yogurt, then mix well.
3. Cover this banana yogurt mixture and leave it for 30 minutes.
4. Meanwhile, mix cinnamon, flour, sugar, baking powder, oat flour, salt, baking soda, coconut oil, cloves, and nutmeg in a mixer.
5. Now slowly add banana mash mixture to the flour and continue mixing until smooth.
6. Fold in nuts and mix gently until evenly incorporated.
7. Spread this banana-nut batter in the prepared loaf pan.
8. Transfer the loaf pan to the Ninja Foodi Digital Air Fry Oven and close the door.
9. Select "Bake" mode by rotating the dial.
10. Press the TIME/SLICE button and change the value to 25 minutes.
11. Press the TEMP/DARKNESS button and change the value to 350 degrees F.
12. Press Start/Pause to begin cooking.
13. Slice and serve.
Serving Suggestion: Serve the bread with fried eggs and crispy bacon.
Variation Tip: Add some crushed oats for a different texture.
Nutritional Information Per Serving:
Calories 331 | Fat 2.5g | Sodium 595mg | Carbs 69g | Fiber 12g | Sugar 12g | Protein 7g

Ham and Cheese Scones

Preparation Time: 15 minutes.
Cooking Time: 25 minutes.
Servings: 6
Ingredients:
- 2 cups all-purpose flour
- 1 tablespoon baking powder
- 2 teaspoons sugar
- 1 teaspoon kosher salt
- 2 tablespoons butter, cubed
- 1 cup ham, diced, cooked
- ¼ cup scallion, chopped
- 4 ounces cheddar cheese, shredded
- ¼ cup milk
- ¾ cup heavy cream

Preparation:
1. Whisk baking powder with flour, sugar, salt, and butter in a mixing bowl.
2. Beat milk, cream, ham, scallion, and cheddar cheese in another bowl.
3. Stir in the flour-butter mixture and mix well until it forms a smooth dough.
4. Place this scones dough on a floured surface and spread it into a 7-inch round sheet.
5. Cut this dough sheet into 6 wedges of equal size.
6. Place these wedges in the cooking pan, lined with parchment paper.
7. Transfer the pan to the Ninja Foodi Digital Air Fry Oven and close the door.
8. Select "Bake" mode by rotating the dial.
9. Press the TIME/SLICE button and change the value to 25 minutes.
10. Press the TEMP/DARKNESS button and change the value to 400 degrees F.
11. Press Start/Pause to begin cooking.
12. When baked, serve the scones with morning eggs.

Serving Suggestion: Serve the scones with the cream cheese dip.
Variation Tip: Add chopped parsley to the scones.
Nutritional Information Per Serving:
Calories 387 | Fat 6g | Sodium 154mg | Carbs 37.4g | Fiber 2.9g | Sugar 15g | Protein 15g

Blueberry-Lemon Scones

Preparation Time: 15 minutes.
Cooking Time: 25 minutes.
Servings: 6
Ingredients:
- 2 cups all-purpose flour
- 1 tablespoon baking powder
- 2 teaspoons sugar
- 1 teaspoon kosher salt
- 2 ounces refined coconut oil
- 1 cup fresh blueberries
- ¼ ounce lemon zest
- 8 ounces coconut milk

Preparation:
1. Blend coconut oil with salt, sugar, baking powder, and flour in a food processor.
2. Transfer this flour mixture to a mixing bowl.
3. Now add coconut milk and lemon zest to the flour mixture, then mix well.
4. Fold in blueberries and mix the prepared dough well until smooth.
5. Spread this blueberry dough into a 7-inch round and place it in a pan.
6. Refrigerate the blueberry dough for 15 minutes, then slice it into 6 wedges.
7. Layer the sheet pan with a parchment sheet.
8. Place the blueberry wedges in the lined sheet pan.
9. Transfer the scones to the Ninja Foodi Digital Air Fry Oven and close the door.
10. Select "Bake" mode by rotating the dial.
11. Press the TIME/SLICE button and change the value to 25 minutes.
12. Press the TEMP/DARKNESS button and change the value to 400 degrees F.
13. Press Start/Pause to begin cooking.
14. Serve fresh.

Serving Suggestion: Serve the scones with blueberry jam.
Variation Tip: Stuff the scones with blueberry jam.
Nutritional Information Per Serving:
Calories 312 | Fat 25g | Sodium 132mg | Carbs 44g | Fiber 3.9g | Sugar 3g | Protein 1.9g

Breakfast Bake

Preparation Time: 15 minutes.
Cooking Time: 50 minutes.
Servings: 6
Ingredients:
- 24 ounces bulk pork sausage
- 1 medium bell pepper, chopped
- 1 medium onion, chopped
- 3 cups frozen hash brown potatoes
- 2 cups shredded Cheddar cheese
- 1 cup Bisquick mix
- 2 cups milk
- ¼ teaspoon pepper
- 4 eggs

Preparation:
1. Whisk Bisquick with milk, eggs, and pepper in a mixer.
2. Sauté pork sausage, onion, and bell pepper in a 10-inch skillet over medium heat.
3. Stir cook until the sausage turns brown in color, then transfer to a casserole dish.
4. Toss in potatoes, 1 ½ cups of cheese, and the Bisquick mixture.
5. Transfer the casserole dish to the Ninja Foodi Digital Air Fry Oven and close the door.
6. Select "Bake" mode by rotating the dial.
7. Press the TIME/SLICE button and change the value to 45 minutes.
8. Press the TEMP/DARKNESS button and change the value to 350 degrees F.
9. Press Start/Pause to begin cooking.
10. Drizzle the remaining cheese over the casserole and bake for 5 minutes.
11. Serve.

Serving Suggestion: Serve the bake with crispy bacon and bread.
Variation Tip: Top egg with fresh herbs or chopped bell pepper.
Nutritional Information Per Serving:
Calories 297 | Fat 15g | Sodium 202mg | Carbs 58.5g | Fiber 4g | Sugar 1g | Protein 33g

Broiled Bacon

Preparation Time: 10 minutes
Cooking Time: 10 minutes
Servings: 6
Ingredients:
- 1 pound bacon

Preparation:
1. Evenly distribute the bacon in the air fry basket.
2. Turn on your Ninja Foodi Digital Air Fry Oven and rotate the knob to select "Air Broil".
3. Select the unit for 5 minutes at LO.
4. With tongs, remove the bacon and place it on a paper towel-lined dish.
5. Allow cooling before serving.
Serving Suggestions: Serve with steamed rice.
Variation Tip: Sprinkle salt and pepper on top.
Nutritional Information per Serving:
Calories: 177 | Fat: 13g | Sat Fat: 5g | Carbohydrates: 1g | Fiber: 0g | Sugar: 0g | Protein: 13g

Peanut Butter Banana Baked Oatmeal

Preparation Time: 5 minutes
Cooking Time: 30 minutes
Servings: 9
Ingredients:
- 1 ½ cups quick-cooking oats
- 1 teaspoon baking powder
- ½ teaspoon sea salt
- 1 teaspoon ground cinnamon
- 2 overripe bananas, mashed
- 1 teaspoon vanilla extract
- ¼ cup pure maple syrup
- 1 large egg lightly beaten
- ¾ cup almond milk unsweetened
- ¼ cup melted creamy peanut butter

Preparation:
1. Select the BAKE function, 350°F, for 25 minutes. While the oven is preheating, prepare a baking pan and the ingredients.
2. Take a small bowl, and mix the baking powder, quick-cooking oats, cinnamon, and sea salt. Set it aside.
3. Take a large bowl and mix the peanut butter with the mashed banana. Add the vanilla extract, egg, and maple syrup. Mix evenly.
4. Next, add in the almond milk and stir to combine.
5. Add the dry ingredients to the wet ingredients and mix well.
6. Empty the combined mixture into the prepared baking pan.
7. Bake it for about 25 minutes. Once done, cut into squares and serve.
Serving Suggestion: Melt peanut butter and drizzle it on top before serving.
Variation Tip: If you want to give it a vegan spin, use chia seeds instead of eggs.
Nutritional Information Per Serving:
Calories: 125 | Fat: 5g | Sodium: 118mg | Carbs: 16.7g | Fiber: 3g | Sugar: 4g | Protein: 5g

Potato & Corned Beef Casserole

Preparation Time: 15 minutes
Cooking Time: 1 hour 20 minutes
Servings: 3
Ingredients:
- 3 Yukon Gold potatoes
- 2 tablespoons unsalted butter
- ½ of onion, chopped
- 2 garlic cloves, minced
- 2 tablespoons vegetable oil
- ½ teaspoon salt
- 12 ounces corned beef
- 3 eggs

Preparation:
1. Press "Power" button of Ninja Foodi Digital Air Fry Oven and turn the dial to select "Bake" mode.
2. Press TIME/SLICE button and again turn the dial to set the cooking time to 30 minutes.
3. Now push TEMP/DARKNESS button and rotate the dial to set the temperature at 350 degrees F.
4. Press "Start/Pause" button to start.
5. When the unit beeps to show that it is preheated, open the oven door and grease the air fry basket.
6. Place the potatoes into the prepared air fry basket and insert in the oven.
7. When cooking time is completed, open the oven door and transfer the potatoes onto a tray.
8. Set aside to cool for about 15 minutes.
9. After cooling, cut the potatoes into ½-inch-thick slices.
10. In a skillet, melt the butter over medium heat and cook the onion and garlic for about 10 minutes.
11. Remove from the heat and place the onion mixture into a casserole dish.
12. Add the potato slices, oil, salt, and corned beef and mix well.
13. Press "Power" button of Ninja Foodi Digital Air Fry Oven and turn the dial to select "Bake" mode.
14. Press TIME/SLICE button and again turn the dial to set the cooking time to 40 minutes.
15. Now push TEMP/DARKNESS button and rotate the dial to set the temperature at 350 degrees F.
16. Press "Start/Pause" button to start.
17. When the unit beeps to show that it is preheated, open the oven door.
18. Arrange the casserole dish over the wire rack and insert in the oven.
19. After 30 minutes of cooking, remove the casserole dish and crack 3 eggs on top.
20. When cooking time is completed, open the oven door and serve immediately.
Serving Suggestions: Serve with fresh baby kale.
Variation Tip: Cut the potatoes in equal-sized slices.
Nutritional Information per Serving:
Calories: 542 | Fat: 35.6g | Sat Fat: 14.1g | Carbohydrates: 33.1g | Fiber: 2.8g | Sugar: 2.3g | Protein: 24.7g

Puff Pastry Danishes

Preparation Time: 30 minutes
Cooking Time: 15 minutes
Servings: 4 to 5
Ingredients:
- 8 ounces cream cheese
- ¼ cup sugar
- 2 tablespoons all-purpose flour
- ½ teaspoon vanilla extract
- 2 large egg yolks
- 1 tablespoon water
- 17.3 ounces frozen puff pastry (thawed)
- 1 rounded tablespoon seedless raspberry jam

Preparation:
1. Select the Bake function, 425°F, for 16 minutes.
2. While the unit is preheating, line the sheet pan with parchment paper and prepare the ingredients.
3. Beat the sugar, cream cheese, flour, and 1 egg yolk in a bowl.
4. In a separate bowl, mix the remaining egg yolk with the water.
5. Lightly flour a surface and lay out the puff pastry sheets. Roll them into 12-inch squares. Cut each into 4-inch squares, and transfer to the sheet pan.
6. Top all the squares with 1 tablespoon of the cream cheese mixture and 1 rounded tablespoon of jam.
7. Bring the two opposite corners of pastry over the filling and seal with the yolk mixture. Use the remaining mixture to brush the tops.
8. Bake the pastries for about 14 to 16 minutes.
Serving Suggestion: Sprinkle with powdered sugar and serve warm.
Variation Tip: You can use the jam of your choice.
Nutritional Information Per Serving:
Calories: 197 | Fat: 12g | Sodium: 130mg | Carbs: 20g | Fiber: 2g | Protein: 3g

Breakfast Casserole

Preparation Time: 15 minutes
Cooking Time: 30 minutes
Servings: 8
Ingredients:
- 8 eggs
- 1 pound pork sausage
- 1 ½ cups whole milk
- 850g frozen hash browns, shredded
- 2 cups cheddar cheese
- 1½ teaspoons salt
- ¼ teaspoon garlic powder

Preparation:
1. Toss the uncooked ground sausage into the pan.
2. Sauté and cook for 6-8 minutes, or until sausage is browned.
3. Mix in the frozen hash browns thoroughly.
4. Mix in 1 cup of cheese.
5. Whisk together the eggs, Cheddar cheese, and spices in a separate basin. Fill the pot with the egg mixture.
6. Place the mixture into the baking dish.
7. Turn on your Ninja Foodi Digital Air Fry Oven and rotate the knob to select "Air Fry."

8. Select the timer for 30 minutes and the temperature for 350 degrees F.
9. Serve while hot.
Serving Suggestions: You can also add olives.
Variation Tip: You can use cream cheese instead of milk.
Nutritional Information per Serving:
Calories: 350 | Fat: 29g | Sat Fat: 12g | Carbohydrates: 1g | Fiber: 1g | Sugar: 1g | Protein: 21g

Sausage Patties

Preparation Time: 5 minutes
Cooking Time: 6 minutes
Servings: 6
Ingredients:
- 1 pound pork sausage patties
- Fennel seeds

Preparation:
2. Prepare the sausage by slicing it into patties or using new patties, then flavor it with fennel seed or your favorite seasoning.
3. Arrange in basket in a uniform layer.
4. Turn on your Ninja Foodi Digital Air Fry Oven and rotate the knob to select "Air Broil".
5. Select the timer for 8 minutes and temperature to LO.
6. Cook for another 4 minutes after carefully flipping the patties.
7. Serve.
Serving Suggestions: Serve with garlic sauce.
Variation Tip: You can use any seasoning.
Nutritional Information per Serving:
Calories: 123 | Fat: 10g | Sat Fat: 3g | Carbohydrates: 1g | Fiber: 0g | Sugar: 0g | Protein: 7g

Breakfast Pizzas with Muffins

Preparation Time: 5 minutes
Cooking Time: 6 minutes
Servings: 3
Ingredients:
- 6 eggs, cooked and scrambled
- 1 pound ground sausage
- ½ cup Colby jack cheese, shredded
- 3 egg muffins, sliced in half
- Olive oil spray

Preparation:
1. Using olive oil cooking spray, spray the air fry basket.
2. Place each half in the basket.
3. Using a light layer of olive oil spray, lightly coat the English muffins and top with scrambled eggs and fried sausages.
4. Add cheese on top of each one.
5. Turn on your Ninja Foodi Digital Air Fry Oven and rotate the knob to select "Bake".
6. Select the timer for 5 minutes and the temperature for 355 degrees F.
7. Serve hot.
Serving Suggestions: Top with fresh parsley.
Variation Tip: You can also add fennel seeds.
Nutritional Information per Serving:
Calories: 429 | Fat: 32g | Sat Fat: 11g | Carbohydrates: 15g | Fiber: 1g | Sugar: 1g | Protein: 20g

Cinnamon Donut Muffins

Preparation Time: 15 minutes
Cooking Time: 20 minutes
Servings: 10
Ingredients:
- 1¾ cups all-purpose flour
- 1½ teaspoon baking powder
- ½ teaspoon salt
- ½ teaspoon ground nutmeg
- ¾ cup sugar
- ⅓ cup canola oil
- 1 large egg, lightly beaten
- ¾ cup 2% milk
- 10 teaspoons seedless strawberry jam

Topping:
- ¼ cup melted butter
- ⅓ cup sugar
- 1 teaspoon ground cinnamon

Preparation:
1. Select the BAKE function, 350°F, for 20 minutes. While the oven is preheating, prepare the ingredients.
2. Mix the baking powder, nutmeg, salt, flour, and cinnamon in a large bowl.
3. In a small bowl, combine the oil, sugar, egg, and milk. Then stir the mixture into the dry ingredients.
4. Grease 10 muffin cups, fill them halfway with the mixture and then top each with 1 teaspoon of jam.
5. Cover with the rest of the batter. Then bake the muffins for about 20 to 25 minutes.
6. For the topping: put the melted butter in a small bowl and combine the sugar with cinnamon in another bowl.
7. Right after taking the muffins out of the oven, dip the tops with butter, cinnamon, and sugar. Then serve warm.

Serving Suggestion: You can drizzle some honey over the muffins before serving.
Variation Tip: You can use some other jam of your choice.
Nutritional Information Per Serving:
Calories: 288 | Fat: 13g | Sodium: 240mg | Carbs: 40g | Fiber: 1g | Sugar: 22g | Protein: 4g

Sheet Pan Breakfast Pizza with Sausage & Potatoes

Preparation Time: 10 minutes
Cooking Time: 25 minutes
Servings: 8
Ingredients:
- 6 egg whites
- 6 eggs
- ½ cup unsweetened almond milk
- ½ cup baby spinach
- 16 ounces turkey breakfast sausage
- 5 cups shredded potato
- 2 tablespoons light cheddar cheese
- Salt and pepper, to taste
- Avocado cooking spray

Preparation:
1. Select the BAKE function, 375°F, for 25 minutes. While the oven is preheating, grease the sheet pan with avocado cooking spray and prepare the ingredients.
2. Add the turkey sausage to a greased skillet over medium heat. Use a spatula to break up the sausage as it cooks. When it's cooked, drain it, and keep it aside.
3. Take a medium bowl and mix the milk, salt, eggs, pepper, and spinach.
4. Lay the shredded potatoes on the prepared sheet pan. Sprinkle the sausage over the potatoes and pour over the egg mixture, spreading it evenly.
5. Top it with the cheese and bake for about 25 to 30 minutes.
6. Take out the sheet pan and slice it into squares before serving.

Serving Suggestion: Serve it alongside some greens.
Variation Tip: You can use any milk of your choice. You can omit cheddar cheese to make it dairy-free.
Nutritional Information Per Serving:
Calories: 179 | Fat: 1.7g | Sodium: 379.8mg | Carbs: 9.8g | Fiber: 1.3g | Sugar: 0.2g | Protein: 14.7g

Air Fryer Breakfast Cookies

Preparation Time: 20 minutes
Cooking Time: 10 minutes/batch
Servings: 2 to 4
Ingredients:
- 1 cup ripe bananas, mashed
- ½ cup chunky peanut butter
- ½ cup honey
- 1 teaspoon vanilla extract
- 1 cup old-fashioned oats
- ½ cup whole-wheat flour
- ¼ cup non-fat dry milk powder
- 2 teaspoons ground cinnamon
- ½ teaspoon salt
- ¼ teaspoon baking soda
- 1 cup dried cranberries or raisins

Preparation:
1. Select the AIR FRY function, 300°F, 10 minutes. Prepare the ingredients while the oven is preheating.
2. In a bowl, mix the honey, peanut butter, and vanilla.
3. Take another bowl, and mix the milk powder, salt, oats, cinnamon, baking soda. Then beat the banana into the mixture, gradually. Stir in the dried cranberries or raisins.
4. Drop the dough onto the air fryer basket on the sheet pan in ¼ cup leaving 2 inches apart. Flatten them to ½ inch thickness.
5. Cook the cookies for about 6 to 8 minutes. Leave them to rest for about 1 minute.

Serving Suggestion: Drizzle with a bit of honey before serving.
Variation Tip: You can try nutmeg or allspice instead of cinnamon.
Nutritional Information Per Serving:
Calories: 212 | Fat: 6g | Sodium: 168mg | Carbs: 38g | Fiber: 4g | Sugar: 25g | Protein: 5g

Air Fryer Candied Bacon

Preparation Time: 5 minutes
Cooking Time: 20 minutes
Servings: 4 to 5
Ingredients:
- 1 tablespoon butter
- ¼ cup white miso paste
- 6 tablespoons honey
- 1 tablespoon rice wine vinegar
- 8 ounces thick-cut bacon

Preparation:
1. Select the AIR FRY function, 390°F, for 20 minutes. While the oven is preheating, prepare the ingredients.
2. Take a small saucepan, and melt the butter in it over medium heat. Increase the heat up to medium-high and add the honey, miso paste, and rice wine vinegar. Stir to combine and bring the mixture to a boil. Remove the pan from the heat, then set it aside.
3. Place the bacon in the air fry basket and air fry, each side for 3 to 4 minutes.
4. Brush a thin layer of miso glaze over one side of the bacon and air fry for 1 more minute.

Serving Suggestion: Serve with sauce or mustard.
Variation Tip: You can use maple syrup instead of honey.
Nutritional Information Per Serving:
Calories: 131 | Fat: 9g | Sodium: 347mg | Carbs: 10g | Fiber: 0g | Sugar: 9g | Protein: 3g

Air Fryer Bacon Crescent Rolls

Preparation Time: 10 minutes
Cooking Time: 10 minutes/batch
Servings: 8
Ingredients:
- 8 ounces refrigerated crescent rolls
- 6 bacon strips, cooked and crumbled
- 1 teaspoon onion powder

Preparation:
1. Select the AIR FRY function, 300°F, for 10 minutes. While the oven is preheating, prepare the ingredients.
2. Unfurl the crescent dough and separate it into 8 triangles. Then set aside 1 tablespoon of the crumbled bacon.
3. Sprinkle the onion powder and remaining bacon over the triangles. Roll them up and sprinkle over with the reserved crumbled bacon. Then press lightly to adhere.
4. Take an ungreased sheet pan and arrange the rolls in a single layer on it, point side down. Put the sheet pan in the air fryer basket and cook for about 8 to 10 minutes.

Serving Suggestion: Serve alongside greens with sauce or mustard.
Variation Tip: Try garlic powder instead of onion powder.
Nutritional Information Per Serving:
Calories: 133 | Fat: 7g | Sodium: 322mg | Carbs: 12g | Fiber: 0g | Sugar: 3g | Protein: 4g

Air Fryer Cheesy Baked Eggs

Preparation Time: 5 minutes
Cooking Time: 16 minutes
Servings: 2
Ingredients:
- 4 large eggs
- 2 ounces smoked Gouda cheese, shredded
- Everything but the Bagel seasoning
- Kosher salt and pepper, to taste

Preparation:
1. Select the AIR FRY function, 400°F, for 16 minutes. While the oven is preheating, prepare the ingredients.
2. Take air fryer-proof ramekin cups and grease them with cooking spray.
3. Add 2 cracked each to each ramekin, and then add 1-ounce Gouda to each.
4. Next, add salt and pepper to taste and sprinkle with the seasoning.
5. Place the ramekins in the air fryer basket and cook for about 16 minutes.

Serving Suggestion: Sprinkle on a little salt and pepper and serve alongside some greens.
Variation Tip: You can try replacing the seasoning with dried onion flakes.
Nutritional Information Per Serving:
Calories: 240 | Fat: 16g | Sodium: 0mg | Carbs: 1g | Fiber: 0g | Sugar: 0g | Protein: 12g

Ube Glazed Air Fryer Donuts

Preparation Time: 5 minutes
Cooking Time: 6 minutes
Servings: 2 to 3
Ingredients:
- 1 cup powdered sugar
- 2 tablespoons milk
- ½ teaspoon Ube extract
- ¼ teaspoon vanilla extract
- 16.3-ounce Flaky Layers Original Biscuits

Preparation:
1. Select the AIR FRY function, 350°F, for 6 minutes. While the oven is preheating, prepare the ingredients.
2. Mix the milk, vanilla extract, Ube extract, and sugar in a bowl.
3. Take the biscuits and place them on a cutting board. With a 1 inch round cookie cutter, cut out the center hole of the donuts.
4. Spray the air fryer basket with a non-stick cooking spray. Place the donuts in the basket, cook for about 3 minutes, flip them over, and cook for another 2 to 3 minutes.
5. Once done, allow the donuts to cool down slightly. Then dip them in the Ube glaze and let them cool completely.

Serving Suggestion: You can serve the donuts with some cream.
Variation Tip: You can use any milk of your choice.
Nutritional Information Per Serving:
Calories: 236 | Fat: 6g | Sodium: 450 | Carbs: 27g | Fiber: 0g | Sugar: 18g | Protein: 4g

Puffed Egg Tarts

Preparation Time: 15 minutes.
Cooking Time: 21 minutes.
Servings: 4
Ingredients:
- ½ (17.3-ounce package) frozen puff pastry, thawed
- ¾ cup Cheddar cheese, shredded
- 4 large eggs
- 1 tablespoon fresh parsley, minced

Preparation:
1. Spread the pastry sheet on a floured surface and cut it into 4 squares of equal size.
2. Place the four squares in the sheet pan of the Ninja Foodi Digital Air Fry Oven.
3. Transfer the sheet to the Ninja Foodi Digital Air Fry Oven and close the door.
4. Select "Air Fry" mode by rotating the dial.
5. Press the TEMP/DARKNESS button and change the value to 300 degrees F.
6. Press the TIME/SLICE button and change the value to 10 minutes, then press Start/Pause to begin cooking.
7. Press the center of each pastry square using the back of a metal spoon.
8. Divide cheese into these indentations and crack one egg into each pastry.
9. Return to the oven and close its oven door.
10. Rotate the dial to select the "Air Fry" mode.
11. Press the TIME/SLICE button and again use the dial to set the cooking time to 11 minutes.
12. Now Press the TEMP/DARKNESS button and rotate the dial to set the temperature at 350 degrees F.
13. Garnish the squares with parsley.
14. Serve warm.
Serving Suggestion: Serve these tarts with crispy bacon on the side.
Variation Tip: Add crumbled bacon on top before baking.
Nutritional Information Per Serving:
Calories 305 | Fat 15g | Sodium 548mg | Carbs 26g | Fiber 2g | Sugar 1g | Protein 19g

Hard Boiled Eggs

Preparation Time: 5 minutes
Cooking Time: 12 minutes
Servings: 6
Ingredients:
- 6 eggs

Preparation:
1. Add the eggs in the air fry basket.
2. Turn on your Ninja Foodi Digital Air Fry Oven and rotate the knob to select "Air Fry".
3. Select the timer for 12 minutes and the temperature for 300 degrees F.
4. After the cooking time has been completed, immerse for 5 minutes in a bowl of icy water.
5. After that, peel and serve.
Serving Suggestions: Serve with bread.
Variation Tip: Sprinkle salt and pepper on top.
Nutritional Information per Serving:
Calories: 72 | Fat: 5g | Sat Fat: 2g | Carbohydrates: 80 | Fiber: 0g | Sugar: 0g | Protein: 6g

Hash Browns

Preparation Time: 5 minutes
Cooking Time: 5 minutes
Servings: 2
Ingredients:
- 4 hash brown patties
- Cooking oil spray

Preparation:
1. Coat the air fry basket with your preferred cooking oil spray.
2. Place the hash brown patties in the oven in an even layer.
3. Spray them with your favorite cooking oil spray.
4. Turn on your Ninja Foodi Digital Air Fry Oven and rotate the knob to select "Air Fry".
5. Select the timer for 5 minutes and the temperature for 390 degrees F.
6. Dish out and serve immediately.
Serving Suggestions: Serve with maple syrup.
Variation Tip: Sprinkle sugar on top.
Nutritional Information per Serving:
Calories: 64 | Fat: 19.1g | Sat Fat: 2.9g | Carbohydrates: 8g | Fiber: 1g | Sugar: 0g | Protein: 1g

Pumpkin Muffins

Preparation Time: 15 minutes.
Cooking Time: 15 minutes.
Servings: 6
Ingredients:
- 1 cup pumpkin puree
- 2 cups oats
- ½ cup honey
- 2 medium eggs, beaten
- 1 teaspoon coconut butter
- 1 tablespoon cocoa nibs
- 1 tablespoon vanilla essence
- 1 teaspoon nutmeg

Preparation:
1. Whisk all ingredients in a mixer until smooth.
2. Divide this pumpkin oat batter into a 12-cup muffin tray.
3. Transfer the tray to the Ninja Foodi Digital Air Fry Oven and close the door.
4. Select "Air Fry" mode by rotating the dial.
5. Press the TIME/SLICE button and change the value to 15 minutes.
6. Press the TEMP/DARKNESS button and change the value to 360 degrees F.
7. Press Start/Pause to begin cooking.
8. Serve fresh.
Serving Suggestion: Serve the pumpkin muffins with morning pudding.
Variation Tip: Add shredded pumpkin flesh for good texture.
Nutritional Information Per Serving:
Calories 234 | Fat 5.1g | Sodium 231mg | Carbs 46g | Fiber 5g | Sugar 2.1g | Protein 7g

German Pancake

Preparation Time: 5 minutes
Cooking Time: 30 minutes
Servings: 8
Ingredients:
- 6 large eggs
- 1 cup 2% milk
- 1 cup all-purpose flour
- ½ teaspoon salt
- 2 tablespoons butter, melted
- Powdered sugar, for serving

Buttermilk syrup:
- ½ cup butter
- 1½ cups sugar
- ¾ cup buttermilk
- 2 tablespoons corn syrup
- 1 teaspoon baking soda
- 2 teaspoons vanilla extract

Preparation:
1. Select the BAKE function, 400°F, for 30 minutes. While the oven is preheating, prepare the ingredients.
2. Put the eggs, 2% milk, flour, and salt in a blender and blend until smooth.
3. Pour the melted butter into a baking dish and coat the surface. Then add the batter and bake for about 20 minutes, uncovered.
4. Meanwhile, to make the buttermilk syrup, put the sugar, butter, corn syrup, buttermilk, and baking soda in a small saucepan, and bring to a boil.
5. Cook for about 7 minutes, then remove from the heat and stir in the vanilla extract.
6. Take out the pancake and sprinkle it with confectioners' sugar.

Serving Suggestion: Serve with syrup and fresh blueberries or strawberries.
Variation Tip: You can fill the pancake with sautéed fruit for a healthy spin.
Nutritional Information Per Serving:
Calories: 428 | Fat: 19g | Sodium: 543mg | Carbs: 56g | Fiber: 0g | Sugar: 42g | Protein: 8g

Egg in Hole

Preparation Time: 5 minutes
Cooking Time: 10 minutes
Servings: 1
Ingredients:
- 1 piece toast
- 1 egg
- Salt and pepper, to taste

Preparation:
1. Use nonstick cooking spray to spray your baking dish.
2. Place a piece of bread on the sheet pan.
3. Remove the bread by poking a hole in it with a cup or a cookie cutter.
4. Into the hole, crack the egg.
5. Turn on your Ninja Foodi Digital Air Fry Oven and rotate the knob to select "Air Fry".
6. Select the timer for 6 minutes and the temperature for 330 degrees F.
7. Dish out and sprinkle with salt and pepper to serve.

Serving Suggestions: Serve with toasted bacon.
Variation Tip: You can also add cheese on top.
Nutritional Information per Serving:
Calories: 136 | Fat: 6g | Sat Fat: 2g | Carbohydrates: 13g | Fiber: 1g | Sugar: 2g | Protein: 8g

Chapter 2 Snack and Appetizer Recipes

Crispy Avocado Fries

Preparation Time: 15 minutes
Cooking Time: 7 minutes
Servings: 2
Ingredients:
- ¼ cup all-purpose flour
- Salt and ground black pepper, as required
- 1 egg
- 1 teaspoon water
- ½ cup panko breadcrumbs
- 1 avocado, peeled, pitted, and sliced into 8 pieces
- Non-stick cooking spray

Preparation:
1. In a shallow bowl, mix the flour, salt, and black pepper together.
2. In a second bowl, mix well egg and water.
3. In a third bowl, put the breadcrumbs.
4. Coat the avocado slices with flour mixture, then dip into egg mixture and finally, coat evenly with the breadcrumbs.
5. Now, spray the avocado slices evenly with cooking spray.
6. Press "Power" button of Ninja Foodi Digital Air Fry Oven and turn the dial to select "Air Fry" mode.
7. Press TIME/SLICE button and again turn the dial to set the cooking time to 7 minutes.
8. Now push TEMP/DARKNESS button and rotate the dial to set the temperature at 400 degrees F.
9. Press "Start/Pause" button to start.
10. When the unit beeps to show that it is preheated, open the oven door.
11. Arrange the avocado fries into the air fry basket and insert in the oven.
12. When cooking time is completed, open the oven door and transfer the avocado fries onto a platter.
13. Serve warm.
Serving Suggestions: Serve with ketchup.
Variation Tip: Make sure to use firm avocados that are not too ripe.
Nutritional Information per Serving:
Calories: 391 | Fat: 23.8g | Sat Fat: 5.6g | Carbohydrates: 24.8g | Fiber: 7.3g | Sugar: 0.8g | Protein: 7g

Roasted Cashews

Preparation Time: 5 minutes
Cooking Time: 5 minutes
Servings: 6
Ingredients:
- 1½ cups raw cashew nuts
- 1 teaspoon butter, melted
- Salt and freshly ground black pepper, as required

Preparation:
1. In a bowl, mix all the ingredients together.
2. Press "Power" button of Ninja Foodi Digital Air Fry Oven and turn the dial to select "Air Fry" mode.
3. Press TIME/SLICE button and again turn the dial to set the cooking time to 5 minutes.

4. Now push TEMP/DARKNESS button and rotate the dial to set the temperature at 355 degrees F.
5. Press "Start/Pause" button to start.
6. When the unit beeps to show that it is preheated, open the oven door.
7. Arrange the cashews into the air fry basket and insert in the oven.
8. Shake the cashews once halfway through.
9. When cooking time is completed, open the oven door and transfer the cashews into a heatproof bowl.
10. Serve warm.
Serving Suggestions: Serve with a sprinkling of little salt.
Variation Tip: Make sure to use raw walnuts.
Nutritional Information per Serving:
Calories: 202 | Fat: 16.5g | Sat Fat: 3.5g | Carbohydrates: 11.2g | Fiber: 1g | Sugar: 1.7g | Protein: 5.3g

Beef Taquitos

Preparation Time: 15 minutes
Cooking Time: 8 minutes
Servings: 6
Ingredients:
- 6 corn tortillas
- 2 cups cooked beef, shredded
- ½ cup onion, chopped
- 1 cup pepper jack cheese, shredded
- Olive oil cooking spray

Preparation:
1. Arrange the tortillas onto a smooth surface.
2. Place the shredded meat over one corner of each tortilla, followed by onion and cheese.
3. Roll each tortilla to secure the filling and secure with toothpicks.
4. Spray each taquito with cooking spray evenly.
5. Arrange the taquitos onto the greased sheet pan.
6. Place the tofu mixture in the greased sheet pan.
7. Press "Power" button of Ninja Foodi Digital Air Fry Oven and turn the dial to select "Air Fry" mode.
8. Press TIME/SLICE button and again turn the dial to set the cooking time to 8 minutes.
9. Now push TEMP/DARKNESS button and rotate the dial to set the temperature at 400 degrees F.
10. Press "Start/Pause" button to start.
11. When the unit beeps to show that it is preheated, open the oven door and insert the sheet pan in oven.
12. When cooking time is completed, open the oven door and transfer the taquitos onto a platter.
13. Serve warm.
Serving Suggestions: Serve with yogurt dip.
Variation Tip: you can use any kind of cooked meat in this recipe.
Nutritional Information per Serving:
Calories: 228 | Fat: 9.6g | Sat Fat: 4.8g | Carbohydrates: 12.3g | Fiber: 1.7g | Sugar: 0.6g | Protein: 22.7g

Persimmon Chips

Preparation Time: 10 minutes
Cooking Time: 10 minutes
Servings: 2
Ingredients:
- 2 ripe persimmons, cut into slices horizontally
- Salt and ground black pepper, as required

Preparation:
1. Arrange the persimmons slices onto the greased sheet pan.
2. Press "Power" button of Ninja Foodi Digital Air Fry Oven and turn the dial to select "Air Fry" mode.
3. Press TIME/SLICE button and again turn the dial to set the cooking time to 10 minutes.
4. Now push TEMP/DARKNESS button and rotate the dial to set the temperature at 400 degrees F.
5. Press "Start/Pause" button to start.
6. When the unit beeps to show that it is preheated, open the oven door.
7. Insert the sheet pan in oven.
8. Flip the chips once halfway through.
9. When cooking time is completed, open the oven door and transfer the chips onto a platter.
10. Serve warm.

Serving Suggestions: Serve with a sprinkling of ground cinnamon.
Variation Tip: You can use these chips in a homemade trail mix.
Nutritional Information per Serving:
Calories: 32 | Fat: 0.1g | Sat Fat: 0g | Carbohydrates: 8.4g | Fiber: 0g | Sugar: 0g | Protein: 0.2g

Carrot Chips

Preparation Time: 15 minutes.
Cooking Time: 15 minutes.
Servings: 8
Ingredients:
- 2 pounds carrots, sliced
- ¼ cup olive oil
- 1 tablespoon sea salt
- 1 teaspoon ground cumin
- 1 teaspoon ground cinnamon

Preparation:
1. Toss the carrot slices with oil, sea salt, cumin, and cinnamon in a large bowl.
2. Grease the sheet pan and spread the carrot slices in it.
3. Transfer the sheet pan to the Ninja Foodi Digital Air Fry Oven and close the door.
4. Select "Bake" mode by rotating the dial.
5. Press the TIME/SLICE button and change the value to 15 minutes.
6. Press the TEMP/DARKNESS button and change the value to 450 degrees F.
7. Press Start/Pause to begin cooking.
8. Flip the chips after 7-8 minutes of cooking and resume baking.
9. Serve fresh.

Serving Suggestion: Serve the chips with tomato ketchup or cheese dip.
Variation Tip: Toss the carrot chips with maple-honey syrup to coat.
Nutritional Information Per Serving:
Calories 182 | Fat 2g | Sodium 350mg | Carbs 12.2g | Fiber 0.7g | Sugar 1g | Protein 4.3g

Potato Chips

Preparation Time: 15 minutes.
Cooking Time: 25 minutes.
Servings: 2
Ingredients:
- 1 medium Russet potato, sliced
- 1 tablespoon canola oil
- ¼ teaspoon sea salt
- ¼ teaspoon black pepper
- 1 teaspoon chopped fresh rosemary

Preparation:
1. Fill a suitable glass bowl with cold water and add sliced potatoes.
2. Leave the potatoes for 20 minutes, then drain them. Pat dry the chips with a paper towel.
3. Toss the potatoes with salt, black pepper, and oil to coat well.
4. Spread the potato slices in the air fry basket evenly.
5. Transfer the basket to the Ninja Foodi Digital Air Fry Oven and close the door.
6. Select "Air Fry" mode by rotating the dial.
7. Press the TIME/SLICE button and change the value to 25 minutes.
8. Press the TEMP/DARKNESS button and change the value to 375 degrees F.
9. Press Start/Pause to begin cooking.
10. Garnish with rosemary.
11. Serve warm.

Serving Suggestion: Serve the chips with tomato sauce.
Variation Tip: Toss the potato chips with paprika.
Nutritional Information Per Serving:
Calories 134 | Fat 3g | Sodium 216mg | Carbs 27g | Fiber 3g | Sugar 4g | Protein 1g

Corn on the Cob

Preparation Time: 5 minutes
Cooking Time: 13 minutes
Servings: 2
Ingredients:
- 2 ears corn
- 2 tablespoons butter, melted
- ½ teaspoon dried parsley
- ¼ teaspoon sea salt
- 2 tablespoons parmesan cheese, shredded

Preparation:
1. Remove any silk from both ears of corn. If desired, cut corns in half.
2. In a mixing dish, combine melted butter, parsley, and sea salt. Using a pastry brush, evenly coat the corn. If used, wrap corn with foil.
3. Place corn inside the sheet pan side by side.
4. Place it inside the oven.
5. Turn on Ninja Foodi Digital Air Fry Oven and rotate the knob to select "Air Roast".
6. Select the timer for 12 minutes and the temperature for 350 degrees F.
7. Remove from the Ninja Foodi Digital Air Fry Oven to serve hot.

Serving Suggestions: Top with fresh parsley.
Variation Tip: You can use any cheese.
Nutritional Information per Serving:
Calories: 199 | Fat: 14g | Sat Fat: 8g | Carbohydrates: 17g | Fiber: 2g | Sugar: 4g | Protein: 5g

Air Fryer Ravioli

Preparation Time: 5 minutes
Cooking Time: 10 minutes
Servings: 2
Ingredients:
- 12 frozen ravioli
- ½ cup buttermilk
- ½ cup Italian breadcrumbs
- Cooking oil

Preparation:
1. Place two bowls next to each other. In one, put the buttermilk, and in the other, put the breadcrumbs.
2. Dip Each ravioli piece in buttermilk and then breadcrumbs, making sure it is well coated.
3. Place each breaded ravioli in a single layer in the air fry basket and spritz the tops halfway through with oil.
4. Place it inside the oven.
5. Turn on Ninja Foodi Digital Air Fry Oven and rotate the knob to select "Air Fry".
6. Select the timer for 7 minutes and the temperature for 400 degrees F.
7. Remove from the Ninja Foodi Digital Air Fry Oven to serve hot.
Serving Suggestions: Top with fresh parsley.
Variation Tip: You can serve with garlic sauce.
Nutritional Information per Serving:
Calories: 481 | Fat: 20g | Sat Fat: 7g | Carbohydrates: 56g | Fiber: 4g | Sugar: 9g | Protein: 20g

Sweet Potato Fries

Preparation Time: 10 minutes
Cooking Time: 15 minutes
Servings: 4
Ingredients:
- 3 sweet potatoes, cut into fries
- 2 tablespoons olive oil
- ½ teaspoon salt
- ¼ teaspoon black pepper
- ½ teaspoon garlic powder

Preparation:
1. Slice sweet potatoes into 1/2-1/4 inch-thick French fry slices.
2. Using olive oil cooking spray, lightly coat the air fry basket.
3. Pour the olive oil, salt, pepper, paprika, and garlic powder over the sweet potatoes in a mixing bowl.
4. To coat them, combine them thoroughly.
5. Place each sweet potato fry in the basket in a uniform layer.
6. Place inside the oven.
7. Turn on Ninja Foodi Digital Air Fry Oven and rotate the knob to select "Air Broil".
8. Select the unit for 12 minutes at LO.
9. Serve immediately after cooking.
Serving Suggestions: Serve with favorite dipping sauce.
Variation Tip: Sprinkle fresh parsley on top.
Nutritional Information per Serving:
Calories: 230 | Fat: 11 | Sat Fat: 2g | Carbohydrates: 30g | Fiber: 4g | Sugar: 6g | Protein: 3g

Pasta Chips

Preparation Time: 15 minutes.
Cooking Time: 10 minutes.
Servings: 4
Ingredients:
- ½ tablespoon olive oil
- ½ tablespoon nutritional yeast
- 1 cup bow tie pasta
- ⅔ teaspoon Italian Seasoning Blend
- ¼ teaspoon salt

Preparation:
1. Cook and boil the pasta in salted water in half of the time as stated on the box, then drain it.
2. Toss the boiled pasta with salt, Italian seasoning, nutritional yeast, and olive oil in a bowl.
3. Spread this pasta in the air fry basket.
4. Transfer the basket to the Ninja Foodi Digital Air Fry Oven and close the door.
5. Select "Air Fry" mode by rotating the dial.
6. Press the TIME/SLICE button and change the value to 5 minutes.
7. Press the TEMP/DARKNESS button and change the value to 390 degrees F.
8. Press Start/Pause to begin cooking.
9. Toss the pasta and continue air frying for another 5 minutes.
10. Enjoy.
Serving Suggestion: Serve the chips with white cheese dip.
Variation Tip: Drizzle white peppers ground on top before baking.
Nutritional Information Per Serving:
Calories 167 | Fat 2g | Sodium 48mg | Carbs 26g | Fiber 2g | Sugar 0g | Protein 1g

Avocado Fries

Preparation Time: 15 minutes.
Cooking Time: 20 minutes.
Servings: 4
Ingredients:
- ½ cup panko breadcrumbs
- ½ teaspoon salt
- 1 avocado, peeled, pitted, and sliced
- 1 cup egg, whisked

Preparation:
1. Toss breadcrumbs with salt in a shallow bowl.
2. First, dip the avocado strips in the egg, then coat them with panko.
3. Spread these slices in the air fry basket.
4. Transfer the sandwich to the Ninja Foodi Digital Air Fry Oven and close the door.
5. Select "Bake" mode by rotating the dial.
6. Press the TIME/SLICE button and change the value to 20 minutes.
7. Press the TEMP/DARKNESS button and change the value to 400 degrees F.
8. Press Start/Pause to begin cooking.
9. Serve fresh.
Serving Suggestion: Serve the fries with chili sauce or mayonnaise dip.
Variation Tip: Coat the fries with crushed cornflakes for more crisp.
Nutritional Information Per Serving:
Calories 110 | Fat 9g | Sodium 318mg | Carbs 19g | Fiber 5g | Sugar 3g | Protein 7g

Fiesta Chicken Fingers

Preparation Time: 15 minutes.
Cooking Time: 12 minutes.
Servings: 4
Ingredients:
• ¾ pound boneless chicken breasts, cut into strips
• ½ cup buttermilk
• ¼ teaspoon pepper
• 1 cup all-purpose flour
• 3 cups corn chips, crushed
• 1 envelope taco seasoning
For Serving:
• Sour cream ranch dip or Fresh salsa
Preparation:
1. Coat the chicken with pepper and flour.
2. Mix corn chips with taco seasoning.
3. Dip the chicken fingers in the buttermilk, then coat with the corn chips.
4. Place the chicken fingers in the air fry basket and spray with cooking oil.
5. Transfer the basket to the Ninja Foodi Digital Air Fry Oven and close the door.
6. Select "Air Fry" mode by rotating the dial.
7. Press the TIME/SLICE button and change the value to 12 minutes.
8. Press the TEMP/DARKNESS button and change the value to 325 degrees F.
9. Press Start/Pause to begin cooking.
10. Flip the Chicken fingers once cooked halfway through, then resume cooking.
11. Serve warm with sour cream ranch dip or fresh salsa.
Serving Suggestion: Serve the chicken fingers with chili garlic sauce.
Variation Tip: Use mayonnaise to coat the fingers for a rich taste.
Nutritional Information Per Serving:
Calories 218 | Fat 12g | Sodium 710mg | Carbs 44g | Fiber 5g | Sugar 3g | Protein 24g

Zucchini Chips

Preparation Time: 10 minutes
Cooking Time: 13 minutes
Servings: 6
Ingredients:
• 2 large zucchinis, sliced
• ¾ cup panko bread crumbs
• 1 teaspoon Old bay
• 1 teaspoon garlic salt
• 1 egg, beaten
• Olive oil spray
Preparation:
1. Combine the Panko and seasoning on a dish and stir well.
2. In a separate bowl, whisk the egg.
3. Dip zucchini slices in the egg one at a time, then coat with the bread crumb mixture on all sides.
4. Using olive oil cooking spray, lightly coat the air fry basket. Place the zucchini in the air fry basket gently.
5. Turn on Ninja Foodi Digital Air Fry Oven and rotate the knob to select "Air Fry".
6. Select the timer for 13 minutes and the temperature for 350 degrees F.
7. Remove and enjoy immediately.

Serving Suggestions: Serve with any sauce.
Variation Tip: You can skip old bay and use pepper.
Nutritional Information per Serving:
Calories: 41 | Fat: 1g | Sat Fat: 1g | Carbohydrates: 6g | Fiber: 1g | Sugar: 1g | Protein: 2g

French Toast Bites

Preparation Time: 5 minutes
Cooking Time: 10 minutes
Servings: 2
Ingredients:
• ½ loaf of brioche bread
• 3 eggs
• 1 tablespoon milk
• 1 teaspoon vanilla
• ½ teaspoon cinnamon
Preparation:
1. In a large mixing bowl, cut half a loaf of bread into cubes.
2. Combine the eggs, milk, vanilla, and cinnamon in a small mixing dish.
3. Pour the mixture over the slices and toss to coat.
4. In greased air fry basket, arrange bread slices in a single layer.
5. Place inside the oven.
6. Turn on Ninja Foodi Digital Air Fry Oven and rotate the knob to select "Air Fry".
7. Select the timer for 10 minutes and the temperature for 390 degrees F.
8. Remove from the Ninja Foodi Digital Air Fry Oven to serve.
Serving Suggestions: Top with maple syrup.
Variation Tip: Sprinkle sugar on top before placing it in the oven.
Nutritional Information per Serving:
Calories: 107 | Fat: 6.8g | Sat Fat: 2.1g | Carbohydrates: 1.9g | Fiber: 0.3g | Sugar: 1.1g | Protein: 8.6g

Air Fryer Blueberry Bread

Preparation Time: 5 minutes
Cooking Time: 30 minutes
Servings: 2 to 4
Ingredients:
• 1 cup milk
• 3 cups all-purpose baking mix
• ¼ cup protein powder
• 3 eggs
• 1½ cups frozen blueberries
Preparation:
1. Select the AIR FRY function, 350°F, for 30 minutes. While the oven is preheating, prepare the ingredients.
2. Mix the milk, baking mix, protein powder, eggs, and blueberries in a large bowl.
3. Empty the mixture into a greased loaf pan and air fry for about 30 minutes.
Serving Suggestion: Drizzle on a little honey before serving.
Variation Tip: You can try using Greek yogurt instead of protein powder.
Nutritional Information Per Serving:
Calories: 140 | Fat: 5g | Sodium: 333mg | Carbs: 18g | Fiber: 17g | Sugar: 1g | Protein: 5g

Crispy Prawns

Preparation Time: 15 minutes
Cooking Time: 8 minutes
Servings: 4
Ingredients:
- 1 egg
- ½ pound nacho chips, crushed
- 12 prawns, peeled and deveined

Preparation:
1. In a shallow dish, beat the egg.
2. In another shallow dish, place the crushed nacho chips.
3. Coat the prawn with the beaten egg and then roll into nacho chips.
4. Press "Power" button of Ninja Foodi Digital Air Fry Oven and turn the dial to select "Air Fry" mode.
5. Press TIME/SLICE button and again turn the dial to set the cooking time to 8 minutes.
6. Now push TEMP/DARKNESS button and rotate the dial to set the temperature at 355 degrees F.
7. Press "Start/Pause" button to start.
8. When the unit beeps to show that it is preheated, open the oven door.
9. Arrange the prawns into the air fry basket and insert in the oven.
10. When cooking time is completed, open the oven door and serve immediately.

Serving Suggestions: Serve alongside your favorite dip.
Variation Tip: Make sure to pat dry the shrimp thoroughly before applying the coating.
Nutritional Information per Serving:
Calories: 386 | Fat: 17g | Sat Fat: 2.9g | Carbohydrates: 36.1g | Fiber: 2.6g | Sugar: 2.2g | Protein: 21g

Potato Croquettes

Preparation Time: 15 minutes
Cooking Time: 8 minutes
Servings: 4
Ingredients:
- 2 medium Russet potatoes, peeled and cubed
- 2 tablespoons all-purpose flour
- ½ cup Parmesan cheese, grated
- 1 egg yolk
- 2 tablespoons fresh chives, minced
- Pinch of ground nutmeg
- Salt and freshly ground black pepper, as needed
- 2 eggs
- ½ cup breadcrumbs
- 2 tablespoons vegetable oil

Preparation:
1. In a pan of a boiling water, add the potatoes and cook for about 15 minutes.
2. Drain the potatoes well and transfer into a large bowl.
3. With a potato masher, mash the potatoes and set aside to cool completely.
4. In the bowl of mashed potatoes, add the flour, Parmesan cheese, egg yolk, chives, nutmeg, salt, and black pepper and mix until well combined.
5. Make small equal-sized balls from the mixture.
6. Now, roll each ball into a cylinder shape.

7. In a shallow dish, crack the eggs and beat well.
8. In another dish, mix together the breadcrumbs and oil.
9. Dip the croquettes in egg mixture and then coat with the breadcrumbs mixture.
10. Press "Power" button of Ninja Foodi Digital Air Fry Oven and turn the dial to select "Air Fry" mode.
11. Press TIME/SLICE button and again turn the dial to set the cooking time to 8 minutes.
12. Now push TEMP/DARKNESS button and rotate the dial to set the temperature at 390 degrees F.
13. Press "Start/Pause" button to start.
14. When the unit beeps to show that it is preheated, open the oven door.
15. Arrange the croquettes in air fry basket and insert in the oven.
16. When cooking time is completed, open the oven door and transfer the croquettes onto a platter.
17. Serve warm.

Serving Suggestions: Serve with mustard sauce.
Variation Tip: Make sure to use dried breadcrumbs.
Nutritional Information per Serving:
Calories: 283 | Fat: 13.4g | Sat Fat: 3.8g | Carbohydrates: 29.9g | Fiber: 3.3g | Sugar: 2.3g | Protein: 11.5g

Tofu Nuggets

Preparation Time: 10 minutes
Cooking Time: 15 minutes
Servings: 4
Ingredients:
- 400g extra firm tofu
- ⅓ cup nutritional yeast
- ¼ cup water
- 1 tablespoon garlic powder
- 1 teaspoon onion powder
- 1 teaspoon sweet paprika
- 1 teaspoon poultry spice

Preparation:
1. Press the tofu for 10 minutes.
2. Add all ingredients to a bowl and stir to combine.
3. Over the bowl, break the tofu into bite-sized chunks. Use your thumb to create rough, rounded edges as you go.
4. Fold the chunks into the paste gently, taking care not to break the tofu.
5. Place the tofu in air fry basket in a single layer.
6. Turn on Ninja Foodi Digital Air Fry Oven and rotate the knob to select "Air Fry".
7. Select the timer for 15 minutes and the temperature for 350 degrees F.
8. Halfway through, pause and shake the basket. Serve immediately or save for later.

Serving Suggestions: Serve with any sauce.
Variation Tip: You can use black pepper instead of paprika.
Nutritional Information per Serving:
Calories: 83 | Fat: 2g | Sat Fat: 1g | Carbohydrates: 6g | Fiber: 2g | Sugar: 1g | Protein: 11g

Cod Nuggets

Preparation Time: 15 minutes
Cooking Time: 8 minutes
Servings: 5
Ingredients:
- 1 cup all-purpose flour
- 2 eggs
- ¾ cup breadcrumbs
- Pinch of salt
- 2 tablespoons olive oil
- 1 pound cod, cut into 1x2½-inch strips

Preparation:
1. In a shallow dish, place the flour.
2. Crack the eggs in a second dish and beat well.
3. In a third dish, mix together the breadcrumbs, salt and oil.
4. Coat the nuggets with flour, then dip into beaten eggs and finally, coat with the breadcrumbs.
5. Press "Power" button of Ninja Foodi Digital Air Fry Oven and turn the dial to select "Air Fry" mode.
6. Press TIME/SLICE button and again turn the dial to set the cooking time to 8 minutes.
7. Now push TEMP/DARKNESS button and rotate the dial to set the temperature at 390 degrees F.
8. Press "Start/Pause" button to start.
9. When the unit beeps to show that it is preheated, open the oven door.
10. Arrange the nuggets in air fry basket and insert in the oven.
11. When cooking time is completed, open the oven door and transfer the nuggets onto a platter.
12. Serve warm.

Serving Suggestions: Enjoy with tartar sauce.
Variation Tip: Use fresh fish.
Nutritional Information per Serving:
Calories: 323 | Fat: 9.2g | Sat Fat: 1.7g | Carbohydrates: 30.9g | Fiber: 1.4g | Sugar: 1.2g | Protein: 27.7g

Pumpkin Fries

Preparation Time: 15 minutes.
Cooking Time: 12 minutes.
Servings: 6
Ingredients:
- ½ cup plain Greek yogurt
- 2 tablespoons maple syrup
- 3 teaspoons chipotle peppers in adobo sauce, minced
- ⅛ teaspoon salt
- 1 medium pie pumpkin
- ¼ teaspoon garlic powder
- ¼ teaspoon ground cumin
- ¼ teaspoon chili powder
- ¼ teaspoon pepper

Preparation:
1. Peel and cut the pumpkin into sticks.
2. Mix garlic powder, cumin, chili powder, salt, and black pepper.
3. Coat the pumpkin sticks with the spice mixture.
4. Spread the pumpkin fries in the air fry basket and spray them with cooking spray.

5. Transfer the basket to the Ninja Foodi Digital Air Fry Oven and close the door.
6. Select "Air Fry" mode by rotating the dial.
7. Press the TIME/SLICE button and change the value to 12 minutes.
8. Press the TEMP/DARKNESS button and change the value to 400 degrees F.
9. Press Start/Pause to begin cooking.
10. Toss the fries once cooked halfway through, then resume cooking.
11. Mix yogurt with maple syrup and adobo sauce in a bowl.
12. Serve fries with the sauce.

Serving Suggestion: Serve the pumpkin chips with tomato ketchup.
Variation Tip: Coat the pumpkin fries with breadcrumbs before cooking.
Nutritional Information Per Serving:
Calories 215 | Fat 16g | Sodium 255mg | Carbs 31g | Fiber 1.2g | Sugar 5g | Protein 4.1g

Air Fryer Pop-Tarts

Preparation Time: 10 minutes
Cooking Time: 11 minutes
Servings: 6
Ingredients:
- 1 (15-ounce) package refrigerated pie crust
- 6 tablespoons grape jelly
- 2 cups powdered sugar
- 2 to 4 tablespoons heavy cream
- 2 tablespoons butter, melted
- 1 teaspoon vanilla extract
- Sprinkles, as required

Preparation:
1. Select the AIR FRY function, 350°F, for 11 minutes. While the oven is preheating, prepare the ingredients.
2. Cut out 12 equal-size rectangles from the pie crust.
3. Place 1 tablespoon of grape jelly in the center of 6 of the rectangles. Spread out the jelly to within ¼ inch of the edge. Moisten the outside using your fingers and some water.
4. Then, place the plain rectangles on top of the jelly rectangles, and press the edges together with a fork.
5. Use a knife to poke a few slits in the top of each pop-tart.
6. Spray the air fryer basket with cooking spray and cook 2 pop-tarts in it at a time.
7. Take out the pop tarts and let them cool completely.
8. To make the icing, mix the powdered sugar, heavy cream, butter, and vanilla extract in a bowl until smooth. Spread over the cooled pop-tarts and then decorate with sprinkles.
9. Let the icing harden in the refrigerator before serving.

Serving Suggestion: Drizzle on some honey along with the sprinkles.
Variation Tip: You can use strawberry jam instead.
Nutritional Information Per Serving:
Calories: 219 | Fat: 11g | Sodium: 174mg | Carbs: 26g | Fiber: 1g | Sugar: 9g | Protein: 3g

Baked Potatoes

Preparation Time: 15 minutes.
Cooking Time: 45 minutes.
Servings: 3
Ingredients:
- 3 russet potatoes, scrubbed and rinsed
- Cooking spray
- ½ teaspoon sea salt
- ½ teaspoon garlic powder

Preparation:
1. Rub the potatoes with salt and garlic powder.
2. Place the potatoes in the air fry basket and spray with cooking spray.
3. Transfer the basket to the Ninja Foodi Digital Air Fry Oven and close the door.
4. Select the "Bake" mode by rotating the dial.
5. Press the TIME/SLICE button and change the value to 45 minutes.
6. Press the TEMP/DARKNESS button and change the value to 350 degrees F.
7. Press Start/Pause to begin cooking.
8. Make a slit on top of potatoes and score the flesh inside.
9. Serve warm.

Serving Suggestion: Serve the baked potatoes with butter sauce or mayo dip.
Variation Tip: Add shredded cheese and crumbled bacon to the toppings.
Nutritional Information Per Serving:
Calories 269 | Fat 5g | Sodium 510mg | Carbs 37g | Fiber 5g | Sugar 4g | Protein 1g

Potato Bread Rolls

Preparation Time: 20 minutes
Cooking Time: 33 minutes
Servings: 8
Ingredients:
- 5 large potatoes, peeled
- 2 tablespoons vegetable oil, divided
- 2 small onions, finely chopped
- 2 green chilies, seeded and chopped
- 2 curry leaves
- ½ teaspoon ground turmeric
- Salt, as required
- 8 bread slices, trimmed

Preparation:
1. In a pan of boiling water, add the potatoes and cook for about 15-20 minutes.
2. Drain the potatoes well and with a potato masher, mash the potatoes.
3. In a skillet, heat 1 teaspoon of oil over medium heat and sauté the onion for about 4-5 minutes.
4. Add the green chilies, curry leaves, and turmeric and sauté for about 1 minute.
5. Add the mashed potatoes and salt and mix well.
6. Remove from the heat and set aside to cool completely.
7. Make 8 equal-sized oval-shaped patties from the mixture.
8. Wet the bread slices completely with water.
9. Press each bread slice between your hands to remove the excess water.
10. Place 1 bread slice in your palm and place 1 patty in the center of the bread.
11. Roll the bread slice in a spindle shape and seal the edges to secure the filling.
12. Coat the roll with some oil.
13. Repeat with the remaining slices, filling and oil.
14. Press "Power" button of Ninja Foodi Digital Air Fry Oven and turn the dial to select "Air Fry" mode.
15. Press TIME/SLICE button and again turn the dial to set the cooking time to 13 minutes.
16. Now push TEMP/DARKNESS button and rotate the dial to set the temperature at 390 degrees F.
17. Press "Start/Pause" button to start.
18. When the unit beeps to show that it is preheated, open the oven door.
19. Arrange the bread rolls into the air fry basket and insert in the oven.
20. When cooking time is completed, open the oven door and transfer the rolls onto a platter.
21. Serve warm.

Serving Suggestions: Serve alongside the ketchup.
Variation Tip: Remove the moisture from bread slices completely.
Nutritional Information per Serving:
Calories: 222 | Fat: 4g | Sat Fat: 0.8g | Carbohydrates: 42.5g | Fiber: 6.2g | Sugar: 3.8g | Protein: 4.8g

Air Fryer Sweet Potato Tots

Preparation Time: 20 minutes
Cooking Time: 1 hour
Servings: 4
Ingredients:
- 14 ounces sweet potatoes, peeled
- 1 tablespoon potato starch
- ⅛ teaspoon garlic powder
- 1¼ teaspoons kosher salt
- ¾ cup no-salt-added ketchup
- Cooking spray

Preparation:
1. Take a medium pot of water and boil it over high heat. Add the potatoes and cook for about 15 minutes. Transfer the potatoes to a plate and let them cool for about 15 minutes.
2. Using the large holes of a box grater, grate the potatoes into a medium bowl. Gently toss them with the potato starch, 1 teaspoon salt, and garlic powder. Then, shape the mixture into tot-shaped cylinders.
3. Select the AIR FRY function, 400°F, for 14 minutes.
4. Coat the air fryer basket with cooking spray. Lay half of the tots in the air fryer basket in a single layer and spray with more cooking spray.
5. Cook the tots for about 12 to 14 minutes, turning them halfway through the cooking time. Repeat the same with the remaining tots.

Serving Suggestion: Sprinkle with salt and serve with ketchup.
Variation Tip: You can try cumin or chives instead of garlic powder.
Nutritional Information Per Serving:
Calories: 78 | Fat: 0g | Sodium: 335mg | Carbs: 19g | Fiber: 2g | Sugar: 2g | Protein: 1g

Air Fried Buffalo Cauliflower Bites

Preparation Time: 10 minutes
Cooking Time: 40 minutes
Servings: 4
Ingredients:
- 3 tablespoons no-salt-added ketchup
- 2 tablespoons hot sauce
- 1 large egg white
- ¾ cup panko
- 3 pounds cauliflower head, cut into florets
- Cooking spray
- ¼ cup reduced-fat sour cream
- 1 tablespoon blue cheese, crumbled
- 1 small garlic clove, grated
- 1 teaspoon red wine vinegar
- ¼ teaspoon black pepper

Preparation:
1. Select the AIR FRY function, 320°F, for 20 minutes. While the oven is preheating, prepare the ingredients.
2. Take a large bowl and whisk together the hot sauce, ketchup, and egg white.
3. Add the cauliflower florets and coat well. Add the panko and coat the florets.
4. Coat the cauliflower with cooking spray and place them in an even layer in the air fryer basket. You'll need to cook in batches.
5. Meanwhile, mix the blue cheese, vinegar, sour cream, garlic, and pepper in a small bowl.
6. Serve the cauliflower bites with the mixed sauce.

Serving Suggestion: Serve with the blue cheese sauce.
Variation Tip: You can try tamarind paste instead of red wine vinegar.
Nutritional Information Per Serving:
Calories: 125 | Fat: 4g | Sodium: 255mg | Carbs: 17g | Fiber: 1g | Sugar: 1g | Protein: 5g

Loaded Potatoes

Preparation Time: 10 minutes
Cooking Time: 25 minutes
Servings: 2
Ingredients:
- 11 ounces baby Yukon Gold potatoes
- 1 teaspoon olive oil
- 2 center-cut bacon slices
- 1½ tablespoons fresh chives, chopped
- 2 tablespoons reduced-fat cheddar cheese, shredded
- 2 tablespoons reduced-fat sour cream
- ⅛ teaspoon kosher salt

Preparation:
1. Select the AIR FRY function, 350°F, for 25 minutes.
2. While the oven is preheating, coat the potatoes with the oil, then transfer them to the air fryer basket. Cook for about 25 minutes, occasionally stirring.
3. Meanwhile, cook the bacon over medium heat in a skillet for about 7 minutes. Remove the bacon and crumble it.
4. Transfer the cooked potatoes to a serving platter and lightly crush them to split.
5. Top with the bacon crumbs, cheese, salt, chives, and sour cream.

Serving Suggestion: Serve with a side salad.
Variation Tip: You can try the recipe with Gouda instead of cheddar cheese.
Nutritional Information Per Serving:
Calories: 199 | Fat: 7g | Sodium: 287mg | Carbs: 26g | Fiber: 4g | Sugar: 3g | Protein: 7g

Salt and Vinegar Cucumber Chips

Preparation Time: 10 minutes
Cooking Time: 3 to 4 hours
Servings: 6
Ingredients:
- 2 medium cucumbers
- 1 tablespoon olive oil
- 1 teaspoon salt
- 2 teaspoons apple cider vinegar

Preparation:
1. Slice the cucumbers very thin. Pat dry the slices with power towels to remove their moisture.
2. Transfer the slices to a large bowl and add the olive oil, apple cider vinegar, and salt. Gently toss to combine.
3. Select the DEHYDRATE function on the oven and dehydrate the cucumber slices for about 3 to 4 hours at 175°F.

Serving Suggestion: Serve with sour cream or mayo.
Variation Tip: You can use white wine vinegar instead of apple cider vinegar.
Nutritional Information Per Serving:
Calories: 29 | Fat: 2g | Sodium: 389mg | Carbs: 1g | Fiber: 1 | Sugar: 1g | Protein: 1g

Tortilla Chips

Preparation Time: 10 minutes
Cooking Time: 3 minutes
Servings: 3
Ingredients:
- 4 corn tortillas, cut into triangles
- 1 tablespoon olive oil
- Salt, to taste

Preparation:
1. Coat the tortilla chips with oil and then sprinkle each side of the tortillas with salt.
2. Press "Power" button of Ninja Foodi Digital Air Fry Oven and turn the dial to select "Air Fry" mode.
3. Press TIME/SLICE button and again turn the dial to set the cooking time to 3 minutes.
4. Now push TEMP/DARKNESS button and rotate the dial to set the temperature at 390 degrees F.
5. Press "Start/Pause" button to start.
6. When the unit beeps to show that it is preheated, open the oven door.
7. Arrange the tortilla chips in air fry basket and insert in the oven.
8. When cooking time is completed, open the oven door and transfer the tortilla chips onto a platter.
9. Serve warm.

Serving Suggestions: Serve with guacamole.
Variation Tip: Use whole grain tortillas.
Nutritional Information per Serving:
Calories: 110 | Fat: 5.6g | Sat Fat: 0.8g | Carbohydrates: 14.3g | Fiber: 2g | Sugar: 0.3g | Protein: 1.8g

Vegan Dehydrated Cookies

Preparation Time: 10 minutes
Cooking Time: 6 hours
Servings: 5 to 8
Ingredients:
- 2 apples
- 4 tablespoons flax seeds
- 1 teaspoon ground cinnamon
- ½ cup almonds
- ½ cup dates
- 4 cups oats

Preparation:
1. Firstly, wash, core, and chop the apples.
2. Place all the ingredients, except the oats, into a food processor and blend for a few seconds.
3. Take a large mixing bowl and place the blended mixture in it, then add 2 cups of oats and blend again. Add the remaining oats and mix with a spoon or your hands.
4. Make the dough into cookies, put them in the air fryer basket and place the basket in the oven.
5. Select the DEHYDRATE function, 115°F, for 6 hours. Turn the cookies over after 4 hours.
Serving Suggestion: Sprinkle some flax seeds on the cookies before serving.
Variation Tip: You can use nutmeg or allspice instead of cinnamon.
Nutritional Information Per Serving:
Calories: 72 | Fat: 1.8g | Sodium: 1mg | Carbs: 12.3g | Fiber: 2g | Sugar: 3.6 | Protein: 2g

Dehydrated Strawberries

Preparation Time: 10 minutes
Cooking Time: 4 hours
Servings: 2
Ingredients:
- 2 cups strawberries, quartered and sliced

Preparation:
1. Select the DEHYDRATE function. Preheat the unit to 195°F.
2. Line the sheet pan with parchment paper. Place the cut strawberries on the baking sheet, cut side up. Place them with some distance in between.
3. Cook for about 2 hours, then flip the strawberries and cook for another 2 hours.
Serving Suggestion: You can serve with almond cream.
Variation Tip: Drizzle some honey over the strawberries.
Nutritional Information Per Serving:
Calories: 53 | Fat: 0.5g | Sodium: 0mg | Carbs: 13g | Fiber: 3g | Sugar: 8g | Protein: 1g

Beet Chips

Preparation Time: 10 minutes
Cooking Time: 15 minutes
Servings: 6
Ingredients:
- 4 medium beetroots, peeled and thinly sliced
- 2 tablespoons olive oil
- ¼ teaspoon smoked paprika
- Salt, to taste

Preparation:
1. In a large bowl and mix all the ingredients together.

2. Press "Power" button of Ninja Foodi Digital Air Fry Oven and turn the dial to select "Air Fry" mode.
3. Press TIME/SLICE button and again turn the dial to set the cooking time to 15 minutes.
4. Now push TEMP/DARKNESS button and rotate the dial to set the temperature at 325 degrees F.
5. Press "Start/Pause" button to start.
6. When the unit beeps to show that it is preheated, open the oven door.
7. Arrange the beet chips into the air fry basket and insert in the oven.
8. Toss the beet chips once halfway through.
9. When cooking time is completed, open the oven door and transfer the beet chips onto a platter.
10. Serve at room temperature.
Serving Suggestions: Serve with a sprinkling of cinnamon.
Variation Tip: For a beautiful presentation, use colorful beets.
Nutritional Information per Serving:
Calories: 70 | Fat: 4.8g | Sat Fat: 0.7g | Carbohydrates: 6.7g | Fiber: 1.4g | Sugar: 5.3g | Protein: 1.1g

Baked Eggplant Sticks

Preparation Time: 10 minutes
Cooking Time: 15 minutes
Servings: 4
Ingredients:
- 10 ounces eggplant, cut into strips
- 1 teaspoon olive oil
- ½ teaspoon kosher salt
- Fresh cracked pepper, to taste
- ½ cup Italian seasoned breadcrumbs
- 2 tablespoons parmesan cheese, grated
- 1 large egg white
- Olive oil spray

Preparation:
1. Select the BAKE function, 450°F, for 15 minutes. While the oven is preheating, prepare the sheet pan with parchment paper and prepare the ingredients.
2. Season the eggplant strips with salt, pepper, and olive oil. Set them aside.
3. Take a bowl and combine the parmesan cheese with the breadcrumbs. Add the egg white to another bowl.
4. Dip the eggplant strips into the egg white and then into the breadcrumb mixture. Place the eggplant strips on the prepared sheet pan. You may need to cook in batches.
5. Spray with more oil, bake for about 10 minutes, turn over, and bake for another 5 minutes.
Serving Suggestion: Serve with marinara sauce.
Variation Tip: You can use gluten-free breadcrumbs for a gluten-free meal.
Nutritional Information Per Serving:
Calories: 87 | Fat: 3g | Sodium: 441mg | Carbs: 12g | Fiber: 2.3g | Sugar: 1g | Protein: 4.5g

Bacon-Wrapped Filled Jalapeno

Preparation Time: 10 minutes
Cooking Time: 15 minutes
Servings: 6
Ingredients:
- 12 jalapenos
- 226g cream cheese
- ½ cup cheddar cheese, shredded
- ¼ teaspoon garlic powder
- ⅛ teaspoon onion powder
- 12 slices bacon, thinly cut
- Salt and pepper, to taste

Preparation:
1. Discard the seeds from the jalapenos by cutting them in half and removing the stems.
2. Combine cream cheese, shredded cheddar cheese, garlic powder, onion powder, salt, and pepper. To blend, stir everything together.
3. Fill each jalapeno just to the top with the cream mixture using a tiny spoon.
4. Turn on Ninja Foodi Digital Air Fry Oven and rotate the knob to select "Bake".
5. Preheat by selecting the timer for 1 minute and temperature for 350 degrees F. Press START/PAUSE to begin.
6. Cut each slice of bacon in half.
7. Wrap one piece of bacon around each half of a jalapeño.
8. In the sheet pan, arrange the bacon-wrapped filled jalapenos in an even layer.
9. Now select the timer for 15 minutes and temperature for 350 degrees F.
10. Serve and enjoy!

Serving Suggestions: Serve with ketchup.
Variation Tip: You can also sprinkle black pepper on top.
Nutritional Information per Serving:
Calories: 188 | Fat: 17g | Sat Fat: 10g | Carbohydrates: 4g | Fiber: 1g | Sugar: 3g | Protein: 5g

Baked Mozzarella Sticks

Preparation Time: 5 minutes
Cooking Time: 8 minutes
Servings: 6
Ingredients:
- ½ cup Italian Style bread crumbs
- ¾ cup panko break crumbs
- ¼ cup parmesan cheese
- 1 tablespoon garlic powder
- 12 mozzarella cheese sticks
- Cooking spray

Preparation:
1. Make mozzarella sticks by freezing them for an hour or two. Take the mozzarella sticks out of the fridge and cut them in half so that each one is 2-3 inches long.
2. Combine the Panko, Italian Style bread crumbs, parmesan cheese, and garlic powder on a dish and stir well.
3. Whisk together the eggs in a separate bowl.
4. Cover the mozzarella stick completely with egg with a fork, then dip and totally cover the mozzarella stick in the breadcrumb mixture.
5. On a nonstick pan, arrange mozzarella sticks in a single layer.

6. Freeze for an hour and take the mozzarella sticks out of the freezer and dip them in the egg and breadcrumb mixture once more.
7. Using cooking spray, lightly coat the sheet pan. Place the cheese sticks.
8. Turn on Ninja Foodi Digital Air Fry Oven and rotate the knob to select "Bake".
9. Select the timer for 10 minutes and the temperature for 360 degrees F.
10. Remove and serve.

Serving Suggestions: Serve with marinara sauce.
Variation Tip: You can use any cheese sticks.
Nutritional Information per Serving:
Calories: 130 | Fat: 8g | Sat Fat: 4g | Carbohydrates: 7g | Fiber: 1g | Sugar: 1g | Protein: 9g

Risotto Bites

Preparation Time: 15 minutes
Cooking Time: 10 minutes
Servings: 4
Ingredients:
- 1½ cups cooked risotto
- 3 tablespoons Parmesan cheese, grated
- ½ egg, beaten
- 1½ ounces mozzarella cheese, cubed
- ⅓ cup breadcrumbs

Preparation:
1. In a bowl, add the risotto, Parmesan and egg and mix until well combined.
2. Make 20 equal-sized balls from the mixture.
3. Insert a mozzarella cube in the center of each ball.
4. With your fingers smooth the risotto mixture to cover the ball.
5. In a shallow dish, place the breadcrumbs.
6. Coat the balls with the breadcrumbs evenly.
7. Press "Power" button of Ninja Foodi Digital Air Fry Oven and turn the dial to select "Air Fry" mode.
8. Press TIME/SLICE button and again turn the dial to set the cooking time to 10 minutes.
9. Now push TEMP/DARKNESS button and rotate the dial to set the temperature at 390 degrees F.
10. Press "Start/Pause" button to start.
11. When the unit beeps to show that it is preheated, open the oven door.
12. Arrange the balls into the air fry basket and insert in the oven.
13. When cooking time is completed, open the oven door and transfer the risotto bites onto a platter.
14. Serve warm.

Serving Suggestions: Serve with blue cheese dip.
Variation Tip: Make sure to use dry breadcrumbs.
Nutritional Information per Serving:
Calories: 340 | Fat: 4.3g | Sat Fat: 2g | Carbohydrates: 62.4g | Fiber: 1.3g | Sugar: 0.7g | Protein: 11.3g

Zucchini Fries

Preparation Time: 10 minutes
Cooking Time: 12 minutes
Servings: 4
Ingredients:
- 1 pound zucchini, sliced into 2½-inch sticks
- Salt, as required
- 2 tablespoons olive oil
- ¾ cup panko breadcrumbs

Preparation:
1. In a colander, add the zucchini and sprinkle with salt. Set aside for about 10 minutes.
2. Gently pat dry the zucchini sticks with the paper towels and coat with oil.
3. In a shallow dish, add the breadcrumbs.
4. Coat the zucchini sticks with breadcrumbs evenly.
5. Press "Power" button of Ninja Foodi Digital Air Fry Oven and turn the dial to select "Air Fry" mode.
6. Press TIME/SLICE button and again turn the dial to set the cooking time to 12 minutes.
7. Now push TEMP/DARKNESS button and rotate the dial to set the temperature at 400 degrees F.
8. Press "Start/Pause" button to start.
9. When the unit beeps to show that it is preheated, open the oven door.
10. Arrange the zucchini fries in air fry basket and insert in the oven.
11. When cooking time is completed, open the oven door and transfer the zucchini fries onto a platter.
12. Serve warm.
Serving Suggestions: Serve with ketchup.
Variation Tip: You can use breadcrumbs of your choice.
Nutritional Information per Serving:
Calories: 151 | Fat: 8.6g | Sat Fat: 1.6g | Carbohydrates: 6.9g | Fiber: 1.3g | Sugar: 2g | Protein: 1.9g

Cheesy Broccoli Bites

Preparation Time: 15 minutes
Cooking Time: 12 minutes
Servings: 5
Ingredients:
- 1 cup broccoli florets
- 1 egg, beaten
- ¾ cup cheddar cheese, grated
- 2 tablespoons Parmesan cheese, grated
- ¾ cup panko breadcrumbs
- Salt and freshly ground black pepper, as needed

Preparation:
1. In a food processor, add the broccoli and pulse until finely crumbled.
2. In a large bowl, mix together the broccoli and remaining ingredients.
3. Make small equal-sized balls from the mixture.
4. Press "Power" button of Ninja Foodi Digital Air Fry Oven and turn the dial to select "Air Fry" mode.
5. Press TIME/SLICE button and again turn the dial to set the cooking time to 12 minutes.

6. Now push TEMP/DARKNESS button and rotate the dial to set the temperature at 350 degrees F.
7. Press "Start/Pause" button to start.
8. When the unit beeps to show that it is preheated, open the oven door.
9. Arrange the broccoli balls into the air fry basket and insert in the oven.
10. When cooking time is completed, open the oven door and transfer the broccoli bites onto a platter.
11. Serve warm.
Serving Suggestions: Serve with your favorite dipping sauce.
Variation Tip: You can use cheese of your choice.
Nutritional Information per Serving:
Calories: 153 | Fat: .2g | Sat Fat: 4.5g | Carbohydrates: 4g | Fiber: 0.5g | Sugar: 0.5g | Protein: 7.1g

Glazed Chicken Wings

Preparation Time: 15 minutes
Cooking Time: 25 minutes
Servings: 4
Ingredients:
- 1½ pounds chicken wingettes and drumettes
- ⅓ cup tomato sauce
- 2 tablespoons balsamic vinegar
- 2 tablespoons maple syrup
- ½ teaspoon liquid smoke
- ¼ teaspoon red pepper flakes, crushed
- Salt, as required

Preparation:
1. Arrange the wings onto the greased sheet pan.
2. Press "Power" button of Ninja Foodi Digital Air Fry Oven and turn the dial to select "Air Fry" mode.
3. Press TIME/SLICE button and again turn the dial to set the cooking time to 25 minutes.
4. Now push TEMP/DARKNESS button and rotate the dial to set the temperature at 380 degrees F.
5. Press "Start/Pause" button to start.
6. When the unit beeps to show that it is preheated, open the oven door and insert the sheet pan in oven.
7. Meanwhile, in a small pan, add the remaining ingredients over medium heat and cook for about 10 minutes, stirring occasionally.
8. When cooking time is completed, open the oven door and place the chicken wings into a bowl.
9. Add the sauce and toss to coat well.
10. Serve immediately.
Serving Suggestions: Serve with your favorite dip.
Variation Tip: Honey can replace the maple syrup.
Nutritional Information per Serving:
Calories: 356 | Fat: 12.7g | Sat Fat: 3.5g | Carbohydrates: 7.9g | Fiber: 0.3g | Sugar: 6.9g | Protein: 49.5g

Air Fried Chicken Wings

Preparation Time: 10 minutes
Cooking Time: 30 minutes
Servings: 2
Ingredients:
- 10 chicken drumettes
- Cooking spray
- 1 tablespoon lower-sodium soy sauce
- ½ teaspoon cornstarch
- 2 teaspoons honey
- 1 teaspoon ground chili paste
- 1 teaspoon garlic, finely chopped
- ½ teaspoon fresh ginger, grated and finely chopped
- 1 teaspoon fresh lime juice
- ⅛ teaspoon kosher salt
- 2 tablespoon scallions, chopped

Preparation:
1. Pat the chicken dry and coat it well with cooking spray. Select the AIR FRY function, 400°F, for 25 minutes. Allow the oven to preheat.
2. Put the chicken drumettes in the air fryer basket and turn them halfway through the cooking time.
3. Take a small skillet and whisk together the cornstarch and soy sauce. Next, add the honey, chili paste, lime juice, ginger, garlic, and salt. Place the skillet over medium heat and bring the mixture to a simmer.
4. Place the chicken in a bowl, add the sauce, toss to coat, and sprinkle with the scallions.

Serving Suggestion: Serve with a side salad.
Variation Tip: You can use coconut aminos instead of soy sauce.
Nutritional Information Per Serving:
Calories: 304 | Fat: 19g | Sodium: 556mg | Carbs: 8g | Fiber: 0g | Sugar: 6g | Protein: 23g

Spicy Spinach Chips

Preparation Time: 10 minutes
Cooking Time: 10 minutes
Servings: 4
Ingredients:
- 2 cups fresh spinach leaves, torn into bite-sized pieces
- ½ tablespoon coconut oil, melted
- ⅛ teaspoon garlic powder
- Salt, as required

Preparation:
1. In a large bowl and mix together all the ingredients.
2. Arrange the spinach pieces onto the greased sheet pan.
3. Press "Power" button of Ninja Foodi Digital Air Fry Oven and turn the dial to select "Air Fry" mode.
4. Press TIME/SLICE button and again turn the dial to set the cooking time to 10 minutes.
5. Now push TEMP/DARKNESS button and rotate the dial to set the temperature at 300 degrees F.
6. Press "Start/Pause" button to start.
7. When the unit beeps to show that it is preheated, open the oven door.
8. Insert the sheet pan in oven.
9. Toss the spinach chips once halfway through.
10. When cooking time is completed, open the oven door and transfer the spinach chips onto a platter.
11. Serve warm.

Serving Suggestions: Serve with a sprinkling of cayenne pepper.
Variation Tip: Make sure to pat dry the spinach leaves before using.
Nutritional Information per Serving:
Calories: 18 | Fat: 1.5g | Sat Fat: 0g | Carbohydrates: 0.5g | Fiber: 0.3g | Sugar: 0.1g | Protein: 0.5g

Chicken & Parmesan Nuggets

Preparation Time: 15 minutes
Cooking Time: 10 minutes
Servings: 6
Ingredients:
- 2 large chicken breasts, cut into 1-inch cubes
- 1 cup breadcrumbs
- ⅓ tablespoon Parmesan cheese, shredded
- 1 teaspoon onion powder
- ¼ teaspoon smoked paprika
- Salt and ground black pepper, as required

Preparation:
1. In a large resealable bag, add all the ingredients.
2. Seal the bag and shake well to coat completely.
3. Press "Power" button of Ninja Foodi Digital Air Fry Oven and turn the dial to select "Air Fry" mode.
4. Press TIME/SLICE button and again turn the dial to set the cooking time to 10 minutes.
5. Now push TEMP/DARKNESS button and rotate the dial to set the temperature at 400 degrees F.
6. Press "Start/Pause" button to start.
7. When the unit beeps to show that it is preheated, open the oven door.
8. Arrange the nuggets into the air fry basket and insert in the oven.
9. When cooking time is completed, open the oven door and transfer the nuggets onto a platter.
10. Serve warm.

Serving Suggestions: Serve with mustard sauce.
Variation Tip: Prefer to use freshly grated cheese.
Nutritional Information per Serving:
Calories: 218 | Fat: 6.6g | Sat Fat: 1.8g | Carbohydrates: 13.3g | Fiber: 0.9g | Sugar: 1.3g | Protein: 24.4g

Onion Rings

Preparation Time: 15 minutes.
Cooking Time: 15 minutes.
Servings: 4
Ingredients:
- ½ cup all-purpose flour
- 1 teaspoon paprika
- 1 teaspoon salt, divided
- ½ cup buttermilk
- 1 egg
- 1 cup panko breadcrumbs
- 2 tablespoons olive oil
- 1 large yellow sweet onion, sliced ½-inch-thick rings

Preparation:
1. Mix flour with paprika and salt on a plate.
2. Coat the onion rings with the flour mixture.
3. Beat egg with buttermilk in a bowl. Dip all the onion rings with the egg mixture.
4. Spread the breadcrumbs in a bowl.
5. Coat the onion rings with breadcrumbs.
6. Place the onion rings in the air fry basket and spray them with cooking oil.
7. Transfer the basket to the Ninja Foodi Digital Air Fry Oven and close the door.
8. Select "Air Fry" mode by rotating the dial.
9. Press the TEMP/DARKNESS button and change the value to 400 degrees F.
10. Press the TIME/SLICE button and change the value to 15 minutes, then press Start/Pause to begin cooking.
11. Serve warm.
Serving Suggestion: Serve the onion rings with chili sauce or mayo dip.
Variation Tip: Coat the onion rings with parmesan cheese.
Nutritional Information Per Serving:
Calories 106 | Fat 5g | Sodium 244mg | Carbs 16g | Fiber 1g | Sugar 1g | Protein 7g

Eggplant Fries

Preparation Time: 15 minutes.
Cooking Time: 10 minutes.
Servings: 4
Ingredients:
- 2 large eggs
- ½ cup grated Parmesan cheese
- ½ cup toasted wheat germ
- 1 teaspoon Italian seasoning
- ¾ teaspoon garlic salt
- 1 (1¼-pound) eggplant, peeled
- Cooking spray
- 1 cup meatless pasta sauce, warmed

Preparation:
1. Cut the eggplant into sticks.
2. Mix parmesan cheese, wheat germ, seasoning, and garlic salt in a bowl.
3. Coat the eggplant sticks with the parmesan mixture.
4. Place the eggplant fries in the air fry basket and spray them with cooking spray.
5. Transfer the basket to the Ninja Foodi Digital Air Fry Oven and close the door.
6. Select "Air Fry" mode by rotating the dial.
7. Press the TIME/SLICE button and change the value to 10 minutes.
8. Press the TEMP/DARKNESS button and change the value to 375 degrees F.
9. Press Start/Pause to begin cooking.
10. Serve warm with marinara sauce.
Serving Suggestion: Serve the eggplant fries with tomato sauce.
Variation Tip: Drizzle paprika on top for more spice.
Nutritional Information Per Serving:
Calories 201 | Fat 7g | Sodium 269mg | Carbs 35g | Fiber 4g | Sugar 12g | Protein 6g

Cauliflower Poppers

Preparation Time: 10 minutes
Cooking Time: 20 minutes
Servings: 6
Ingredients:
- 3 tablespoons olive oil
- 1 teaspoon paprika
- ½ teaspoon ground cumin
- ¼ teaspoon ground turmeric
- Salt and ground black pepper, as required
- 1 medium head cauliflower, cut into florets

Preparation:
1. In a bowl, place all ingredients and toss to coat well.
2. Place the cauliflower mixture in the greased sheet pan.
3. Press "Power" button of Ninja Foodi Digital Air Fry Oven and turn the dial to select the "Bake" mode.
4. Press TIME/SLICE button and again turn the dial to set the cooking time to 20 minutes.
5. Now push TEMP/DARKNESS button and rotate the dial to set the temperature at 450 degrees F.
6. Press "Start/Pause" button to start.
7. When the unit beeps to show that it is preheated, open the oven door and insert the sheet pan in oven.
8. Flip the cauliflower mixture once halfway through.
9. When cooking time is completed, open the oven door and transfer the cauliflower poppers onto a platter.
10. Serve warm.
Serving Suggestions: Serve with a squeeze of lemon juice.
Variation Tip: Feel free to use spices of your choice.
Nutritional Information per Serving:
Calories: 73 | Fat: 7.1g | Sat Fat: 1g | Carbohydrates: 2.7g | Fiber: 1.3g | Sugar: 1.1g | Protein: 1g

Chapter 3 Vegetable & Sides Recipes

Sweet & Spicy Parsnips

Preparation Time: 15 minutes
Cooking Time: 44 minutes
Servings: 5
Ingredients:
- 1½ pounds parsnip, peeled and cut into 1-inch chunks
- 1 tablespoon butter, melted
- 2 tablespoons honey
- 1 tablespoon dried parsley flakes, crushed
- ¼ teaspoon red pepper flakes, crushed
- Salt and ground black pepper, as required

Preparation:
1. In a large bowl, mix together the parsnips and butter.
2. Press "Power" button of Ninja Foodi Digital Air Fry Oven and turn the dial to select "Air Fry" mode.
3. Press TIME/SLICE button and again turn the dial to set the cooking time to 44 minutes.
4. Now push TEMP/DARKNESS button and rotate the dial to set the temperature at 355 degrees F.
5. Press "Start/Pause" button to start.
6. When the unit beeps to show that it is preheated, open the oven door.
7. Arrange the parsnip chunks into the greased air fry basket and insert in the oven.
8. Meanwhile, in another large bowl, mix together the remaining ingredients.
9. After 40 minutes of cooking, press "Start/Pause" button to pause the unit.
10. Transfer the parsnip chunks into the bowl of honey mixture and toss to coat well.
11. Again, arrange the parsnip chunks into the air fry basket and insert in the oven.
12. When cooking time is completed, open the oven door and serve hot.
Serving Suggestions: Serve with garlic bread.
Variation Tip: Make sure to cut the parsnip into uniform-sized chunks.
Nutritional Information per Serving:
Calories: 149 | Fat: 2.7g | Sat Fat: 1.5g | Carbohydrates: 31.5g | Fiber: 6.7g | Sugar: 13.5g | Protein: 1.7g

Cauliflower in Buffalo Sauce

Preparation Time: 10 minutes
Cooking Time: 12 minutes
Servings: 4
Ingredients:
- 1 large head cauliflower, cut into bite-size florets
- 1 tablespoon olive oil
- 2 teaspoons garlic powder
- Salt and ground black pepper, as required
- ⅔ cup warm buffalo sauce

Preparation:
1. In a large bowl, add cauliflower florets, olive oil, garlic powder, salt and pepper and toss to coat.
2. Press "Power" button of Ninja Foodi Digital Air Fry Oven and turn the dial to select "Air Fry" mode.
3. Press TIME/SLICE button and again turn the dial to set the cooking time to 12 minutes.
4. Now push TEMP/DARKNESS button and rotate the dial to set the temperature at 375 degrees F.
5. Press "Start/Pause" button to start.
6. When the unit beeps to show that it is preheated, open the oven door.
7. Arrange the cauliflower florets in the air fry basket and insert in the oven.
8. After 7 minutes of cooking, coat the cauliflower florets with buffalo sauce.
9. When cooking time is completed, open the oven door and serve hot.
Serving Suggestions: Serve with the garnishing of scallions.
Variation Tip: Use best quality buffalo sauce.
Nutritional Information per Serving:
Calories: 183 | Fat: 17.1g | Sat Fat: 4.3g | Carbohydrates: 5.9g | Fiber: 1.8g | Sugar: 1.0g | Protein: 1.6g

Beans & Veggie Burgers

Preparation Time: 15 minutes
Cooking Time: 22 minutes
Servings: 4
Ingredients:
- 1 cup cooked black beans
- 2 cups boiled potatoes, peeled, and mashed
- 1 cup fresh spinach, chopped
- 1 cup fresh mushrooms, chopped
- 2 teaspoons Chile lime seasoning
- Olive oil cooking spray

Preparation:
1. In a large bowl, add the beans, potatoes, spinach, mushrooms, and seasoning and with your hands, mix until well combined.
2. Make 4 equal-sized patties from the mixture.
3. Spray the patties with cooking spray evenly.
4. Press "Power" button of Ninja Foodi Digital Air Fry Oven and turn the dial to select "Air Fry" mode.
5. Press TIME/SLICE button and again turn the dial to set the cooking time to 22 minutes.
6. Now push TEMP/DARKNESS button and rotate the dial to set the temperature at 370 degrees F.
7. Press "Start/Pause" button to start.
8. When the unit beeps to show that it is preheated, open the oven door.
9. Arrange the patties in the greased air fry basket and insert in the oven.
10. Flip the patties once after 12 minutes.
11. When cooking time is completed, open the oven door and remove the air fry basket from the oven.
Serving Suggestions: Serve with avocado and tomato salad.
Variation Tip: Feel free to add seasoning of your choice.
Nutritional Information per Serving:
Calories: 113 | Fat: 0.4g | Sat Fat: 0g | Carbohydrates:23.1g | Fiber: 6.2g | Sugar: 1.7g | Protein: 6g

Stuffed Eggplants

Preparation Time: 20 minutes
Cooking Time: 11 minutes
Servings: 4
Ingredients:
- 4 small eggplants, halved lengthwise
- 1 teaspoon fresh lime juice
- 1 teaspoon vegetable oil
- 1 small onion, chopped
- ¼ teaspoon garlic, chopped
- ½ of small tomato, chopped
- Salt and ground black pepper, as required
- 1 tablespoon cottage cheese, chopped
- ¼ of green bell pepper, seeded and chopped
- 1 tablespoon tomato paste
- 1 tablespoon fresh cilantro, chopped

Preparation:
1. Carefully cut a slice from one side of each eggplant lengthwise.
2. With a small spoon, scoop out the flesh from each eggplant, leaving a thick shell.
3. Transfer the eggplant flesh into a bowl.
4. Drizzle the eggplants with lime juice evenly.
5. Press "Power" button of Ninja Foodi Digital Air Fry Oven and turn the dial to select "Air Fry" mode.
6. Press TIME/SLICE button and again turn the dial to set the cooking time to 3 minutes.
7. Now push TEMP/DARKNESS button and rotate the dial to set the temperature at 320 degrees F.
8. Press "Start/Pause" button to start.
9. When the unit beeps to show that it is preheated, open the oven door.
10. Arrange the hollowed eggplants into the greased air fry basket and insert in the oven.
11. Meanwhile, in a skillet, heat the oil over medium heat and sauté the onion and garlic for about 2 minutes.
12. Add the eggplant flesh, tomato, salt, and black pepper and sauté for about 2 minutes.
13. Stir in the cheese, bell pepper, tomato paste, and cilantro and cook for about 1 minute.
14. Remove the pan of the veggie mixture from heat.
15. When the cooking time is completed, open the oven door and arrange the cooked eggplants onto a plate.
16. Stuff each eggplant with the veggie mixture.
17. Close each with its cut part.
18. Again arrange the eggplants shells into the greased air fry basket and insert into the oven.
19. Press "Power" button of Ninja Foodi Digital Air Fry Oven and turn the dial to select "Air Fry" mode.
20. Press TIME/SLICE button and again turn the dial to set the cooking time to 8 minutes.
21. Now push TEMP/DARKNESS button and rotate the dial to set the temperature at 320 degrees F.
22. Press "Start/Pause" button to start.
23. When cooking time is completed, open the oven door and transfer the eggplants onto serving plates.
24. Serve hot.

Serving Suggestions: Serve with the topping f feta cheese.

Variation Tip: Clean the eggplant by running under cold running water.
Nutritional Information per Serving:
Calories: 131 | Fat: 2g | Sat Fat: 0.3g | Carbohydrates: 27.8g | Fiber: 5.3g | Sugar: 4.3g | Protein: 5.1g

Vegetable Casserole

Preparation Time: 15 minutes.
Cooking Time: 42 minutes.
Servings: 6
Ingredients:
- 2 cups peas
- 8 ounces mushrooms, sliced
- 4 tablespoons all-purpose flour
- 1 ½ cups celery, sliced
- 1 ½ cups carrots, sliced
- ½ teaspoon mustard powder
- 2 cups milk
- Salt and black pepper, to taste
- 7 tablespoons butter
- 1 cup breadcrumbs
- ½ cup Parmesan cheese, grated

Preparation:
1. Grease and rub a casserole dish with butter and keep it aside.
2. Add carrots, onion, and celery to a saucepan, then fill it with water.
3. Cover this pot and cook for 10 minutes, then stir in peas.
4. Cook for 4 minutes, then strain the vegetables.
5. Now melt 1 tablespoon of butter in the same saucepan and toss in mushrooms to sauté.
6. Once the mushrooms are soft, transfer them to the vegetables.
7. Prepare the sauce by melting 4 tablespoons of butter in a suitable saucepan.
8. Stir in mustard and flour, then stir cook for 2 minutes.
9. Gradually pour in the milk and stir cook until thickened, then add salt and black pepper.
10. Add vegetables and mushrooms to the flour milk mixture and mix well.
11. Spread this vegetable blend in the casserole dish evenly.
12. Toss the breadcrumbs with the remaining butter and spread it on top of vegetables.
13. Top this casserole dish with cheese.
14. Transfer the dish to the Ninja Foodi Digital Air Fry Oven and close the door.
15. Select "Air Fry" mode by rotating the dial.
16. Press the TIME/SLICE button and change the value to 25 minutes.
17. Press the TEMP/DARKNESS button and change the value to 350 degrees F.
18. Press Start/Pause to begin cooking.
19. Serve warm.

Serving Suggestion: Serve the vegetable casserole with a tortilla.
Variation Tip: Add broccoli florets to the mixture and then cook.
Nutritional Information Per Serving:
Calories 338 | Fat 24g | Sodium 620mg | Carbs 18.3g | Fiber 2.4g | Sugar 1.2g | Protein 5.4g

Broccoli Casserole

Preparation Time: 15 minutes.
Cooking Time: 45 minutes.
Servings: 6
Ingredients:
- 1 cup mayonnaise
- 10 ½ ounces cream of celery soup
- 2 large eggs, beaten
- 20 ounces chopped broccoli
- 2 tablespoons onion, minced
- 1 cup Cheddar cheese, grated
- 1 tablespoon Worcestershire sauce
- 1 teaspoon seasoned salt
- Black pepper, to taste
- 2 tablespoons butter

Preparation:
1. Whisk mayonnaise with eggs, condensed soup in a large bowl.
2. Stir in salt, black pepper, Worcestershire sauce, and cheddar cheese.
3. Spread broccoli and onion in a greased casserole dish.
4. Top the veggies with the mayonnaise mixture.
5. Transfer this broccoli casserole to the Ninja Foodi Digital Air Fry Oven and close its oven door.
6. Rotate the Ninja Foodi dial to select the "Bake" mode.
7. Press the TIME/SLICE button and again use the dial to set the cooking time to 45 minutes.
8. Now Press the TEMP/DARKNESS button and rotate the dial to set the temperature at 350 degrees F.
9. Slice and serve warm.

Serving Suggestion: Serve the broccoli casserole with spaghetti or any other pasta.
Variation Tip: Top the casserole with a pepperoni slice before cooking.
Nutritional Information Per Serving:
Calories 341 | Fat 24g | Sodium 547mg | Carbs 26.4g | Fiber 1.2g | Sugar 1g | Protein 10.3g

Brussels Sprouts Gratin

Preparation Time: 15 minutes.
Cooking Time: 35 minutes.
Servings: 6
Ingredients:
- 1 pound Brussels sprouts
- 1 garlic clove, cut in half
- 3 tablespoons butter, divided
- 2 tablespoons shallots, minced
- 2 tablespoons all-purpose flour
- Kosher salt, to taste
- Freshly ground black pepper
- 1 dash ground nutmeg
- 1 cup milk
- ½ cup fontina cheese, shredded
- 1 strip of bacon, cooked and crumbled
- ½ cup fine bread crumbs

Preparation:
1. Trim the Brussels sprouts and remove their outer leaves.
2. Slice the sprouts into quarters, then rinse them under cold water.
3. Grease a gratin dish with cooking spray and rub it with garlic halves.
4. Boil salted water in a suitable pan, then add Brussels sprouts.
5. Cook the sprouts for 3 minutes, then immediately drain.
6. Place a suitable saucepan over medium-low heat and melt 2 tablespoons of butter in it.
7. Toss in shallots and sauté until soft, then stir in flour, nutmeg, ½ teaspoons of salt, and black pepper.
8. Stir cook for 2 minutes, then gradually add milk and a half and half cream.
9. Mix well and add bacon along with shredded cheese.
10. Fold in Brussels sprouts and transfer this mixture to the casserole dish.
11. Toss breadcrumbs with 1 tablespoon butter and spread over the casserole.
12. Transfer the gratin to the Ninja Foodi Digital Air Fry Oven and close the door.
13. Select "Bake" mode by rotating the dial.
14. Press the TIME/SLICE button and change the value to 25 minutes.
15. Press the TEMP/DARKNESS button and change the value to 350 degrees F.
16. Press Start/Pause to begin cooking.
17. Enjoy!

Serving Suggestion: Serve the gratin with mashed potatoes.
Variation Tip: Add crushed crackers on top for a crunchy taste.
Nutritional Information Per Serving:
Calories 378 | Fat 3.8g | Sodium 620mg | Carbs 33.3g | Fiber 2.4g | Sugar 1.2g | Protein 14g

Asparagus with Garlic and Parmesan

Preparation Time: 5 minutes
Cooking Time: 10 minutes
Servings: 4
Ingredients:
- 1 bundle asparagus
- 1 teaspoon olive oil
- ⅛ teaspoon garlic salt
- 1 tablespoon parmesan cheese
- Pepper to taste

Preparation:
1. Clean the asparagus and dry it. To remove the woody stalks, cut 1 inch off the bottom.
2. In a sheet pan, arrange asparagus in a single layer and spray with oil.
3. On top of the asparagus, evenly sprinkle garlic salt. Season with salt and pepper, then sprinkle with Parmesan cheese.
4. Turn on Ninja Foodi Digital Air Fry Oven and rotate the knob to select "Air Fry".
5. Select the timer for 10 minutes and the temperature for 350 degrees F.
6. Enjoy right away.

Serving Suggestions: Sprinkle more parmesan cheese before serving.
Variation Tip: You can also sprinkle some paprika.
Nutritional Information per Serving:
Calories: 18 | Fat: 2g | Sat Fat: 1g | Carbohydrates: 1g | Fiber: 0g | Sugar: 0g | Protein: 1g

Broccoli with Cauliflower

Preparation Time: 15 minutes
Cooking Time: 20 minutes
Servings: 4
Ingredients:
- 1½ cups broccoli, cut into 1-inch pieces
- 1½ cups cauliflower, cut into 1-inch pieces
- 1 tablespoon olive oil
- Salt, as required

Preparation:
1. In a bowl, add the vegetables, oil, and salt and toss to coat well.
2. Press "Power" button of Ninja Foodi Digital Air Fry Oven and turn the dial to select "Air Fry" mode.
3. Press TIME/SLICE button and again turn the dial to set the cooking time to 20 minutes.
4. Now push TEMP/DARKNESS button and rotate the dial to set the temperature at 375 degrees F.
5. Press "Start/Pause" button to start.
6. When the unit beeps to show that it is preheated, open the oven door.
7. Arrange the veggie mixture into the greased air fry basket and insert in the oven.
8. When cooking time is completed, open the oven door and serve hot.
Serving Suggestions: Serve with the drizzling of lemon juice.
Variation Tip: You can add spices according to your taste.
Nutritional Information per Serving:
Calories: 51 | Fat: 3.7g | Sat Fat: 0.5g | Carbohydrates: 4.3g | Fiber: 1.8g | Sugar: 1.5g | Protein: 1.7g

Veggie Rice

Preparation Time: 15 minutes
Cooking Time: 18 minutes
Servings: 2
Ingredients:
- 2 cups cooked white rice
- 1 tablespoon vegetable oil
- 2 teaspoons sesame oil, toasted and divided
- 1 tablespoon water
- Salt and ground white pepper, as required
- 1 large egg, lightly beaten
- ½ cup frozen peas, thawed
- ½ cup frozen carrots, thawed
- 1 teaspoon soy sauce
- 1 teaspoon Sriracha sauce
- ½ teaspoon sesame seeds, toasted

Preparation:
1. In a large bowl, add the rice, vegetable oil, one teaspoon of sesame oil, water, salt, and white pepper and mix well.
2. Transfer rice mixture into a lightly greased sheet pan.
3. Press "Power" button of Ninja Foodi Digital Air Fry Oven and turn the dial to select "Air Fry" mode.
4. Press TIME/SLICE button and again turn the dial to set the cooking time to 18 minutes.
5. Now push TEMP/DARKNESS button and rotate the dial to set the temperature at 380 degrees F.
6. Press "Start/Pause" button to start.
7. When the unit beeps to show that it is preheated, open the oven door.
8. Place the pan over the wire rack and insert in the oven.
9. While cooking, stir the mixture once after 12 minutes.
10. After 12 minutes of cooking, press "Start/Pause" to pause cooking.
11. Remove the pan from oven and place the beaten egg over rice.
12. Again, insert the pan in the oven and press "Start/Pause" to resume cooking.
13. After 16 minutes of cooking, press "Start/Pause" to pause cooking.
14. Remove the pan from and stir in the peas and carrots.
15. Again, insert the pan in the oven and press "Start/Pause" to resume cooking.
16. Meanwhile, in a bowl, mix together the soy sauce, Sriracha sauce, sesame seeds and the remaining sesame oil.
17. When cooking time is completed, open the oven door and transfer the rice mixture into a serving bowl.
18. Drizzle with the sauce mixture and serve.
Serving Suggestions: Serve with yogurt sauce.
Variation Tip: Thaw the vegetables completely before cooking.
Nutritional Information per Serving:
Calories: 443 | Fat: 16.4g | Sat Fat: 3.2g | Carbohydrates: 62.3g | Fiber: 3.6g | Sugar: 3.6g | Protein: 10.1g

Vinegar Green Beans

Preparation Time: 10 minutes
Cooking Time: 20 minutes
Servings: 2
Ingredients:
- 1 (10-ounce) bag frozen cut green beans
- ¼ cup nutritional yeast
- 3 tablespoons balsamic vinegar
- Salt and ground black pepper, as required

Preparation:
1. In a bowl, add the green beans, nutritional yeast, vinegar, salt, and black pepper and toss to coat well.
2. Press "Power" button of Ninja Foodi Digital Air Fry Oven and turn the dial to select "Air Fry" mode.
3. Press TIME/SLICE button and again turn the dial to set the cooking time to 20 minutes.
4. Now push TEMP/DARKNESS button and rotate the dial to set the temperature at 400 degrees F.
5. Press "Start/Pause" button to start.
6. When the unit beeps to show that it is preheated, open the oven door.
7. Arrange the green beans into the greased air fry basket and insert in the oven.
8. When cooking time is completed, open the oven door and serve hot.
Serving Suggestions: Serve with the garnishing of sesame seeds.
Variation Tip: Balsamic vinegar can be replaced with lemon juice.
Nutritional Information per Serving:
Calories: 115 | Fat: 1.3g | Sat Fat: 0.2g | Carbohydrates: 18.5g | Fiber: 9.3g | Sugar: 1.8g | Protein: 11.3g

Tofu in Sweet & Sour Sauce

Preparation Time: 20 minutes
Cooking Time: 20 minutes
Servings: 4
Ingredients:
For Tofu:
- 1 (14-ounce) block firm tofu, pressed and cubed
- ½ cup arrowroot flour
- ½ teaspoon sesame oil

For Sauce:
- 4 tablespoons low-sodium soy sauce
- 1½ tablespoons rice vinegar
- 1½ tablespoons chili sauce
- 1 tablespoon agave nectar
- 2 large garlic cloves, minced
- 1 teaspoon fresh ginger, peeled and grated
- 2 scallions (green part), chopped

Preparation:
1. In a bowl, mix together the tofu, arrowroot flour, and sesame oil.
2. Press "Power" button of Ninja Foodi Digital Air Fry Oven and turn the dial to select "Air Fry" mode.
3. Press TIME/SLICE button and again turn the dial to set the cooking time to 20 minutes.
4. Now push TEMP/DARKNESS button and rotate the dial to set the temperature at 360 degrees F.
5. Press "Start/Pause" button to start.
6. When the unit beeps to show that it is preheated, open the oven door.
7. Arrange the tofu cubes in greased air fry basket and insert in the oven.
8. Flip the tofu cubes once halfway through.
9. Meanwhile, for the sauce: in a bowl, add all the ingredients except scallions and beat until well combined.
10. When cooking time is completed, open the oven door and remove the tofu.
11. Transfer the tofu into a skillet with sauce over medium heat and cook for about 3 minutes, stirring occasionally.
12. Garnish with scallions and serve hot.
Serving Suggestions: Serve with plain boiled rice.
Variation Tip: None.
Nutritional Information per Serving:
Calories: 115 | Fat: 4.8g | Sat Fat: 1g | Carbohydrates: 10.2g | Fiber: 1.7g | Sugar: 5.6g | Protein: 0.1g

Cheesy Kale

Preparation Time: 10 minutes
Cooking Time: 15 minutes
Servings: 3
Ingredients:
- 1 pound fresh kale, tough ribs removed and chopped
- 3 tablespoons olive oil
- Salt and ground black pepper, as required
- 1 cup goat cheese, crumbled
- 1 teaspoon fresh lemon juice

Preparation:
1. In a bowl, add the kale, oil, salt, and black pepper and mix well.
2. Press "Power" button of Ninja Foodi Digital Air Fry Oven and turn the dial to select "Air Fry" mode.
3. Press TIME/SLICE button and again turn the dial to set the cooking time to 15 minutes.
4. Now push TEMP/DARKNESS button and rotate the dial to set the temperature at 340 degrees F.
5. Press "Start/Pause" button to start.
6. When the unit beeps to show that it is preheated, open the oven door and grease the air fry basket.
7. Arrange the kale into air fry basket and insert in the oven.
8. When cooking time is completed, open the oven door and immediately transfer the kale mixture into a bowl.
9. Stir in the cheese and lemon juice and serve hot.
Serving Suggestions: Serve with a garnishing of lemon zest.
Variation Tip: Goat cheese can be replaced with feta.
Nutritional Information per Serving:
Calories: 327 | Fat: 24.7g | Sat Fat: 9.5g | Carbohydrates: 17.9g | Fiber: 2.3g | Sugar: 2g | Protein: 11.6g

Sweet Potato Casserole

Preparation Time: 15 minutes.
Cooking Time: 35 minutes.
Servings: 6
Ingredients:
- 3 cups sweet potatoes, mashed and cooled
- 1 ½ cups brown sugar, packed
- 2 large eggs, beaten
- 1 teaspoon vanilla extract
- ½ cup milk
- ¾ cup butter, melted
- ⅓ cup flour
- 4 ounces pecans, chopped

Preparation:
1. Mix the sweet potato mash with vanilla extract, milk, eggs, 1 cup of brown sugar, and ½ cup of melted butter in a large bowl.
2. Spread this sweet potato mixture in a casserole dish.
3. Now whisk remaining sugar and butter with flour in a separate bowl.
4. Fold in pecan, then top the sweet potatoes mixed with this pecan mixture.
5. Transfer the dish to the Ninja Foodi Digital Air Fry Oven and close the door.
6. Select "Bake" mode by rotating the dial.
7. Press the TIME/SLICE button and change the value to 35 minutes.
8. Press the TEMP/DARKNESS button and change the value to 350 degrees F.
9. Press Start/Pause to begin cooking.
10. Slice and serve!
Serving Suggestion: Serve the sweet potato casserole with roasted pecans.
Variation Tip: Add breadcrumbs on top before baking for a crispy texture.
Nutritional Information Per Serving:
Calories 353 | Fat 3g | Sodium 510mg | Carbs 32g | Fiber 3g | Sugar 4g | Protein 4g

Parmesan Broccoli

Preparation Time: 10 minutes
Cooking Time: 15 minutes
Servings: 8
Ingredients:
- 2 pounds broccoli, cut into 1-inch florets
- 2 tablespoons butter
- Salt and ground black pepper, as required
- ¼ cup Parmesan cheese, grated

Preparation:
1. In a pan of boiling water, add the broccoli and cook for about 3-4 minutes.
2. Drain the broccoli well.
3. In a bowl, place the broccoli, cauliflower, oil, salt, and black pepper and toss to coat well.
4. Press "Power" button of Ninja Foodi Digital Air Fry Oven and turn the dial to select "Air Fry" mode.
5. Press TIME/SLICE button and again turn the dial to set the cooking time to 15 minutes.
6. Now push TEMP/DARKNESS button and rotate the dial to set the temperature at 400 degrees F.
7. Press "Start/Pause" button to start.
8. When the unit beeps to show that it is preheated, open the oven door.
9. Arrange the broccoli mixture in air fry basket and insert in the oven.
10. Toss the broccoli mixture once halfway through.
11. When cooking time is completed, open the oven door and transfer the veggie mixture into a large bowl.
12. Immediately stir in the cheese and serve immediately.
Serving Suggestions: Serve with a drizzling of lemon juice.
Variation Tip: Choose broccoli heads with tight, green florets and firm stalks.
Nutritional Information per Serving:
Calories: 73 | Fat: 3.9g | Sat Fat: 2.1g | Carbohydrates: 7.5g | Fiber: 3g | Sugar: 1.9g | Protein: 4.2g

Fried Tortellini

Preparation Time: 15 minutes.
Cooking Time: 10 minutes.
Servings: 8
Ingredients:
- 1 (9-ounce) package cheese tortellini
- 1 cup Panko breadcrumbs
- ⅓ cup Parmesan, grated
- 1 teaspoon dried oregano
- ½ teaspoon garlic powder
- ½ teaspoon crushed red pepper flakes
- Kosher salt, to taste
- Freshly ground black pepper, to taste
- 1 cup all-purpose flour
- 2 large eggs

Preparation:
1. Boil tortellini according to salted boiling water according to package's instructions, then drain.
2. Mix panko with garlic powder, black pepper, salt, red pepper flakes, oregano, Parmesan in a small bowl.
3. Beat eggs in one bowl and spread flour on a plate.

4. Coat the tortellini with the flour, dip into the eggs and then coat with the panko mixture.
5. Spread the tortellini in the air fry basket and spray them with cooking oil.
6. Transfer the basket to the Ninja Foodi Digital Air Fry Oven and close the door.
7. Select "Air Fry" mode by rotating the dial.
8. Press the TIME/SLICE button and change the value to 10 minutes.
9. Press the TEMP/DARKNESS button and change the value to 400 degrees F.
10. Press Start/Pause to begin cooking.
Serving Suggestion: Serve the tortellini with tomato sauce on the side.
Variation Tip: Use crushed cornflakes to coat the tortellini.
Nutritional Information Per Serving:
Calories 151 | Fat 19g | Sodium 412mg | Carbs 23g | Fiber 0.3g | Sugar 1g | Protein 3g

Broccoli Cheese Casserole

Preparation Time: 15 minutes
Cooking Time: 30 minutes
Servings: 10
Ingredients:
- 2 bunches broccoli
- ¼ cup water
- 1 large egg, lightly beaten
- 10½ ounces cream of chicken soup
- ½ cup mayonnaise
- ½ cup sour cream
- 8 ounces sharp cheddar cheese, shredded
- ½ small onion, chopped
- 1 teaspoon salt

For the topping:
- 1 cup Ritz crackers, crushed
- 2 tablespoons butter, melted

Preparation:
1. Select the BAKE function, 350°F, for 30 minutes. While the oven is preheating, prepare an air fryer-safe casserole dish with non-stick spray.
2. Wash and dry the broccoli before cutting it into florets. Place the florets into a large microwave-safe bowl with the water. Tightly cover the bowl with plastic wrap and microwave for about 5 minutes, then let it stand for 2 minutes before draining.
3. Take a large bowl, and combine the rest of the ingredients except the butter and crackers. Next, add the broccoli to the bowl and mix to coat. Place the broccoli in the prepared baking dish. Bake for 20 minutes
4. Meanwhile, in a small bowl, mix the crackers and butter. Take the casserole out of the oven and sprinkle with the topping. Cook for another 10 minutes.
Serving Suggestion: Sprinkle with some cheese and serve with a green salad.
Variation Tip: You can use cheddar cheese substitutes like Colby cheese or gouda.
Nutritional Information Per Serving:
Calories: 287 | Fat: 24g | Sodium: 722mg | Carbs: 11.41g | Fiber: 3.26g | Sugar: 3.26g | Protein: 11g

Tofu with Broccoli

Preparation Time: 15 minutes
Cooking Time: 15 minutes
Servings: 2
Ingredients:
- 8 ounces block firm tofu, pressed and cubed
- 1 small head broccoli, cut into florets
- 1 tablespoon canola oil
- 1 tablespoon nutritional yeast
- ¼ teaspoon dried parsley
- Salt and ground black pepper, as required

Preparation:
1. In a bowl, mix together the tofu, broccoli and the remaining ingredients.
2. Press "Power" button of Ninja Foodi Digital Air Fry Oven and turn the dial to select "Air Fry" mode.
3. Press TIME/SLICE button and again turn the dial to set the cooking time to 15 minutes.
4. Now push TEMP/DARKNESS button and rotate the dial to set the temperature at 390 degrees F.
5. Press "Start/Pause" button to start.
6. When the unit beeps to show that it is preheated, open the oven door.
7. Arrange the tofu mixture into the greased air fry basket and insert in the oven.
8. Flip the tofu mixture once halfway through.
9. When cooking time is completed, open the oven door and serve hot.

Serving Suggestions: Serve with the garnishing of sesame seeds.
Variation Tip: Cut the broccoli in small florets.
Nutritional Information per Serving:
Calories: 206 | Fat: 13.1g | Sat Fat: 1.6g | Carbohydrates: 12.1g | Fiber: 5.4g | Sugar: 2.6g | Protein: 15g

Cauliflower Tots

Preparation Time: 5 minutes
Cooking Time: 10 minutes
Servings: 4
Ingredients:
- Cooking spray
- 450g cauliflower tots

Preparation:
1. Using nonstick cooking spray, coat the air fry basket.
2. Place as many cauliflower tots as you can in the air fry basket, ensuring sure they do not touch, and air fry in batches if needed.
3. Turn on Ninja Foodi Digital Air Fry Oven and rotate the knob to select "Air Fry".
4. Select the timer for 6 minutes and the temperature for 400 degrees F.
5. Pull the basket out, flip the tots, and cook for another 3 minutes, or until browned and cooked through.
6. Remove from the Ninja Foodi Digital Air Fry Oven to serve.

Serving Suggestions: Serve with garlic sauce.
Variation Tip: You can top with parmesan cheese.
Nutritional Information per Serving:
Calories: 147 | Fat: 6g | Sat Fat: 0.7g | Carbohydrates: 20g | Fiber: 6g | Sugar: 1.6g | Protein: 2g

Roasted Green Beans

Preparation Time: 5 minutes
Cooking Time: 15 minutes
Servings: 4
Ingredients:
- 2 tablespoons lard
- 290g whole green beans
- 1 tablespoon minced garlic
- 2 tablespoons pimentos, diced
- Garlic powder, to taste
- Onion powder, to taste
- Salt, to taste

Preparation:
1. In a stovetop pot, melt the lard.
2. Sauté until the green beans are bright green and glossy, then add the additional ingredients.
3. Using parchment paper, line the air fry basket.
4. Arrange the greens in a single layer on the air fry basket.
5. Turn on Ninja Foodi Digital Air Fry Oven and rotate the knob to select "Air Fry".
6. Select the timer for 15 minutes and the temperature at 390 degrees F.
7. Remove from the Ninja Foodi Digital Air Fry Oven to serve.

Serving Suggestions: Sprinkle some sesame seeds on top.
Variation Tip: You can also add pinch of black pepper.
Nutritional Information per Serving:
Calories: 91 | Fat: 7g | Sat Fat: 3g | Carbohydrates: 6g | Fiber: 2g | Sugar: 3g | Protein: 2g

Vegetable Nachos

Preparation Time: 10 minutes
Cooking Time: 5 minutes
Servings: 3
Ingredients:
- 8 ounces Tortilla chips
- ½ cup Grilled chicken
- 1 can (15 ounces) Black beans, drained, rinsed
- 1 cup White queso
- ½ cup Grape tomatoes, halved
- ⅓ cup Green onion, diced

Preparation:
1. Use foil to line the air fry basket.
2. Using a nonstick spray, coat the surface.
3. Assemble the nachos by layering the chips, chicken, and beans on top.
4. Place a layer of queso on top.
5. Add tomatoes and onions to the top.
6. Turn on Ninja Foodi Digital Air Fry Oven and rotate the knob to select "Air Fry".
7. Select the timer for 5 minutes and the temperature for 355 degrees F.
8. Remove from the Ninja Foodi Digital Air Fry Oven to serve.

Serving Suggestions: Top with some fresh parsley.
Variation Tip: You can add cheese.
Nutritional Information per Serving:
Calories: 43 | Fat: 1.3g | Sat Fat: 0.4g | Carbohydrates: 7.3g | Fiber: 1.2g | Sugar: 1.6g | Protein: 1.9g

Garlic Parmesan Roasted Asparagus

Preparation Time: 5 minutes
Cooking Time: 8 minutes
Servings: 4
Ingredients:
- ½ pound fresh asparagus
- ½ teaspoon salt
- ½ teaspoon fresh ground black pepper
- 3 cloves garlic, minced
- 2 to 3 tablespoons parmesan cheese, grated
- Olive oil spray

Preparation:
1. Select the AIR ROAST function, 425°F, for 8 minutes. While the oven is preheating, prepare the ingredients.
2. Line an air fryer-appropriate rimmed baking sheet with aluminum foil. Set it aside.
3. Rinse the asparagus and trim off their woody ends. Lay them out on the prepared baking sheet.
4. Lightly coat the asparagus with the olive oil spray. Sprinkle them with the garlic, salt, pepper, and parmesan cheese. Mix well with your hands, and spread them in a single layer again. Give them one more coat of olive oil.
5. Cook the asparagus for about 8 minutes.
Serving Suggestion: Sprinkle with salt, pepper, and more cheese before serving.
Variation Tip: Try using vegetable oil instead of olive oil.
Nutritional Information Per Serving:
Calories: 24 | Fat: 1g | Sodium: 332mg | Carbs: 3g | Fiber: 1g | Sugar: 1g | Protein: 2g

Garlic Parmesan Roasted Potatoes

Preparation Time: 10 minutes
Cooking Time: 30 minutes
Servings: 6
Ingredients:
- 3 pounds red potatoes, quartered
- 2 tablespoons olive oil
- 5 cloves garlic, minced
- 1 teaspoon dried thyme
- ½ teaspoon dried oregano
- ½ teaspoon dried basil
- ⅓ cup parmesan, freshly grated
- Kosher salt, to taste
- Freshly ground black pepper, to taste
- 2 tablespoons unsalted butter

Preparation:
1. Select the AIR ROAST function, 400°F, for 35 minutes. Allow the oven to preheat.
2. Grease the sheet pan and place the potatoes onto it. Then, add the garlic, basil, olive oil, thyme, parmesan, and oregano. Season with salt and pepper and gently toss to combine.
3. Put it into the oven and cook for about 25 to 35 minutes. When done, stir in the butter and let it melt. You may need to cook in batches.
Serving Suggestion: Garnish with chopped parsley before serving, about 2 to 3 tablespoons.
Variation Tip: You can experiment with different types of herbs and cheese.

Nutritional Information Per Serving:
Calories: 259 | Fat: 10g | Sodium: 98.9mg | Carbs: 36.5g | Fiber: 4.5g | Sugar: 2.3g | Protein: 6.6g

Baked Potato

Preparation Time: 5 minutes
Cooking Time: 45 minutes
Servings: 4
Ingredients:
- 4 russet potatoes
- 1½ tablespoons olive oil
- 1½ tablespoons sea salt

Preparation:
1. Poke each potato, massage it all over with olive oil and sea salt.
2. Place the potato in the sheet pan.
3. Turn on Ninja Foodi Digital Air Fry Oven and rotate the knob to select "Bake".
4. Select the timer for 40 minutes and the temperature for 350 degrees F.
5. Remove the baked potatoes from the Ninja Foodi, split them in half, and top them with chosen toppings!
Serving Suggestions: Top with chopped green onions.
Variation Tip: You can also add cheese on top.
Nutritional Information per Serving:
Calories: 213 | Fat: 5g | Sat Fat: 1g | Carbohydrates: 37g | Fiber: 4g | Sugar: 2g | Protein: 5g

Roast Cauliflower and Broccoli

Preparation Time: 15 minutes.
Cooking Time: 10 minutes.
Servings: 4
Ingredients:
- ½ pound broccoli, florets
- ½ pound cauliflower, florets
- 1 tablespoon olive oil
- Black pepper, to taste
- Salt, to taste
- ⅓ cup water

Preparation:
1. Toss all the veggies with seasoning in a large bowl.
2. Spread these vegetables in the air fry basket.
3. Transfer the basket to the Ninja Foodi Digital Air Fry Oven and close the door.
4. Select "Air Fry" mode by rotating the dial.
5. Press the TIME/SLICE button and change the value to 10 minutes.
6. Press the TEMP/DARKNESS button and change the value to 400 degrees F.
7. Press Start/Pause to begin cooking.
8. Serve warm.
Serving Suggestion: Serve the roasted cauliflower with white rice.
Variation Tip: Add green beans to the mixture before baking.
Nutritional Information Per Serving:
Calories 318 | Fat 15.7g | Sodium 124mg | Carbs 7g | Fiber 0.1g | Sugar 0.3g | Protein 4.9g

Cauliflower Au Gratin

Preparation Time: 5 minutes
Cooking Time: 30 minutes
Servings: 8
Ingredients:
- 6 tablespoons butter
- 4 ounces cooked ham
- 1 to 2 garlic cloves, minced
- 1 head cauliflower, cut into florets
- 1½ cups heavy whipping cream
- 2 tablespoons all-purpose flour
- ¼ teaspoon salt
- ¼ teaspoon pepper
- Dash cayenne pepper
- 1½ cups Swiss cheese, shredded

Preparation:
1. Select the AIR BROIL function on HI. Prepare the ingredients while the oven is preheating.
2. Melt the butter in a large skillet. Add the garlic and then sauté for about 2 minutes.
3. Add the cauliflower, and cook until it's crisp. Combine the cream with the flour and stir it into the skillet. Mix well.
4. Next, add the salt, pepper, and cayenne pepper, then cook until the mixture is thickened and bubbly. Cook and stir for 1 more minute.
5. Transfer the mixture to a baking dish. Sprinkle with the cheese and cooked ham and broil for about 2 to 4 minutes.

Serving Suggestion: Sprinkle with minced parsley before serving, about 2 to 3 tablespoons.
Variation Tip: You can add chopped asparagus along with the cauliflower.
Nutritional Information Per Serving:
Calories: 351 | Fat: 32g | Sodium: 362mg | Carbs: 7g | Fiber: 2g | Sugar: 3g | Protein: 11g

Air Fryer Roasted Cauliflower

Preparation Time: 10 minutes
Cooking Time: 25 minutes
Servings: 2
Ingredients:
- 3 cloves garlic
- 1 tablespoon peanut oil
- ½ teaspoon salt
- ½ teaspoon smoked paprika
- 4 cups cauliflower florets

Preparation:
1. Select the AIR FRY function, 400°F, for 25 minutes. While the oven is preheating, grease the air fryer basket with cooking oil and prepare the ingredients.
2. Cut and smash the garlic, then place it in a bowl with the salt, oil, and paprika. Then add the cauliflower florets and coat them well.
3. Transfer the coated cauliflower to the greased air fryer basket.
4. Cook for about 15 minutes, shaking every 5 minutes.

Serving Suggestion: Sprinkle with salt and pepper and chopped fresh herbs of your choice.
Variation Tip: Try adding a seasoning of your choice for added flavor.
Nutritional Information Per Serving:
Calories: 118 | Fat: 7g | Sodium: 642.3 | Carbs: 12.3g | Fiber: 5.3g | Sugar: 5g | Protein: 4.3g

Scalloped Potatoes

Preparation Time: 30 minutes
Cooking Time: 45 minutes
Servings: 6
Ingredients:
- 3 pounds potatoes, thinly sliced
- ½ onion, thinly sliced
- 9 tablespoons all-purpose flour
- 6 tablespoons butter
- Salt and ground black pepper, to taste
- 3 cups whole milk

Preparation:
1. Select the BAKE function, 375°F, for 1 hour. While the oven is preheating, prepare an air fryer-safe baking dish by greasing it. Then, prepare the ingredients.
2. Spread about ⅓ of the potato slices into the prepared baking dish and top with ⅓ of the onion slices. Sprinkle with 3 tablespoons of flour.
3. Arrange 2 tablespoons of butter on top of the flour and season it with salt and pepper. Repeat the layering twice.
4. In a saucepan, heat the milk and pour it in the baking dish over the mixture, enough to cover the top layer of potatoes.
5. The bake time is about 45 minutes to 1 hour.

Serving Suggestion: Serve with cream or mustard alongside some greens.
Variation Tip: Try introducing a seasoning of your choice to the recipe.
Nutritional Information Per Serving:
Calories: 396 | Fat: 15g | Sodium: 170mg | Carbs: 55g | Fiber: 5.5g | Sugar: 7.7g | Protein: 9.8g

Creamy Roast Mushrooms

Preparation Time: 5 minutes
Cooking Time: 20 minutes
Servings: 4
Ingredients:
- 35 ounces button mushrooms
- 2 tablespoons olive oil
- 4 tablespoons creme fraiche
- Salt and pepper, to taste

Preparation:
1. Select the AIR ROAST function, 395°F, for 20 minutes. While the oven is preheating, prepare the ingredients.
2. Pour the olive oil into a baking dish, then add the mushrooms and toss to combine.
3. Top the mushrooms with the creme fraiche and cook for about 20 minutes.
4. Lastly, stir the mushrooms to coat them in the creamy sauce evenly. Add salt and pepper as you like.

Serving Suggestion: Garnish with fresh parsley before serving.
Variation Tip: You can replace creme fraiche with sour cream.
Nutritional Information Per Serving:
Calories: 108k | Fat: 10g | Sodium: 20mg | Carbs: 4g | Fiber: 1g | Sugar: 2g | Protein: 3g

Soy Sauce Green Beans

Preparation Time: 10 minutes
Cooking Time: 10 minutes
Servings: 2
Ingredients:
- 8 ounces fresh green beans, trimmed and cut in half
- 1 tablespoon soy sauce
- 1 teaspoon sesame oil

Preparation:
1. In a bowl, mix together the green beans, soy sauce and sesame oil.
2. Press "Power" button of Ninja Foodi Digital Air Fry Oven and turn the dial to select "Air Fry" mode.
3. Press TIME/SLICE button and again turn the dial to set the cooking time to 10 minutes.
4. Now push TEMP/DARKNESS button and rotate the dial to set the temperature at 390 degrees F.
5. Press "Start/Pause" button to start.
6. When the unit beeps to show that it is preheated, open the oven door.
7. Arrange the green beans in air fry basket and insert in the oven.
8. When cooking time is completed, open the oven door and serve hot.

Serving Suggestions: Serve with the garnishing of sesame seeds.
Variation Tip: You can add seasoning of your choice.
Nutritional Information per Serving:
Calories: 62 | Fat: 2.6g | Sat Fat: 0.4g | Carbohydrates: 8.8g | Fiber: 4g | Sugar: 1.7g | Protein: 2.6g

Spicy Potato

Preparation Time: 15 minutes
Cooking Time: 25 minutes
Servings: 4
Ingredients:
- 2 cups water
- 6 russet potatoes, peeled and cubed
- ½ tablespoon extra-virgin olive oil
- ½ of onion, chopped
- 1 tablespoon fresh rosemary, chopped
- 1 garlic clove, minced
- 1 jalapeño pepper, chopped
- ½ teaspoon garam masala powder
- ¼ teaspoon ground cumin
- ¼ teaspoon red chili powder
- Salt and ground black pepper, as required

Preparation:
1. In a large bowl, add the water and potatoes and set aside for about 30 minutes.
2. Drain well and pat dry with the paper towels.
3. In a bowl, add the potatoes and oil and toss to coat well.
4. Press "Power" button of Ninja Foodi Digital Air Fry Oven and turn the dial to select "Air Fry" mode.
5. Press TIME/SLICE button and again turn the dial to set the cooking time to 5 minutes.
6. Now push TEMP/DARKNESS button and rotate the dial to set the temperature at 330 degrees F.
7. Press "Start/Pause" button to start.
8. When the unit beeps to show that it is preheated, open the oven door.

9. Arrange the potato cubes in air fry basket and insert in the oven.
10. Remove from oven and transfer the potatoes into a bowl.
11. Add the remaining ingredients and toss to coat well.
12. Press "Power" button of Ninja Foodi Digital Air Fry Oven and turn the dial to select "Air Fry" mode.
13. Press TIME/SLICE button and again turn the dial to set the cooking time to 20 minutes.
14. Now push TEMP/DARKNESS button and rotate the dial to set the temperature at 390 degrees F.
15. Press "Start/Pause" button to start.
16. When the unit beeps to show that it is preheated, open the oven door.
17. Arrange the potato mixture in air fry basket and insert in the oven.
18. When cooking time is completed, open the oven door and serve hot.

Serving Suggestions: Serve with plain bread.
Variation Tip: Adjust the ratio of spices.
Nutritional Information per Serving:
Calories: 274 | Fat: 2.3g | Sat Fat: 0.4g | Carbohydrates: 52.6g | Fiber: 8.5g | Sugar: 4.4g | Protein: 5.7g

Roasted Vegetables

Preparation Time: 15 minutes.
Cooking Time: 15 minutes.
Servings: 6
Ingredients:
- 2 medium bell peppers cored, chopped
- 2 medium carrots, peeled and sliced
- 1 small zucchini, ends trimmed, sliced
- 1 medium broccoli, florets
- ½ red onion, peeled and diced
- 2 tablespoons olive oil
- 1 ½ teaspoons Italian seasoning
- 2 garlic cloves, minced
- Salt and freshly ground black pepper
- 1 cup grape tomatoes
- 1 tablespoon fresh lemon juice

Preparation:
1. Toss all the veggies with olive oil, Italian seasoning, salt, black pepper, and garlic in a large salad bowl.
2. Spread this broccoli-zucchini mixture in the sheet pan.
3. Transfer the pan to the Ninja Foodi Digital Air Fry Oven and close the door.
4. Select "Bake" mode by rotating the dial.
5. Press the TIME/SLICE button and change the value to 15 minutes.
6. Press the TEMP/DARKNESS button and change the value to 400 degrees F.
7. Press Start/Pause to begin cooking.
8. Serve warm with lemon juice on top.
9. Enjoy.

Serving Suggestion: Serve the roasted vegetables with guacamole on the side.
Variation Tip: Add olives or sliced mushrooms to the vegetable mixture.
Nutritional Information Per Serving:
Calories 346 | Fat 15g | Sodium 220mg | Carbs 4.3g | Fiber 2.4g | Sugar 1.2g | Protein 12.4g

Parmesan Carrot

Preparation Time: 10 minutes
Cooking Time: 20 minutes
Servings: 2
Ingredients:
- 3 carrots
- 1 tablespoon olive oil
- 1 clove garlic, crushed
- 2 tablespoons parmesan cheese, grated
- ¼ teaspoon red pepper, crushed

Preparation:
1. Stir in the crushed garlic with olive oil.
2. Carrots should be washed and dried. Cut the tops in half and remove the tops. Then, to make flat surfaces, cut each half in half.
3. Toss the carrot fries with the garlic and olive oil mixture.
4. Combine the parmesan, red pepper, and black pepper in a mixing bowl. Half of the mixture should be sprinkled over the carrot fries that have been coated.
5. Toss in the remaining parmesan mixture and repeat.
6. Arrange the carrot fries in an equal layer in an air fry basket or on a sheet pan.
7. Turn on Ninja Foodi Digital Air Fry Oven and rotate the knob to select "Air Fry".
8. Select the timer for 20 minutes and the temperature for 350 degrees F.
9. Remove from the Ninja Foodi Digital Air Fry Oven to serve.

Serving Suggestions: Sprinkle more parmesan cheese before serving.
Variation Tip: You can also add a pinch of cayenne pepper.
Nutritional Information per Serving:
Calories: 106 | Fat: 7g | Sat Fat: 1.1g | Carbohydrates: 10g | Fiber: 3g | Sugar: 5g | Protein: 1.2g

Wine Braised Mushrooms

Preparation Time: 10 minutes
Cooking Time: 32 minutes
Servings: 6
Ingredients:
- 1 tablespoon butter
- 2 teaspoons Herbs de Provence
- ½ teaspoon garlic powder
- 2 pounds fresh mushrooms, quartered
- 2 tablespoons white wine

Preparation:
1. In a frying pan, mix together the butter, Herbs de Provence, and garlic powder over medium-low heat and stir fry for about 2 minutes.
2. Stir in the mushrooms and remove from the heat.
3. Transfer the mushroom mixture into a sheet pan.
4. Press "Power" button of Ninja Foodi Digital Air Fry Oven and turn the dial to select "Air Fry" mode.
5. Press TIME/SLICE button and again turn the dial to set the cooking time to 30 minutes.
6. Now push TEMP/DARKNESS button and rotate the dial to set the temperature at 320 degrees F.

7. Press "Start/Pause" button to start.
8. When the unit beeps to show that it is preheated, open the oven door.
9. Arrange the pan over the wire rack and insert in the oven.
10. After 25 minutes of cooking, stir the wine into mushroom mixture.
11. When cooking time is completed, open the oven door and serve hot.

Serving Suggestions: Serve with a garnishing of fresh herbs.
Variation Tip: White wine can be replaced with broth.
Nutritional Information per Serving:
Calories: 54 | Fat: 2.4g | Sat Fat: 1.2g | Carbohydrates: 5.3g | Fiber: 1.5g | Sugar: 2.7g | Protein: 4.8g

Eggplant Parmesan

Preparation Time: 5 minutes
Cooking Time: 20 minutes
Servings: 2
Ingredients:
- 1 medium eggplant
- 2 eggs, beaten
- ¼ cup panko breadcrumbs
- 1 cup mozzarella cheese
- 2 cups marinara sauce
- Olive oil spray
- 2 tablespoons parmesan cheese

Preparation:
1. Peel the eggplant and cut it into 1/4-inch slices.
2. In a shallow plate, place the breadcrumbs.
3. Whisk the eggs in a small bowl.
4. Dip the eggplant slices in the egg mixture gently. After that, cover both sides in breadcrumbs.
5. Fill your air fry basket with eggplant in a single layer. Using an olive oil spray, coat the tops of the slices.
6. Turn on Ninja Foodi Digital Air Fry Oven and rotate the knob to select "Air Roast".
7. Select the timer for 12 minutes and the temperature for 400 degrees F.
8. Flip your eggplant slices after 8 minutes and drizzle the tops with olive oil.
9. Cook for another 4 minutes after spraying the tops of your eggplant.
10. Spread marinara sauce evenly over the top of your eggplant rounds and sprinkle with mozzarella and parmesan cheese.
11. Rotate the knob to select "Air Fry".
12. Set the time for 3 minutes and temperature for 350 degrees F.
13. Dish out to serve hot.

Serving Suggestions: Top with some fresh parsley.
Variation Tip: You can also lay a slice of low-fat mozzarella cheese on top and broil for 3 minutes.
Nutritional Information per Serving:
Calories: 69 | Fat: 2g | Sat Fat: 0.1g | Carbohydrates: 6.3g | Fiber: 2g | Sugar: 2.6g | Protein: 5.9g

Air Fryer Stuffed Sweet Potatoes

Preparation Time: 20 minutes
Cooking Time: 45 minutes
Servings: 4
Ingredients:
- 2 medium sweet potatoes
- 1 teaspoon olive oil
- 1 cup cooked spinach, chopped
- 1 cup cheddar cheese, shredded
- 1 green onion, chopped
- ¼ cup fresh cranberries
- ⅓ cup chopped pecans
- 2 tablespoons butter
- ¼ teaspoon kosher salt
- ¼ teaspoon pepper

Preparation:
1. Select the AIR FRY function, 400°F, for 45 minutes. While the oven is preheating, prepare the ingredients.
2. Lightly coat the potatoes with the olive oil. Place them in the air fryer basket and cook for about 30 to 40 minutes.
3. When cooked, cut the potatoes in half, lengthwise. Then, scoop out their pulp, leaving a ¼ inch thick shell.
4. Take a large bowl and mash the potato pulp. Then mix ¾ cup cheese, spinach, onion, butter, pecans, salt, pepper, and cranberries. Spoon the mixture into the potato shells.
5. Reduce the oven temperature to 360°F. Place the filled potato halves in the air fryer basket, cut side up, and cook for about 10 minutes.
6. Sprinkle with the remaining cheese and cook for about 1 to 2 minutes.
Serving Suggestion: Serve with sour cream.
Variation Tip: You can experiment by adding or replacing some veggies.
Nutritional Information Per Serving:
Calories 376 | Fat: 25g | Sodium: 489mg | Carbs: 28g | Fiber: 5g | Sugar: 10g | Protein: 12g

Stuffed Peppers

Preparation Time: 15 minutes
Cooking Time: 15 minutes
Servings: 6
Ingredients:
- 6 green bell peppers
- 1 pound lean ground beef
- 1 tablespoon olive oil
- ¼ cup green onion, diced
- ¼ cup fresh parsley
- ½ teaspoon ground sage
- ½ teaspoon garlic salt
- 1 cup rice, cooked
- 1 cup marinara sauce to taste
- ¼ cup mozzarella cheese, shredded

Preparation:
1. Cook the ground beef in a medium sized skillet until it is well done.
2. Return the beef to the pan after draining it.
3. Combine the olive oil, green onion, parsley, sage, and salt in a large mixing bowl and add to the skillet with beef.
4. Add the cooked rice and marinara sauce in the skillet and stir this rice-beef mixture thoroughly.

5. Remove the tops off each pepper and discard the seeds.
6. Scoop the mixture into each pepper and place it in the air fry basket.
7. Turn on Ninja Foodi Digital Air Fry Oven and rotate the knob to select "Air Fry".
8. Select the timer for 10 minutes and temperature for 355 degrees F.
9. Dish out to serve and enjoy.
Serving Suggestions: Top with some fresh parsley.
Variation Tip: You can use any cheese.
Nutritional Information per Serving:
Calories: 296 | Fat: 13g | Sat Fat: 4g | Carbohydrates: 19g | Fiber: 2g | Sugar: 6g | Protein: 25g

Air Fryer Sweet and Roasted Carrots

Preparation Time: 5 minutes
Cooking Time: 20 minutes
Servings: 2
Ingredients:
- Cooking spray
- 1 tablespoon melted butter
- 1 tablespoon hot honey
- 1 teaspoon orange zest, grated
- ½ teaspoon ground cardamom
- ½ pound baby carrots, sliced
- 1 tablespoon freshly squeezed orange juice
- Pinch of salt
- Ground black pepper, to taste

Preparation:
1. Select the AIR FRY function, 400°F, for 20 minutes. While the oven is preheating, grease the air fryer basket with cooking spray and prepare the ingredients.
2. Take a mixing bowl and combine the honey, cardamom, orange zest, and butter. Take out 1 tablespoon of the sauce and keep it aside in a separate bowl.
3. Add the sliced carrots to the remaining sauce and toss well to coat. Transfer the carrots to the air fryer basket.
4. Cook the carrots for 15 to 20 minutes, tossing them every 7 minutes.
5. Mix the orange juice with the sauce kept aside, then toss the carrots to combine.
Serving Suggestion: Season with salt and pepper and serve.
Variation Tip: You can try using almond cream instead of orange juice.
Nutritional Information Per Serving:
Calories: 129k | Fat: 6g | Sodium: 206.4mg | Carbs: 19.3g | Fiber: 3.5g | Sugar: 14.6g | Protein: 1g

Green Tomatoes

Preparation Time: 15 minutes
Cooking Time: 7 minutes
Servings: 4
Ingredients:
- 3 green tomatoes
- ½ teaspoon salt
- ½ cup flour
- 2 eggs
- ⅓ cup cornmeal
- ⅓ cup breadcrumbs
- ⅛ teaspoon paprika

Preparation:
1. Slice the green tomatoes into 1/4-inch slices and generously coat with salt. Allow for at least 5 minutes of resting time.
2. Put the flour in one bowl, the egg (whisked) in the second, and the cornmeal, breadcrumbs, and paprika in the third bowl to make a breading station.
3. Using a paper towel, pat green tomato slices dry.
4. Dip each tomato slice into the flour, then the egg, and finally the cornmeal mixture, making sure the tomato slices are completely covered.
5. Place them in air fry basket in a single layer.
6. Turn on Ninja Foodi Digital Air Fry Oven and rotate the knob to select "Air Fry".
7. Select the timer for 9 minutes and the temperature for 380 degrees F.
8. Cook for 7-9 minutes, flipping and spritzing with oil halfway through.
Serving Suggestions: Sprinkle more parmesan cheese before serving.
Variation Tip: You can also add a pinch of cayenne pepper.
Nutritional Information per Serving:
Calories: 186 | Fat: 4g | Sat Fat: 1g | Carbohydrates: 31g | Fiber: 3g | Sugar: 4g | Protein: 8g

Vegan Cakes

Preparation Time: 15 minutes.
Cooking Time: 15 minutes.
Servings: 8
Ingredients:
- 4 potatoes, diced and boiled
- 1 bunch green onions
- 1 lime, zest, and juice
- 1½-inch knob of fresh ginger
- 1 tablespoon tamari
- 4 tablespoons red curry paste
- 4 sheets nori
- 1 (398 grams) can heart of palm, drained
- ¾ cup canned artichoke hearts, drained
- Black pepper, to taste
- Salt, to taste

Preparation:
1. Add potatoes, green onions, lime zest, juice, and the rest of the ingredients to a food processor.
2. Press the pulse button and blend until smooth.

3. Make 8 small patties out of this mixture.
4. Place the patties in the air fry basket.
5. Transfer the basket to the Ninja Foodi Digital Air Fry Oven and close the door.
6. Select "Air Fry" mode by rotating the dial.
7. Press the TIME/SLICE button and change the value to 15 minutes.
8. Press the TEMP/DARKNESS button and change the value to 400 degrees F.
9. Press Start/Pause to begin cooking.
10. Serve warm.
Serving Suggestion: Serve the vegan cakes with roasted asparagus.
Variation Tip: Add boiled quinoa to the cake mixture.
Nutritional Information Per Serving:
Calories 324 | Fat 5g | Sodium 432mg | Carbs 13.1g | Fiber 0.3g | Sugar 1g | Protein 5.7g

Quinoa Burgers

Preparation Time: 10 minutes
Cooking Time: 10 minutes
Servings: 4
Ingredients:
- ½ cup cooked and cooled quinoa
- 1 cup rolled oats
- 2 eggs, lightly beaten
- ¼ cup white onion, minced
- ¼ cup feta cheese, crumbled
- Salt and ground black pepper, as required
- Olive oil cooking spray

Preparation:
1. In a large bowl, add all ingredients and mix until well combined.
2. Make 4 equal-sized patties from the mixture.
3. Lightly spray the patties with cooking spray.
4. Press "Power" button of Ninja Foodi Digital Air Fry Oven and turn the dial to select "Air Fry" mode.
5. Press TIME/SLICE button and again turn the dial to set the cooking time to 10 minutes.
6. Now push TEMP/DARKNESS button and rotate the dial to set the temperature at 400 degrees F.
7. Press "Start/Pause" button to start.
8. When the unit beeps to show that it is preheated, open the oven door.
9. Arrange the patties into the greased air fry basket and insert in the oven.
10. Flip the patties once halfway through.
11. When cooking time is completed, open the oven door and transfer the patties onto a platter.
12. Serve warm.
Serving Suggestions: Serve with green sauce.
Variation Tip: For crispy texture, refrigerate the patties for at least 15 minutes before cooking.
Nutritional Information per Serving:
Calories: 215 | Fat: 6.6g | Sat Fat: 2.5g | Carbohydrates: 28.7g | Fiber: 3.7g | Sugar: 1.1g | Protein: 9.9g

Chapter 4 Fish and Seafood Recipes

Herbed Shrimp

Preparation Time: 15 minutes
Cooking Time: 7 minutes
Servings: 3
Ingredients:
- 4 tablespoons salted butter, melted
- 1 tablespoon fresh lemon juice
- 1 tablespoon garlic, minced
- 2 teaspoons red pepper flakes, crushed
- 1 pound shrimp, peeled and deveined
- 2 tablespoons fresh basil, chopped
- 1 tablespoon fresh chives, chopped
- 2 tablespoons chicken broth

Preparation:
1. In a 7-inch round baking pan, place butter, lemon juice, garlic, and red pepper flakes and mix well.
2. Press "Power" button of Ninja Foodi Digital Air Fry Oven and turn the dial to select the "Air Fry" mode.
3. Press TIME/SLICE button and again turn the dial to set the cooking time to 7 minutes.
4. Now push TEMP/DARKNESS button and rotate the dial to set the temperature at 325 degrees F.
5. Press "Start/Pause" button to start.
6. When the unit beeps to show that it is preheated, open the oven door and place the pan over wire rack.
7. Insert the wire rack in oven.
8. After 2 minutes of cooking in the pan, stir in the shrimp, basil, chives, and broth.
9. When cooking time is completed, open the oven door and stir the mixture.
10. Serve hot.
Serving Suggestions: Serve with the garnishing of scallion.
Variation Tip: Use fresh shrimp.
Nutritional Information per Serving:
Calories: 327 | Fat: 18.3g | Sat Fat: 10.6g | Carbohydrates: 4.2g | Fiber: 0.5g | Sugar: 0.3g | Protein: 35.3g

Tangy Sea Bass

Preparation Time: 10 minutes
Cooking Time: 12 minutes
Servings: 2
Ingredients:
- 2 (5-ounce) sea bass fillets
- 1 garlic clove, minced
- 1 teaspoon fresh dill, minced
- 1 tablespoon olive oil
- 1 tablespoon balsamic vinegar
- Salt and ground black pepper, as required

Preparation:
1. In a large resealable bag, add all the ingredients.
2. Seal the bag and shake well to mix.
3. Refrigerate to marinate for at least 30 minutes.
4. Remove the fish fillets from bag and shake off the excess marinade.
5. Arrange the fish fillets onto the greased sheet pan in a single layer.

6. Press "Power" button of Ninja Foodi Digital Air Fry Oven and turn the dial to select "Bake" mode.
7. Press TIME/SLICE button and again turn the dial to set the cooking time to 12 minutes.
8. Now push TEMP/DARKNESS button and rotate the dial to set the temperature at 450 degrees F.
9. Press "Start/Pause" button to start.
10. When the unit beeps to show that it is preheated, open the oven door and insert the sheet pan in oven.
11. Open the Flip the fish fillets once halfway through.
12. When cooking time is completed, open the oven door and serve hot.
Serving Suggestions: Serve with fresh salad.
Variation Tip: Rinse fish with cool, running water and pat it dry.
Nutritional Information per Serving:
Calories: 241 | Fat: 10.7g | Sat Fat: 1.9g | Carbohydrates: 0.9g | Fiber: 0.1g | Sugar: 0.1g | Protein: 33.7g

Salmon with Prawns

Preparation Time: 15 minutes
Cooking Time: 18 minutes
Servings: 4
Ingredients:
- 4 (4-ounce) salmon fillets
- 2 tablespoons olive oil
- ½ pound cherry tomatoes, chopped
- 8 large prawns, peeled and deveined
- 2 tablespoons fresh lemon juice
- 2 tablespoons fresh thyme, chopped

Preparation:
1. In the bottom of a greased baking pan, place salmon fillets and tomatoes in a greased baking dish in a single layer and drizzle with the oil.
2. Arrange the prawns on top in a single layer.
3. Drizzle with lemon juice and sprinkle with thyme.
4. Press "Power" button of Ninja Foodi Digital Air Fry Oven and turn the dial to select "Air Fry" mode.
5. Press TIME/SLICE button and again turn the dial to set the cooking time to 18 minutes.
6. Now push TEMP/DARKNESS button and rotate the dial to set the temperature at 390 degrees F.
7. Press "Start/Pause" button to start.
8. When the unit beeps to show that it is preheated, open the oven door.
9. Arrange the baking pan into the air fry basket and insert in the oven.
10. When cooking time is completed, open the oven door and serve immediately.
Serving Suggestions: Serve with pasta of your choice.
Variation Tip: Make sure to use fresh salmon and prawns.
Nutritional Information per Serving:
Calories: 239 | Fat: 14.5g | Sat Fat: 2.2g | Carbohydrates: 3.4g | Fiber: 1.2g | Sugar: 1.7g | Protein: 25.2g

Crispy Catfish

Preparation Time: 15 minutes
Cooking Time: 15 minutes
Servings: 5
Ingredients:
- 5 (6-ounce) catfish fillets
- 1 cup milk
- 2 teaspoons fresh lemon juice
- ½ cup yellow mustard
- ½ cup cornmeal
- ¼ cup all-purpose flour
- 2 tablespoons dried parsley flakes
- ¼ teaspoon red chili powder
- ¼ teaspoon cayenne pepper
- ¼ teaspoon onion powder
- ¼ teaspoon garlic powder
- Salt and ground black pepper, as required
- Olive oil cooking spray

Preparation:
1. In a large bowl, place the catfish, milk, and lemon juice and refrigerate for about 15 minutes.
2. In a shallow bowl, add the mustard.
3. In another bowl, mix together the cornmeal, flour, parsley flakes and spices.
4. Remove the catfish fillets from milk mixture and with paper towels, pat them dry.
5. Coat each fish fillet with mustard and then roll into cornmeal mixture.
6. Then, spray each fillet with the cooking spray.
7. Press "Power" button of Ninja Foodi Digital Air Fry Oven and turn the dial to select "Air Fry" mode.
8. Press TIME/SLICE button and again turn the dial to set the cooking time to 15 minutes.
9. Now push TEMP/DARKNESS button and rotate the dial to set the temperature at 400 degrees F.
10. Press "Start/Pause" button to start.
11. When the unit beeps to show that it is preheated, open the oven door.
12. Arrange the catfish fillets into the greased air fry basket and insert in the oven.
13. After 10 minutes of cooking, flip the fillets and spray with the cooking spray.
14. When cooking time is completed, open the oven door and serve hot.
Serving Suggestions: Serve with cheese sauce.
Variation Tip: Use freshly squeezed lemon juice.
Nutritional Information per Serving:
Calories: 340 | Fat: 15.5g | Sat Fat: 3.1g | Carbohydrates: 18.3g | Fiber: 2g | Sugar: 2.7g | Protein: 30.9g

Salmon with Broccoli

Preparation Time: 15 minutes
Cooking Time: 12 minutes
Servings: 2
Ingredients:
- 1½ cups small broccoli florets
- 2 tablespoons vegetable oil, divided
- Salt and ground black pepper, as required
- 1 (½-inch) piece fresh ginger, grated
- 1 tablespoon soy sauce
- 1 teaspoon rice vinegar
- 1 teaspoon light brown sugar
- ¼ teaspoon cornstarch
- 2 (6-ounce) skin-on salmon fillets

Preparation:
1. In a bowl, mix together the broccoli, 1 tablespoon of oil, salt, and black pepper.
2. In another bowl, mix well the ginger, soy sauce, vinegar, sugar, and cornstarch.
3. Coat the salmon fillets with remaining oil and then with the ginger mixture.
4. Press "Power" button of Ninja Foodi Digital Air Fry Oven and turn the dial to select "Air Fry" mode.
5. Press TIME/SLICE button and again turn the dial to set the cooking time to 12 minutes.
6. Now push TEMP/DARKNESS button and rotate the dial to set the temperature at 375 degrees F.
7. Press "Start/Pause" button to start.
8. When the unit beeps to show that it is preheated, open the oven door.
9. Arrange the broccoli florets into the greased air fry basket and top with the salmon fillets.
10. Insert the basket in the oven.
11. When cooking time is completed, remove basket from oven and cool for 5 minutes before serving.
Serving Suggestions: Serve with the garnishing of lemon zest.
Variation Tip: Use low-sodium soy sauce.
Nutritional Information per Serving:
Calories: 385 | Fat: 24.4g | Sat Fat: 4.2g | Carbohydrates: 7.8g | Fiber: 2.1g | Sugar: 3g | Protein: 35.6g

Parmesan Flounder

Preparation Time: 15 minutes.
Cooking Time: 20 minutes.
Servings: 4
Ingredients:
- ¼ cup olive oil
- 4 fillets flounder
- Kosher salt, to taste
- Freshly ground black pepper
- ½ cup Parmesan, grated
- ¼ cup bread crumbs
- 4 garlic cloves, minced
- Juice and zest of 1 lemon

Preparation:
1. Mix parmesan, breadcrumbs, and all the ingredients in a bowl and coat the flounder well.
2. Place the fish in a sheet pan.
3. Transfer the fish to the Ninja Foodi Digital Air Fry Oven and close the door.
4. Select "Bake" mode by rotating the dial.
5. Press the TIME/SLICE button and change the value to 20 minutes.
6. Press the TEMP/DARKNESS button and change the value to 425 degrees F.
7. Press Start/Pause to begin cooking.
8. Serve warm.
Serving Suggestion: Serve the flounder with fresh greens and yogurt dip.
Variation Tip: Drizzle cheddar cheese on top for a rich taste.
Nutritional Information Per Serving:
Calories 351 | Fat 4g | Sodium 236mg | Carbs 9.1g | Fiber 0.3g | Sugar 0.1g | Protein 36g

Cajun Salmon

Preparation Time: 10 minutes
Cooking Time: 7 minutes
Servings: 2
Ingredients:
- 2 (7-ounce) (¾-inch thick) salmon fillets
- 1 tablespoon Cajun seasoning
- ½ teaspoon sugar
- 1 tablespoon fresh lemon juice

Preparation:
1. Sprinkle the salmon fillets with Cajun seasoning and sugar evenly.
2. Press "Power" button of Ninja Foodi Digital Air Fry Oven and turn the dial to select "Air Fry" mode.
3. Press TIME/SLICE button and again turn the dial to set the cooking time to 7 minutes.
4. Now push TEMP/DARKNESS button and rotate the dial to set the temperature at 355 degrees F.
5. Press "Start/Pause" button to start.
6. When the unit beeps to show that it is preheated, open the oven door.
7. Arrange the salmon fillets, skin-side up in the greased air fry basket and insert in the oven.
8. When cooking time is completed, open the oven door and transfer the salmon fillets onto a platter.
9. Drizzle with the lemon juice and serve hot.
Serving Suggestions: Serve with mashed cauliflower.
Variation Tip: Adjust the ratio of Cajun seasoning according to your taste.
Nutritional Information per Serving:
Calories: 268 | Fat: 12.3g | Sat Fat: 1.8g | Carbohydrates: 1.2g | Fiber: 0g | Sugar: 1.2g | Protein: 36.8g

Cod with Sauce

Preparation Time: 15 minutes
Cooking Time: 15 minutes
Servings: 2
Ingredients:
- 2 (7-ounce) cod fillets
- Salt and ground black pepper, as required
- ¼ teaspoon sesame oil
- 1 cup water
- 5 little squares rock sugar
- 5 tablespoons light soy sauce
- 1 teaspoon dark soy sauce
- 2 scallions (green part), sliced
- ¼ cup fresh cilantro, chopped
- 3 tablespoons olive oil
- 5 ginger slices

Preparation:
1. Season each cod fillet evenly with salt, and black pepper and drizzle with sesame oil.
2. Set aside at room temperature for about 15-20 minutes.
3. Press "Power" button of Ninja Foodi Digital Air Fry Oven and turn the dial to select "Air Fry" mode.
4. Press TIME/SLICE button and again turn the dial to set the cooking time to 12 minutes.
5. Now push TEMP/DARKNESS button and rotate the dial to set the temperature at 355 degrees F.

6. Press "Start/Pause" button to start.
7. When the unit beeps to show that it is preheated, open the oven door.
8. Arrange the cod fillets into the greased air fry basket and insert in the oven.
9. Meanwhile, in a small pan, add the water and bring it to a boil.
10. Add the rock sugar and both soy sauces and cook until sugar is dissolved, stirring continuously.
11. Remove from the heat and set aside.
12. Remove the cod fillets from oven and transfer onto serving plates.
13. Top each fillet with scallion and cilantro.
14. In a small frying pan, heat the olive oil over medium heat and sauté the ginger slices for about 2-3 minutes.
15. Remove the frying pan from heat and discard the ginger slices.
16. When cooking time is completed, open the oven door and transfer the cod fillets onto serving plates.
17. Carefully pour the hot oil evenly over cod fillets.
18. Top with the sauce mixture and serve.
Serving Suggestions: Serve with boiled rice.
Variation Tip: For best result, use toasted sesame oil.
Nutritional Information per Serving:
Calories: 380 | Fat: 23.4g | Sat Fat: 3.1g | Carbohydrates: 5g | Fiber: 0.8g | Sugar: 1.1g | Protein: 38.3g

Spicy Bay Scallops

Preparation Time: 15 minutes.
Cooking Time: 8 minutes.
Servings: 4
Ingredients:
- 1 pound bay scallops rinsed and patted dry
- 2 teaspoons smoked paprika
- 2 teaspoons chili powder
- 2 teaspoons olive oil
- 1 teaspoon garlic powder
- ¼ teaspoon ground black pepper
- ⅛ teaspoon cayenne red pepper

Preparation:
1. Scallops with paprika, chili powder, olive oil, garlic powder, black pepper, and red pepper in a bowl.
2. Place the scallops in the air fry basket.
3. Transfer the basket to the Ninja Foodi Digital Air Fry Oven and close the door.
4. Select "Air Fry" mode by rotating the dial.
5. Press the TIME/SLICE button and change the value to 8 minutes.
6. Press the TEMP/DARKNESS button and change the value to 400 degrees F.
7. Press Start/Pause to begin cooking.
8. Enjoy.
Serving Suggestion: Serve the scallops with crispy onion rings on the side.
Variation Tip: Coat the scallops with breadcrumbs for a crispy texture.
Nutritional Information Per Serving:
Calories 476 | Fat 17g | Sodium 1127mg | Carbs 4g | Fiber 1g | Sugar 3g | Protein 29g

Prawns in Butter Sauce

Preparation Time: 15 minutes
Cooking Time: 6 minutes
Servings: 2
Ingredients:
- ½ pound large prawns, peeled and deveined
- 1 large garlic clove, minced
- 1 tablespoon butter, melted
- 1 teaspoon fresh lemon zest, grated

Preparation:
1. In a bowl, add all the ingredients and toss to coat well.
2. Set aside at room temperature for about 30 minutes.
3. Arrange the prawn mixture into a sheet pan.
4. Press "Power" button of Ninja Foodi Digital Air Fry Oven and turn the dial to select "Bake" mode.
5. Press TIME/SLICE button and again turn the dial to set the cooking time to 6 minutes.
6. Now push TEMP/DARKNESS button and rotate the dial to set the temperature at 450 degrees F.
7. Press "Start/Pause" button to start.
8. When the unit beeps to show that it is preheated, open the oven door.
9. Arrange the pan over the wire rack and insert in the oven.
10. When cooking time is completed, open the oven door and serve immediately.

Serving Suggestions: Serve with fresh salad.
Variation Tip: Avoid shrimp that smells like ammonia.
Nutritional Information per Serving:
Calories: 189 | Fat: 7.7g | Sat Fat: 4.2g | Carbohydrates: 2.4g | Fiber: 0.1g | Sugar: 0.1g | Protein: 26g

Cod Burgers

Preparation Time: 15 minutes
Cooking Time: 7 minutes
Servings: 4
Ingredients:
- ½ pound cod fillets
- ½ teaspoon fresh lime zest, grated finely
- ½ egg
- ½ teaspoon red chili paste
- Salt, to taste
- ½ tablespoon fresh lime juice
- 3 tablespoons coconut, grated and divided
- 1 small scallion, chopped finely
- 1 tablespoon fresh parsley, chopped

Preparation:
1. In a food processor, add cod filets, lime zest, egg, chili paste, salt and lime juice and pulse until smooth.
2. Transfer the cod mixture into a bowl.
3. Add 1½ tablespoons coconut, scallion and parsley and mix until well combined.
4. Make 4 equal-sized patties from the mixture.
5. In a shallow dish, place the remaining coconut.
6. Coat the patties in coconut evenly.
7. Press "Power" button of Ninja Foodi Digital Air Fry Oven and turn the dial to select "Air Fry" mode.
8. Press TIME/SLICE button and again turn the dial to set the cooking time to 7 minutes.

9. Now push TEMP/DARKNESS button and rotate the dial to set the temperature at 375 degrees F.
10. Press "Start/Pause" button to start.
11. When the unit beeps to show that it is preheated, open the oven door.
12. Arrange the patties into the greased air fry basket and insert in the oven.
13. When cooking time is completed, open the oven door and serve hot.

Serving Suggestions: Serve alongside the dipping sauce.
Variation Tip: Use unsweetened coconut.
Nutritional Information per Serving:
Calories: 70 | Fat: 2.4g | Sat Fat: 1.3g | Carbohydrates: 1.1g | Fiber: 0.4g | Sugar: 0.5g | Protein: 11g

Crispy Cod

Preparation Time: 15 minutes
Cooking Time: 15 minutes
Servings: 4
Ingredients:
- 4 (4-ounce) (¾-inch thick) cod fillets
- Salt, as required
- 2 tablespoons all-purpose flour
- 2 eggs
- ½ cup panko breadcrumbs
- 1 teaspoon fresh dill, minced
- ½ teaspoon dry mustard
- ½ teaspoon lemon zest, grated
- ½ teaspoon onion powder
- ½ teaspoon paprika
- Olive oil cooking spray

Preparation
1. Season the cod fillets with salt generously.
2. In a shallow bowl, place the flour.
3. Crack the eggs in a second bowl and beat well.
4. In a third bowl, mix together the panko, dill, lemon zest, mustard and spices.
5. Coat each cod fillet with the flour, then dip into beaten eggs and finally, coat with panko mixture.
6. Press "Power" button of Ninja Foodi Digital Air Fry Oven and turn the dial to select "Air Fry" mode.
7. Press TIME/SLICE button and again turn the dial to set the cooking time to 15 minutes.
8. Now push TEMP/DARKNESS button and rotate the dial to set the temperature at 400 degrees F.
9. Press "Start/Pause" button to start.
10. When the unit beeps to show that it is preheated, open the oven door and grease the air fry basket.
11. Place the cod fillets into the prepared air fry basket and insert in the oven.
12. Flip the cod fillets once halfway through.
13. When cooking time is completed, open the oven door and serve hot.

Serving Suggestions: Serve with steamed green beans.
Variation Tip: Make sure you remove all the fish scales before cooking.
Nutritional Information per Serving:
Calories: 190 | Fat: 4.3g | Sat Fat: 1.1g | Carbohydrates: 5.9g | Fiber: 0.4g | Sugar: 0.4g | Protein: 24g

Nuts Crusted Salmon

Preparation Time: 15 minutes
Cooking Time: 15 minutes
Servings: 2
Ingredients:
- 2 (6-ounce) skinless salmon fillets
- Salt and ground black pepper, as required
- 3 tablespoons walnuts, chopped finely
- 3 tablespoons quick-cooking oats, crushed
- 2 tablespoons olive oil

Preparation:
1. Rub the salmon fillets with salt and black pepper evenly.
2. In a bowl, mix together the walnuts, oats and oil.
3. Arrange the salmon fillets onto the greased sheet pan in a single layer.
4. Place the oat mixture over salmon fillets and gently, press down.
5. Press "Power" button of Ninja Foodi Digital Air Fry Oven and turn the dial to select the "Bake" mode.
6. Press TIME/SLICE button and again turn the dial to set the cooking time to 15 minutes.
7. Now push TEMP/DARKNESS button and rotate the dial to set the temperature at 400 degrees F.
8. Press "Start/Pause" button to start.
9. When the unit beeps to show that it is preheated, open the oven door.
10. Insert the sheet pan in oven.
11. When cooking time is completed, open the oven door and serve hot.
Serving Suggestions: Serve with steamed asparagus.
Variation Tip: Walnuts can be replaced with pecans.
Nutritional Information per Serving:
Calories: 446 | Fat: 319g | Sat Fat: 4g | Carbohydrates: 6.4g | Fiber: 1.6g | Sugar: 0.2g | Protein: 36.8g

Spiced Shrimp

Preparation Time: 15 minutes
Cooking Time: 5 minutes
Servings: 3
Ingredients:
- 1 pound tiger shrimp
- 3 tablespoons olive oil
- 1 teaspoon old bay seasoning
- ½ teaspoon cayenne pepper
- ½ teaspoon smoked paprika
- Salt, as required

Preparation:
1. In a large bowl, add all the ingredients and stir to combine.
2. Press "Power" button of Ninja Foodi Digital Air Fry Oven and turn the dial to select "Air Fry" mode.
3. Press TIME/SLICE button and again turn the dial to set the cooking time to 5 minutes.
4. Now push TEMP/DARKNESS button and rotate the dial to set the temperature at 390 degrees F.
5. Press "Start/Pause" button to start.
6. When the unit beeps to show that it is preheated, open the oven door.

7. Arrange the shrimp into the greased air fry basket and insert in the oven.
8. When cooking time is completed, open the oven door and serve hot.
Serving Suggestions: Serve with fresh greens.
Variation Tip: You can use seasoning of your choice.
Nutritional Information per Serving:
Calories: 272 | Fat: 15.7g | Sat Fat: 2.5g | Carbohydrates: 0.4g | Fiber: 0.2g | Sugar: 0.1g | Protein: 31.7g

Salmon Burgers

Preparation Time: 15 minutes
Cooking Time: 22 minutes
Servings: 6
Ingredients:
- 3 large russet potatoes, peeled and cubed
- 1 (6-ounce) cooked salmon fillet
- 1 egg
- ¾ cup frozen vegetables (of your choice), parboiled and drained
- 2 tablespoons fresh parsley, chopped
- 1 teaspoon fresh dill, chopped
- Salt and ground black pepper, as required
- 1 cup breadcrumbs
- ¼ cup olive oil

Preparation:
1. In a pan of boiling water, cook the potatoes for about 10 minutes.
2. Drain the potatoes well.
3. Transfer the potatoes into a bowl and mash with a potato masher.
4. Set aside to cool completely.
5. In another bowl, add the salmon and flake with a fork.
6. Add the cooked potatoes, egg, parboiled vegetables, parsley, dill, salt, and black pepper and mix until well combined.
7. Make 6 equal-sized patties from the mixture.
8. Coat patties with breadcrumb evenly and then drizzle with the oil evenly.
9. Press "Power" button of Ninja Foodi Digital Air Fry Oven and turn the dial to select "Air Fry" mode.
10. Press TIME/SLICE button and again turn the dial to set the cooking time to 12 minutes.
11. Now push TEMP/DARKNESS button and rotate the dial to set the temperature at 355 degrees F.
12. Press "Start/Pause" button to start.
13. When the unit beeps to show that it is preheated, open the oven door.
14. Arrange the patties in greased air fry basket and insert in the oven.
15. Flip the patties once halfway through.
16. When cooking time is completed, open the oven door and serve hot.
Serving Suggestions: Serve your favorite dipping sauce.
Variation Tip: You can use herbs of your choice in this recipe.
Nutritional Information per Serving:
Calories: 334 | Fat: 12.1g | Sat Fat: 2g | Carbohydrates: 45.2g | Fiber: 6.3g | Sugar: 4g | Protein: 12.5g

Buttered Crab Shells

Preparation Time: 15 minutes
Cooking Time: 20 minutes
Servings: 4
Ingredients:
- 4 soft crab shells, cleaned
- 1 cup buttermilk
- 3 eggs
- 2 cups panko breadcrumb
- 2 teaspoons seafood seasoning
- 1½ teaspoons lemon zest, grated
- 2 tablespoons butter, melted

Preparations:
1. In a shallow bowl, place the buttermilk.
2. In a second bowl, whisk the eggs.
3. In a third bowl, mix together the breadcrumbs, seafood seasoning, and lemon zest.
4. Soak the crab shells into the buttermilk for about 10 minutes.
5. Now, dip the crab shells into beaten eggs and then, coat with the breadcrumb mixture.
6. Press "Power" button of Ninja Foodi Digital Air Fry Oven and turn the dial to select "Air Fry" mode.
7. Press TIME/SLICE button and again turn the dial to set the cooking time to 10 minutes.
8. Now push TEMP/DARKNESS button and rotate the dial to set the temperature at 375 degrees F.
9. Press "Start/Pause" button to start.
10. When the unit beeps to show that it is preheated, open the oven door and grease the air fry basket.
11. Place the crab shells into the prepared air fry basket and insert in the oven.
12. When cooking time is completed, open the oven door and transfer the crab shells onto serving plates.
13. Drizzle crab shells with the melted butter and serve immediately.
Serving Suggestions: Serve alongside the lemon slices.
Variation Tip: Use seasoning of your choice.
Nutritional Information per Serving:
Calories: 549 | Fat: 17.3g | Sat Fat: 7g | Carbohydrates: 11.5g | Fiber: 0.3g | Sugar: 3.3g | Protein: 53.5g

Scallops with Capers Sauce

Preparation Time: 10 minutes
Cooking Time: 6 minutes
Servings: 2
Ingredients:
- 10 (1-ounce) sea scallops, cleaned and patted very dry
- Salt and ground black pepper, as required
- ¼ cup extra-virgin olive oil
- 2 tablespoons fresh parsley, finely chopped
- 2 teaspoons capers, finely chopped
- 1 teaspoon fresh lemon zest, finely grated
- ½ teaspoon garlic, finely chopped

Preparation:
1. Season each scallop evenly with salt and black pepper.
2. Press "Power" button of Ninja Foodi Digital Air Fry Oven and turn the dial to select "Air Fry" mode.
3. Press TIME/SLICE button and again turn the dial to set the cooking time to 6 minutes.
4. Now push TEMP/DARKNESS button and rotate the dial to set the temperature at 400 degrees F.
5. Press "Start/Pause" button to start.
6. When the unit beeps to show that it is preheated, open the oven door and grease the air fry basket.
7. Place the scallops into the prepared air fry basket and insert in the oven.
8. Meanwhile, for the sauce: in a bowl, mix the remaining ingredients.
9. When cooking time is completed, open the oven door and transfer the scallops onto serving plates.
10. Top with the sauce and serve immediately.
Serving Suggestions: Serve with a garnishing of fresh herbs.
Variation Tip: Avoid shiny, wet or soft scallops.
Nutritional Information per Serving:
Calories: 344 | Fat: 26.3g | Sat Fat: 3.7g | Carbohydrates: 4.2g | Fiber: 0.3g | Sugar: 0.1g | Protein: 24g

Lobster Tail Casserole

Preparation Time: 15 minutes.
Cooking Time: 16 minutes.
Servings: 6
Ingredients:
- 1 pound salmon fillets, cut into 8 equal pieces
- 16 large sea scallops
- 16 large prawns, peeled and deveined
- 8 East Coast lobster tails split in half
- ⅓ cup butter
- ¼ cup white wine
- ¼ cup lemon juice
- 2 tablespoons chopped fresh tarragon
- 2 medium garlic cloves, minced
- ½ teaspoon paprika
- ¼ teaspoon ground cayenne pepper

Preparation:
1. Whisk butter with lemon juice, wine, garlic, tarragon, paprika, salt, and cayenne pepper in a small saucepan.
2. Stir cook this mixture over medium heat for 1 minute.
3. Toss scallops, salmon fillet, and prawns in the Ninja baking dish and pour the butter mixture on top.
4. Transfer the dish to the Ninja Foodi Digital Air Fry Oven and close the door.
5. Select "Bake" mode by rotating the dial.
6. Press the TIME/SLICE button and change the value to 15 minutes.
7. Press the TEMP/DARKNESS button and change the value to 450 degrees F.
8. Press Start/Pause to begin cooking.
9. Serve warm.
Serving Suggestion: Serve the casserole with fresh greens and chili sauce on the side.
Variation Tip: Add breadcrumbs on top for a crispy touch.
Nutritional Information Per Serving:
Calories 457 | Fat 19g | Sodium 557mg | Carbs 9g | Fiber 1.8g | Sugar 1.2g | Protein 32.5g

Fish Newburg with Haddock

Preparation Time: 15 minutes.
Cooking Time: 29 minutes.
Servings: 4
Ingredients:
- 1 ½ pounds haddock fillets
- Salt and freshly ground black pepper
- 4 tablespoons butter
- 1 tablespoon & 2 teaspoons flour
- ¼ teaspoon sweet paprika
- ¼ teaspoon ground nutmeg
- Dash cayenne pepper
- ¾ cup heavy cream
- ½ cup milk
- 3 tablespoons dry sherry
- 2 large egg yolks
- 4 pastry shells

Preparation:
1. Rub haddock with black pepper and salt, then place in a sheet pan.
2. Place the spiced haddock in the pastry shell and close it like a colzone.
3. Drizzle 1 tablespoon of melted butter on top. Transfer the pan to the Ninja Foodi Digital Air Fry Oven and close the door.
4. Select "Bake" mode by rotating the dial.
5. Press the TIME/SLICE button and change the value to 25 minutes.
6. Press the TEMP/DARKNESS button and change the value to 350 degrees F.
7. Press Start/Pause to begin cooking.
8. Meanwhile, melt 3 tablespoons of butter in a suitable saucepan over low heat.
9. Stir in nutmeg, cayenne, paprika, and salt, then mix well.
10. Add flour to the spice butter and whisk well to avoid lumps.
11. Cook for 2 minutes, then add milk and cream. Mix well and cook until thickens.
12. Beat egg yolks with sherry in a bowl and stir in a ladle of cream mixture.
13. Mix well and return the mixture to the saucepan.
14. Cook the mixture on low heat for 2 minutes.
15. Add the baked wrapped haddock to the sauce and cook until warm.
16. Serve warm.
Serving Suggestion: Serve the haddock with fried rice.
Variation Tip: Drizzle parmesan cheese on top before cooking.
Nutritional Information Per Serving:
Calories 421 | Fat 7.4g | Sodium 356mg | Carbs 9.3g | Fiber 2.4g | Sugar 5g | Protein 37.2g

Scallops with Spinach

Preparation Time: 15 minutes
Cooking Time: 10 minutes
Servings: 2
Ingredients:
- ¾ cup heavy whipping cream
- 1 tablespoon tomato paste
- 1 teaspoon garlic, minced
- 1 tablespoon fresh basil, chopped
- Salt and ground black pepper, as required
- 8 jumbo sea scallops
- Olive oil cooking spray
- 1 (12-ounce) package frozen spinach, thawed and drained

Preparation:
1. In a bowl, place the cream, tomato paste, garlic, basil, salt, and black pepper and mix well.
2. Spray each scallop evenly with cooking spray and then, sprinkle with a little salt and black pepper.
3. In the bottom of a baking pan, place the spinach.
4. Arrange scallops on top of the spinach in a single layer and top with the cream mixture evenly.
5. Press "Power" button of Ninja Foodi Digital Air Fry Oven and turn the dial to select "Air Fry" mode.
6. Press TIME/SLICE button and again turn the dial to set the cooking time to 10 minutes.
7. Now push TEMP/DARKNESS button and rotate the dial to set the temperature at 350 degrees F.
8. Press "Start/Pause" button to start.
9. When the unit beeps to show that it is preheated, open the oven door.
10. Place the pan into the prepared air fry basket and insert in the oven.
11. When cooking time is completed, open the oven door and serve hot.
Serving Suggestions: Serve with crusty bread.
Variation Tip: Spinach can be replaced with kale.
Nutritional Information per Serving:
Calories: 309 | Fat: 18.8g | Sat Fat: 10.6g | Carbohydrates: 12.3g | Fiber: 4.1g | Sugar: 1.7g | Protein: 26.4g

Seafood Medley Mix

Preparation Time: 5 minutes
Cooking Time: 15 minutes
Servings: 1
Ingredients:
- ½ pound frozen seafood medley
- Oil or cooking spray
- Salt and black pepper, to taste

Preparation:
1. Take an air fry basket and evenly spray with a cooking spray.
2. Put frozen seafood medley in the air fry basket.
3. Turn on your Ninja Foodi Digital Air Fry Oven and rotate the knob to select "Air Fry".
4. Select the timer for 15 minutes and temperature for 400 degrees F.
5. Season the seafood medley with salt and pepper.
6. Serve and enjoy!
Serving Suggestions: Serve it with crispy garlic bread.
Variation Tip: Drizzle little bit of butter and lemon on top.
Nutritional Information per Serving:
Calories: 323 | Fat: 15.6g | Sat Fat: 3.8g | Carbohydrates: 5.1g | Fiber: 0g | Sugar: 0g | Protein: 32.4g

Maple Bacon Salmon

Preparation Time: 15 minutes.
Cooking Time: 29 minutes.
Servings: 4
Ingredients:
Salmon
- 1 lemon, sliced
- 1 (2 ¼-pound) skin-on salmon fillet
- 2 ½ teaspoons salt, black pepper, and garlic seasoning
- 1 tablespoon Dijon mustard
- ⅓ cup olive oil
- 2 tablespoons lemon juice
- 2 tablespoons maple syrup
- Chopped chives for garnish

Candied Bacon
- 3 tablespoons maple syrup
- 1 tablespoon packed brown sugar
- ¼ teaspoon salt, black pepper and garlic seasoning

Preparation:
1. Place lemon slices in a sheet pan and top them with salmon.
2. Drizzle salt, black pepper, and garlic seasoning on top.
3. Mix mustard, oil, maple syrup, lemon juice, salt, black pepper, and seasoning in a bowl.
4. Pour this sauce over the salmon.
5. Transfer the pan to the Ninja Foodi Digital Air Fry Oven and close the door.
6. Select "Air Fry" mode by rotating the dial.
7. Press the TIME/SLICE button and change the value to 25 minutes.
8. Press the TEMP/DARKNESS button and change the value to 350 degrees F.
9. Press Start/Pause to begin cooking.
10. Meanwhile, mix brown sugar, salt, black pepper, and garlic seasoning in a bowl.
11. Sauté bacon in a skillet until crispy and pour the sugar syrup on top.
12. Cook for 4 minutes until the liquid is absorbed.
13. Allow the bacon to cool and then crumble it.
14. Garnish the salmon with crumbled bacon and chopped chives.
15. Serve warm.
Serving Suggestion: Serve the salmon with roasted broccoli florets.
Variation Tip: Drizzle lemon butter on top before cooking.
Nutritional Information Per Serving:
Calories 415 | Fat 15g | Sodium 634mg | Carbs 4.3g | Fiber 1.4g | Sugar 1g | Protein 23.3g

Crispy Flounder

Preparation Time: 15 minutes
Cooking Time: 12 minutes
Servings: 3
Ingredients:
- 1 egg
- 1 cup dry Italian breadcrumb
- ¼ cup olive oil
- 3 (6-ounce) flounder fillets

Preparation:
1. In a shallow bowl, beat the egg.
2. In another bowl, add the breadcrumbs and oil and mix until a crumbly mixture is formed.
3. Dip the flounder fillets into the beaten egg and then coat with the breadcrumb mixture.
4. Press "Power" button of Ninja Foodi Digital Air Fry Oven and turn the dial to select "Air Fry" mode.
5. Press TIME/SLICE button and again turn the dial to set the cooking time to 12 minutes.
6. Now push TEMP/DARKNESS button and rotate the dial to set the temperature at 355 degrees F.
7. Press "Start/Pause" button to start.
8. When the unit beeps to show that it is preheated, open the oven door and grease the air fry basket.
9. Place the flounder fillets into the prepared air fry basket and insert in the oven.
10. When cooking time is completed, open the oven door and serve hot.
Serving Suggestions: Serve with potato chips.
Variation Tip: To avoid gluten, use crushed pork rinds instead of breadcrumbs.
Nutritional Information per Serving:
Calories: 508 | Fat: 22.8g | Sat Fat: 3.9g | Carbohydrates: 26.5g | Fiber: 1.8g | Sugar: 2.5g | Protein: 47.8g

Baked Sardines with Garlic and Oregano

Preparation Time: 15 minutes.
Cooking Time: 45 minutes.
Servings: 4
Ingredients:
- 2 pounds fresh sardines
- Salt and black pepper to taste
- 2 tablespoons Greek oregano
- 6 cloves garlic, thinly sliced
- ½ cup olive oil
- ½ cup freshly squeezed lemon juice
- ½ cup water

Preparation:
1. Mix salt, black pepper, oregano, garlic, olive oil, lemon juice, and water in a baking pan.
2. Spread the sardines in the marinade and rub well.
3. Leave the sardines for 10 minutes to marinate.
4. Transfer the pan to the Ninja Foodi Digital Air Fry Oven and close the door.
5. Select "Air Fry" mode by rotating the dial.
6. Press the TIME/SLICE button and change the value to 45 minutes.
7. Press the TEMP/DARKNESS button and change the value to 355 degrees F.
8. Press Start/Pause to begin cooking.
9. Serve warm.
Serving Suggestion: Serve the sardines with crispy bread and sautéed veggies.
Variation Tip: Add chili flakes on top for more spice.
Nutritional Information Per Serving:
Calories 392 | Fat 16g | Sodium 466mg | Carbs 3.9g | Fiber 0.9g | Sugar 0.6g | Protein 48g

Rum-Glazed Shrimp

Preparation Time: 10 minutes.
Cooking Time: 5 minutes.
Servings: 4
Ingredients:
- 1 ½ pounds shrimp, peeled and deveined
- 3 tablespoons olive oil
- ⅓ cup sweet chili sauce
- ¼ cup soy sauce
- ¼ Captain Morgan Spiced Rum
- 2 garlic cloves, minced
- Juice of 1 lime
- ½ teaspoon crushed red pepper flakes
- 1 green onion, thinly sliced

Preparation:
1. Mix shrimp with all the ingredients in a bowl.
2. Cover and marinate the shrimp for 30 minutes.
3. Spread the glazed shrimp in a sheet pan.
4. Transfer the pan to the Ninja Foodi Digital Air Fry Oven and close the door.
5. Select "Bake" mode by rotating the dial.
6. Press the TIME/SLICE button and change the value to 5 minutes.
7. Press the TEMP/DARKNESS button and change the value to 375 degrees F.
8. Press Start/Pause to begin cooking.
9. Serve warm.

Serving Suggestion: Serve the shrimp with sautéed asparagus.
Variation Tip: Spread the shrimp on top of the lettuce leaves.
Nutritional Information Per Serving:
Calories 378 | Fat 7g | Sodium 316mg | Carbs 6.2g | Fiber 0.3g | Sugar 0.3g | Protein 26g

Air Fried Fish Sticks

Preparation Time: 6 minutes
Cooking Time: 15 minutes
Servings: 1
Ingredients:
- ½ pound fish fillets
- ¼ teaspoon ground black pepper, divided
- 1 egg
- ¼ cup flour
- ½ teaspoon salt, divided
- ½ cup breadcrumbs, dried

Preparation:
1. Take a bowl and add flour, salt and pepper.
2. In a second bowl, whisk the egg. In another bowl, add breadcrumbs.
3. Dredge the fish in flour, then dip in egg and lastly coat with breadcrumbs.
4. Once they are done, put them in an air fry basket.
5. Turn on your Ninja Foodi Digital Air Fry Oven and rotate the knob to select "Air Fry".
6. Select the timer for about 10 to 15 minutes and temperature for 400 degrees F.
7. Serve and enjoy!

Serving Suggestions: Serve with fresh lemon juice.
Variation Tip: You can season fish with salt beforehand.
Nutritional Information per Serving:
Calories: 918 | Fat: 35.4g | Sat Fat: 8.5g | Carbohydrates: 101.9g | Fiber: 4.5g | Sugar: 3.8g | Protein: 49.3g

Garlic Shrimp with Lemon

Preparation Time: 5 minutes
Cooking Time: 12 minutes
Servings: 1
Ingredients:
- ½ pound raw shrimp
- ⅛ teaspoon garlic powder
- Salt and black pepper, to taste
- Vegetable oil, to coat shrimp
- Chili flakes
- Lemon wedges
- Parsley

Preparation:
1. Take a bowl and coat the shrimp with vegetable oil.
2. Add garlic powder, pepper and salt and toss to coat well.
3. Now, transfer shrimp to a plate or air fry basket.
4. Turn on your Ninja Foodi Digital Air Fry Oven and rotate the knob to select "Air Fry".
5. Select the timer for about 12 minutes and temperature for 400 degrees F.
6. Transfer shrimp to a bowl and add lemon wedges.
7. Sprinkle parsley and chili flakes evenly on top.
8. Serve and enjoy!

Serving Suggestions: Serve it with macaroni salad.
Variation Tip: Try not to cook for too long otherwise it can get dry.
Nutritional Information per Serving:
Calories: 398 | Fat: 17.9g | Sat Fat: 2.2g | Carbohydrates: 4.7g | Fiber: 0.4g | Sugar: 0.4g | Protein: 51.9g

Lemon Pepper Shrimp

Preparation Time: 5 minutes
Cooking Time: 8 minutes
Servings: 4
Ingredients:
- 2 lemons, juiced
- ½ tablespoon lemon pepper
- 2 tablespoons olive oil
- ½ teaspoon paprika
- ½ teaspoon garlic powder
- 1½ pounds shrimp

Preparation:
1. Take a bowl, add all the ingredients together and mix well.
2. Add shrimp and toss to coat well.
3. Turn on your Ninja Foodi Digital Air Fry Oven and rotate the knob to select "Air Fry".
4. Select the timer for about 6 to 8 minutes and temperature for 400 degrees F.
5. Place shrimp in the air fry basket and cook until pink.
6. Serve and enjoy!

Serving Suggestions: Serve with lemon slices.
Variation Tip: You can also add a couple drops of tabasco with olive oil.
Nutritional Information per Serving:
Calories: 274 | Fat: 10g | Sat Fat: 1.9g | Carbohydrates: 6.2g | Fiber: 1.2g | Sugar: 0.9g | Protein: 39.3g

Buttered Trout

Preparation Time: 10 minutes
Cooking Time: 10 minutes
Servings: 2
Ingredients:
- 2 (6-ounce) trout fillets
- Salt and ground black pepper, as required
- 1 tablespoon butter, melted

Preparation:
1. Season each trout fillet with salt and black pepper and then coat with the butter.
2. Arrange the trout fillets onto the greased sheet pan in a single layer.
3. Press "Power" button of Ninja Foodi Digital Air Fry Oven and turn the dial to select "Air Fry" mode.
4. Press TIME/SLICE button and again turn the dial to set the cooking time to 10 minutes.
5. Now push TEMP/DARKNESS button and rotate the dial to set the temperature at 360 degrees F.
6. Press "Start/Pause" button to start.
7. When the unit beeps to show that it is preheated, open the oven door.
8. Insert the sheet pan in oven.
9. Flip the fillets once halfway through.
10. When cooking time is completed, open the oven door and serve hot.

Serving Suggestions: Serve with your favorite salad.
Variation Tip: Rinse the trout thoroughly.
Nutritional Information per Serving:
Calories: 374 | Fat: 20.2g | Sat Fat: 6.2g | Carbohydrates: 0g | Fiber: 0g | Sugar: 0g | Protein: 45.4g

Greek Baked Bonito with Herbs and Potatoes

Preparation Time: 30 minutes
Cooking Time: 1 hour 30 minutes
Servings: 6
Ingredients:
- 3-pound whole bonito
- Sea salt, to taste
- Freshly ground black pepper, to taste
- 2 teaspoons Greek oregano
- 5 to 6 cloves garlic, sliced
- 2½ pounds potatoes
- Cooking spray
- ½ cup olive oil
- 6 tablespoons freshly squeezed lemon juice
- 1⅓ cups water

Preparation:
1. Select the BAKE function, 355°F, for 1 hour, 30 minutes. While the oven is preheating, prepare the ingredients.
2. Remove and discard the fish's head and intestines. Cut along the back, remove the bloodline, and cut the fish in half lengthwise.
3. Rinse and pat the fish dry. Sprinkle with the salt, pepper, and 1 teaspoon of oregano. Then, insert the sliced garlic into the meatiest parts of the fish.
4. Next, peel the potatoes and cut them into equal-sized wedge-shaped pieces. Sprinkle salt, pepper, and the remaining oregano over the potatoes.
5. Use the cooking spray to lightly spray a large roasting pan (one that is air fryer-appropriate). Add the fish, skin side down, and put the potatoes around it.
6. Take a small bowl, and whisk together the lemon juice and oil. Pour the mixture over the fish and potatoes and add the water.
7. Bake the fillets for 1½ hours in the preheated oven.

Serving Suggestion: Garnish with some greens and serve it alongside the baked potatoes.
Variation Tip: You can combine chipotle chilies, Mexican oregano, crushed garlic, lime juice, salt, and olive oil to make a paste. Use this for a Mexican flavor.
Nutritional Information Per Serving:
Calories: 1000 | Fat: 24g | Sodium: 16057mg | Carbs: 42g | Fiber: 4g | Sugar: 2g | Protein: 147g

Fish Casserole

Preparation Time: 10 minutes
Cooking Time: 40 minutes
Servings: 3
Ingredients:
- ½ tablespoon unsalted butter, softened
- ¼ teaspoon salt
- 1 pound white fish fillet
- ¼ teaspoon pepper
- ½ sweet onion, thinly sliced
- 2 teaspoons extra-virgin olive oil, divided
- ¼ teaspoon dry thyme
- 1 pinch nutmeg
- 1 bread slice, crusts removed
- ¼ teaspoon paprika
- ⅛ teaspoon garlic powder
- ½ cup shredded Swiss cheese

Preparation:
1. Turn on your Ninja Foodi Digital Air Fry Oven and rotate the knob to select "Bake".
2. Preheat by selecting the timer for 3 minutes and temperature for 400 degrees F.
3. Arrange fish fillet on a dish and season with salt and pepper.
4. Take a pan and heat oil over medium-high heat. Add onion and cook until it starts to brown.
5. Stir in thyme and nutmeg.
6. Spread the onion mixture over fish.
7. In a food processor, add bread slice, paprika, garlic powder and a little oil.
8. Process until we have a moist mixture.
9. Sprinkle crumbs over the onion mixture.
10. Add cheese on top of casserole and place inside the Ninja Foodi Digital Air Fry Oven.
11. Select the timer for about 18 to 22 minutes and temperature for 400 degrees F.
12. Serve warm.

Serving Suggestions: Serve with rice or with potatoes.
Variation Tip: You can also add a tablespoon of lemon juice.
Nutritional Information per Serving:
Calories: 389 | Fat: 21.6g | Sat Fat: 6.7g | Carbohydrates: 4.6g | Fiber: 0.6g | Sugar: 1.2g | Protein: 42.4g

Baked Sole with Mint and Ginger

Preparation Time: 10 minutes
Cooking Time: 15 minutes
Servings: 4
Ingredients:
- 2 pounds petrale sole fillets
- 1 bunch fresh mint
- 2 pieces ginger, peeled and chopped
- 1 tablespoon vegetable oil
- ½ teaspoon salt
- ¼ teaspoon freshly ground black pepper

Preparation:
1. Select the BAKE function, 375°F, for 15 minutes. While the oven is preheating, prepare the ingredients.
2. Rinse and pat dry the fillets, then arrange them on an air fryer-safe rimmed baking pan.
3. Place the ginger, salt, pepper, mint, and oil in a blender and blend to make a smooth paste.
4. Rub the fillets evenly with the mint-ginger paste. Bake the fish for about 15 minutes.

Serving Suggestion: You can serve the fish with some roasted veggies.
Variation Tip: You can try using canola oil.
Nutritional Information Per Serving:
Calories: 230 | Fat: 9g | Sodium: 1089mg | Carbs: 1g | Fiber: 1g | Sugar: 0g | Protein: 35g

Crispy Air Fryer Fish Tacos

Preparation Time: 25 minutes
Cooking Time: 10 minutes
Servings: 2 to 4
Ingredients:
- 1 cup panko breadcrumbs
- 1¼ teaspoons garlic powder
- 1½ teaspoons chili powder
- ½ teaspoon onion powder
- 1 teaspoon ground cumin
- ¾ teaspoon kosher salt
- ¼ teaspoon black pepper
- 24 ounces barramundi
- 1 large egg
- 2 tablespoons water
- 16 flour tortillas

For the salsa:
- 2 tablespoons lime juice
- 2 teaspoons honey
- 1 small garlic clove, grated
- ½ teaspoon kosher salt
- ½ teaspoon ground cumin
- ½ teaspoon chili powder
- 2 tablespoons olive oil
- 5 cups cabbage, shredded
- Diced jalapeño, diced
- 1 cup pineapple, chopped
- ¼ cup fresh cilantro, chopped
- ¼ cup red onion, diced

Preparation:
1. Select the AIR FRY function, 380°F, for 10 minutes. While the oven is preheating, start preparing the ingredients.
2. Take a shallow bowl and mix the panko, chili powder, garlic powder, salt, onion powder, cumin, and black pepper. Stir to combine.
3. Take another shallow bowl and combine the egg and water. Pat the fish dry using paper towels and cut the fish into pieces. Then sprinkle it with salt and pepper.
4. First, dip the fish pieces into the egg mixture, then coat in the breadcrumb mixture. Make sure the breadcrumbs are pressed into the fish.
5. Add half of the fillets to the air fryer basket and spray with olive oil spray. Cook for about 4 minutes, turn over, spray with oil spray, and cook for another 2 minutes. Repeat for the next batch.
6. Meanwhile, whisk together the honey, cumin, garlic, lime juice, olive oil, and chili powder in a medium bowl. Then, add the jalapeño, cilantro, cabbage, pineapple, and red onion. Toss to combine, then season with salt and pepper.
7. Warm the tortillas in the microwave or over an open flame. Add a little slaw to the tortillas. Top with the cooked fish and cover with some more slaw.

Serving Suggestion: Serve with sour cream and a squeeze of lime juice.
Variation Tip: Try experimenting with the ingredients of salsa for added flavors.
Nutritional Information Per Serving:
Calories: 82 | Fat: 3g | Sodium: 162mg | Carbs: 5g | Fiber: 1g | Sugar: 2g | Protein: 9g

Lobster Tails with Lemon-Garlic Butter

Preparation Time: 5 minutes
Cooking Time: 10 minutes
Servings: 1
Ingredients:
- 2 tablespoons butter
- ½ teaspoon lemon zest
- 1 lobster tail
- ½ clove garlic, grated
- ½ teaspoon parsley, chopped
- Salt, to taste
- Fresh ground black pepper, to taste

Preparation:
1. Cut the lobster tail lengthwise through the center of the hard top shell.
2. Cut to the bottom of the shell and spread the tail halves apart.
3. Place the lobster tail in the air fry basket.
4. Take a saucepan and melt butter on medium heat.
5. Add garlic and lemon zest and cook for 30 seconds.
6. Now, pour the butter mixture onto lobster tail.
7. Turn on your Ninja Foodi Digital Air Fry Oven and rotate the knob to select "Air Fry".
8. Select the timer for about 5 to 7 minutes and temperature for 380 degrees F.
9. Let it cook and serve with parsley as topping.

Serving Suggestions: Serve with lemon wedges on side.
Variation Tip: You can use small piece of foil to hold in the butter mixture.
Nutritional Information per Serving:
Calories: 337 | Fat: 24.3g | Sat Fat: 14.9g | Carbohydrates: 0.8g | Fiber: 0.1g | Sugar: 0.1g | Protein: 27.9g

Beer-Battered Fish

Preparation Time: 15 minutes.
Cooking Time: 15 minutes.
Servings: 4
Ingredients:
- 1 ½ cups all-purpose flour
- kosher salt, to taste
- ½ teaspoon Old Bay seasoning
- 1 (12-ounce) bottle lager
- 1 large egg, beaten
- 2 pounds cod, cut into 12 pieces
- freshly ground black pepper
- vegetable oil for frying
- lemon wedges, for serving

Preparation:
1. Mix flour with old bay, salt, egg, and beer in a bowl.
2. Rub the cod with black pepper and salt.
3. Coat the codfish with the beer batter and place it in the air fry basket.
4. Transfer the basket to the Ninja Foodi Digital Air Fry Oven and close the door.
5. Select "Air Fry" mode by rotating the dial.
6. Press the TIME/SLICE button and change the value to 15 minutes
7. Press the TEMP/DARKNESS button and change the value to 350 degrees F.
8. Press Start/Pause to begin cooking.
9. Serve warm.

Serving Suggestion: Serve the fish with potato fries and tomato ketchup.
Variation Tip: Rub the fish with lemon juice before coating.
Nutritional Information Per Serving:
Calories 428 | Fat 17g | Sodium 723mg | Carbs 21g | Fiber 2.5g | Sugar 2g | Protein 43g

Baked Swordfish

Preparation Time: 10 minutes
Cooking Time: 25 minutes
Servings: 4
Ingredients:
- 4 ounces mushrooms
- 1 cup onion
- 1 rib celery
- ½ green bell pepper
- 2 tablespoons olive oil
- 2 tablespoons lemon juice
- Dash of kosher salt
- Dash of black pepper
- 1½ pounds swordfish
- ½ teaspoon Creole seasoning blend
- 2 bay leaves
- 1 dozen grape tomatoes
- 3 to 4 tablespoons water or broth

Preparation:
1. Select the BAKE function, 400°F, for 25 minutes. While the oven is preheating, prepare the ingredients.
2. Rinse and thoroughly dry the mushrooms, then slice them thinly.
3. Peel and cut the onion in half and slice thinly. Clean and dice the half bell pepper.
4. Place a skillet over medium flame to heat the olive oil. Add the mushrooms, onion, celery, and bell pepper. Cook, occasionally stirring, for about 8 to 10 minutes.

5. Next, add the lemon juice, salt, and pepper, then stir to combine.
6. Prepare a large shallow baking pan with non-stick cooking spray. Lay half of the mushrooms and onion mixture in it and arrange the swordfish steaks on top of them.
7. Sprinkle with the Creole seasoning. Place a piece of bay leaf on every steak.
8. Scatter the sliced tomatoes over the fish steaks, then sprinkle with the remaining mushroom and onion mixture. Drizzle with water or broth.
9. Cover and bake the fish for about 20 to 25 minutes.

Serving Suggestion: Serve the fish on a bed of rice or alongside roasted potatoes.
Variation Tip: You can try Italian seasoning instead of Creole seasoning.
Nutritional Information Per Serving:
Calories: 399 | Fat: 21g | Sodium: 284mg | Carbs: 10g | Fiber: 3g | Sugar: 0g | Protein: 42g

Breaded Shrimp

Preparation Time: 8 minutes
Cooking Time: 7 minutes
Servings: 2
Ingredients:
- ¼ teaspoon garlic powder
- ¼ teaspoon onion powder
- ¼ teaspoon salt
- ½ pound raw shrimp
- 1 egg
- 2 teaspoons flour
- ½ teaspoon corn starch
- 1 tablespoon water
- 6 tablespoons fine breadcrumbs
- 6 tablespoons panko breadcrumbs

Preparation:
1. Take a small bowl, add flour, corn starch, garlic powder, onion powder and salt.
2. Add shrimp in the bowl and toss to coat well.
3. In a second bowl, whisk in the egg.
4. Mix the panko breadcrumbs and fine breadcrumbs together in another bowl.
5. Now, take seasoned shrimp, dip in the egg and place in the breadcrumbs mixture.
6. Lightly grease the air fry basket.
7. Turn on your Ninja Foodi Digital Air Fry Oven and rotate the knob to select "Air Fry".
8. Select the timer for about 7 minutes and temperature for 370 degrees F.
9. Place the coated shrimp to the air fry basket and let it cook.
10. Serve and enjoy!

Serving Suggestions: Serve it with tartar sauce or a dipping sauce of your choice.
Variation Tip: Try to rinse shrimp using cold water beforehand.
Nutritional Information per Serving:
Calories: 1351 | Fat: 26.6g | Sat Fat: 10.3g | Carbohydrates: 54.3g | Fiber: 1.3g | Sugar: 1g | Protein: 37.7g

Scallops with Chanterelles

Preparation Time: 10 minutes
Cooking Time: 15 minutes
Servings: 3
Ingredients:
- 1 tablespoon balsamic vinegar
- ½ pound scallops
- 3 tablespoons butter
- ½ tomato, peeled, seeded, and chopped
- 1 tablespoon butter
- ¼ pound chanterelle mushrooms

Preparation:
1. Take a pan and add half tablespoon butter over medium heat.
2. Stir in chanterelles and cook for 5 to 8 minutes.
3. Transfer to a bowl.
4. Add remaining butter in the same pan over low heat and cook for 5 minutes.
5. Stir in tomato and balsamic vinegar and cook for 2 minutes.
6. Stir the tomato mixture into mushrooms.
7. Turn on your Ninja Foodi Digital Air Fry Oven and rotate the knob to select "Air Broil".
8. Select the timer for about 2 minutes per side and temperature for HI.
9. Serve warm and enjoy!

Serving Suggestions: Serve with mashed potatoes and green onions.
Variation Tip: Use extra chanterelles on top.
Nutritional Information per Serving:
Calories: 361 | Fat: 16.7g | Sat Fat: 9.1g | Carbohydrates: 22.2g | Fiber: 9.9g | Sugar: 0.8g | Protein: 23.7g

Broiled Scallops

Preparation Time: 5 minutes
Cooking Time: 8 minutes
Servings: 2
Ingredients:
- 1 pound bay scallops
- 1 tablespoon lemon juice
- 1 tablespoon butter, melted
- ½ tablespoon garlic salt

Preparation:
1. Turn on your Ninja Foodi Digital Air Fry Oven and rotate the knob to select "Air Broil".
2. Rinse scallop and place in a pan.
3. Season with garlic salt, butter and lemon juice.
4. Select the timer for about 8 minutes and temperature for HI.
5. Remove from oven and serve warm.

Serving Suggestions: Serve with margarine on side.
Variation Tip: You can use extra melted butter.

Nutritional Information per Serving:
Calories: 259 | Fat: 7.6g | Sat Fat: 3.9g | Carbohydrates: 7g | Fiber: 0.2g | Sugar: 0.7g | Protein: 38.5g

Garlic Butter Salmon Bites

Preparation Time: 6 minutes
Cooking Time: 10 minutes
Servings: 2
Ingredients:
- 1 tablespoon lemon juice

- 2 tablespoons butter
- ½ tablespoon garlic, minced
- ½ teaspoon pepper
- 4 oz. salmon
- ½ teaspoon salt
- ½ tablespoon apple cider or rice vinegar

Preparation:
1. Take a large bowl and add everything except salmon and whisk together until well combined.
2. Slice the salmon into small cubes and marinade them into the mixture.
3. Cover the bowl with plastic wrap and refrigerate it for about an hour.
4. Now, spread out the marinated salmon cubes into the air fry basket.
5. Turn on your Ninja Foodi Digital Air Fry Oven and rotate the knob to select "Air Fry".
6. Select the timer for 10 minutes and temperature for 350 degrees F.
7. Wait till the salmon is finely cooked.
8. Serve and enjoy!

Serving Suggestions: Serve with cheese on top.
Variation Tip: You can also coat salmon using bread crumbs for a fine taste.
Nutritional Information per Serving:
Calories: 159 | Fat: 12.2g | Sat Fat: 6g | Carbohydrates: 1.7g | Fiber: 0.2g | Sugar: 0.6g | Protein: 11.3g

Baked Tilapia with Buttery Crumb Topping

Preparation Time: 15 minutes.
Cooking Time: 16 minutes.
Servings: 4
Ingredients:
- 4 tilapia fillets
- Salt and black pepper to taste
- 1 cup bread crumbs
- 3 tablespoons butter, melted
- ½ teaspoon dried basil

Preparation:
1. Rub the tilapia fillets with black pepper and salt, then place them in the sheet pan.
2. Mix butter, breadcrumbs, and seasonings in a bowl.
3. Sprinkle the breadcrumbs mixture on top of the tilapia.
4. Transfer the fish to the Ninja Foodi Digital Air Fry Oven and close the door.
5. Select "Bake" mode by rotating the dial.
6. Press the TIME/SLICE button and change the value to 15 minutes.
7. Press the TEMP/DARKNESS button and change the value to 375 degrees F.
8. Press Start/Pause to begin cooking.
9. Switch to "AIR BROIL" at "HI" and cook for 1 minute.
10. Serve warm.

Serving Suggestion: Serve the tilapia with vegetable rice.
Variation Tip: Add crushed corn flakes on top for more crispiness.
Nutritional Information Per Serving:
Calories 558 | Fat 9g | Sodium 994mg | Carbs 1g | Fiber 0.4g | Sugar 3g | Protein 16g

Brown Sugar and Garlic Air Fryer Salmon

Preparation Time: 5 minutes
Cooking Time: 10 minutes
Servings: 4
Ingredients:
- 1 pound salmon
- Salt and pepper, to taste
- 2 tablespoons brown sugar
- 1 teaspoon chili powder
- ½ teaspoon paprika
- 1 teaspoon Italian seasoning
- 1 teaspoon garlic powder

Preparation:
1. Select the AIR FRY function, 400°F, for 10 minutes. While the oven is preheating, prepare the ingredients.
2. Season the salmon with salt and pepper.
3. Take a small bowl and add the chili powder, Italian seasoning, brown sugar, paprika, and garlic powder. Rub the mixture on the salmon.
4. Put the salmon in the air fryer basket, skin side down, and cook for about 10 minutes.

Serving Suggestion: You can use cayenne pepper instead of paprika.
Variation Tip: You can add asparagus to the recipe.
Nutritional Information Per Serving:
Calories: 190 | Fat: 7.7g | Sodium: 61mg | Carbs: 7g | Fiber: 1g | Sugar: 6g | Protein: 23g

Air Fried Fish Cakes

Preparation Time: 5 minutes
Cooking Time: 10 minutes
Servings: 1
Ingredients:
- ½ pound white fish, finely chopped
- ⅓ cup panko breadcrumbs
- 2 tablespoons cilantro, chopped
- 1 tablespoon chili sauce
- Cooking spray
- ½ egg
- 1 tablespoon mayonnaise
- ⅛ teaspoon ground pepper
- 1 pinch of salt

Preparation:
1. Take a bowl and add all ingredients together until well combined.
2. Shape the mixture into cakes.
3. Grease the air fry basket using cooking spray.
4. Turn on your Ninja Foodi Digital Air Fry Oven and rotate the knob to select "Air Fry".
5. Select the timer for about 10 minutes and temperature for 400 degrees F.
6. Let the fish cakes cook until they are golden brown.
7. Serve and enjoy!

Serving Suggestions: Serve with lemon wedges to enhance taste.
Variation Tip: Squeeze out any excess moisture before adding fish to the mixture.
Nutritional Information per Serving:
Calories: 517 | Fat: 17g | Sat Fat: 4.3g | Carbohydrates: 9.7g | Fiber: 0.3g | Sugar: 1.4g | Protein: 57.6g

Baked Oysters

Preparation Time: 5 minutes
Cooking Time: 25 minutes
Servings: 4 to 6
Ingredients:
- 24 shucked oysters
- Creole seasoning, to taste
- ½ cup parmesan cheese, grated
- ½ cup sharp cheddar cheese, grated
- 2 tablespoons fresh parsley, chopped

Preparation:
1. Select the BAKE function, 375°F, for 15 minutes. While the oven is preheating, prepare the ingredients.
2. Take a large, air fryer-safe, rimmed baking sheet and line it with a crinkled-up foil sheet.
3. Transfer the oysters to the prepared baking sheet.
4. Sprinkle the oysters with some Creole seasoning and top each with 1 teaspoon of each cheese.
5. Bake the oysters for about 15 minutes.

Serving Suggestion: Sprinkle with fresh parsley before serving.
Variation Tip: You can experiment by using Italian seasoning instead of Creole seasoning.
Nutritional Information Per Serving:
Calories: 114 | Fat: 5g | Sodium: 283mg | Carbs: 5.3g | Fiber: 0.2g | Sugar: 1.3g | Protein: 11.6g

Buttery Baked Lobster Tails

Preparation Time: 10 minutes
Cooking Time: 6 minutes
Servings: 4
Ingredients:
- 4 (6 to 8 ounces) fresh lobster tails
- 4 tablespoons unsalted butter, melted
- 3 cloves garlic, minced
- 1 teaspoon sweet or smoked paprika
- ½ teaspoon salt
- ½ teaspoon ground black pepper
- 1 tablespoon fresh parsley, chopped

Preparation:
1. Select the AIR BROIL function on HI. Allow the oven to preheat.
2. Place the lobster tails on the sheet pan.
3. Cut the lobster along their middle with kitchen shears towards the fins of their tails. Avoid cutting through the fin.
4. Gently open the shell and pull the meat out without detaching it. Close the empty shells and place the meat on top of the seam.
5. Take a mixing bowl, and combine the garlic, salt, pepper, melted butter, parsley, and paprika.
6. Brush the tops of the tails with the butter mixture.
7. Broil the tails for about 6 to 8 minutes.

Serving Suggestion: Serve with lemon wedges and more butter sauce.
Variation Tip: Try using celery leaves instead of parsley.
Nutritional Information Per Serving:
Calories: 144k | Fat: 12g | Sodium: 593mg | Carbs: 2g | Fiber: 1g | Sugar: 1g | Protein: 8g

Seafood Casserole

Preparation Time: 15 minutes.
Cooking Time: 20 minutes.
Servings: 8
Ingredients:
- 8 ounces haddock, skinned and diced
- 1 pound scallops
- 1 pound large shrimp, peeled and deveined
- 3 to 4 garlic cloves, minced
- ½ cup heavy cream
- ½ cup Swiss cheese, shredded
- 2 tablespoons Parmesan, grated
- Paprika, to taste
- Sea salt and black pepper, to taste

Preparation:
1. Toss shrimp, scallops, and haddock chunks in the sheet pan greased with cooking spray.
2. Drizzle salt, black pepper, and minced garlic over the seafood mix.
3. Top this seafood with cream, Swiss cheese, paprika, and Parmesan cheese.
4. Transfer the dish to the Ninja Digital Air Fryer Oven and close its oven door.
5. Select "Bake" mode by rotating the dial.
6. Press the TIME/SLICE button and change the value to 20 minutes.
7. Press the TEMP/DARKNESS button and change the value to 375 degrees F.
8. Press Start/Pause to begin cooking.
9. Serve warm.

Serving Suggestion: Serve the seafood casserole with fresh vegetable salad.
Variation Tip: Add alfredo sauce to the casserole for better taste.
Nutritional Information Per Serving:
Calories 548 | Fat 13g | Sodium 353mg | Carbs 31g | Fiber 0.4g | Sugar 1g | Protein 29g

Fish in Yogurt Marinade

Preparation Time: 15 minutes.
Cooking Time: 10 minutes.
Servings: 2
Ingredients:
- 1 cup plain Greek yogurt
- Finely grated zest of 1 lemon
- 1 tablespoon lemon juice
- 1 tablespoon finely minced garlic
- 3 tablespoons fresh oregano leaves
- 1 teaspoon ground cumin
- ¼ teaspoon ground allspice
- ½ teaspoon salt
- ½ teaspoon freshly ground black pepper
- 1½ pounds perch filets

Preparation:
1. Mix lemon zest, yogurt, garlic, cumin, oregano, black pepper, salt, and all spices in a shallow pan.
2. Add fish to this marinade, mix well to coat then cover it with a plastic wrap.
3. Marinate for 15 minutes in the refrigerator, then uncover.
4. Transfer the fish pan to the Ninja Foodi Digital Air Fry Oven and close the door.
5. Select "Bake" mode by rotating the dial.
6. Press the TIME/SLICE button and change the value to 10 minutes.

7. Press the TEMP/DARKNESS button and change the value to 450 degrees F.
8. Press Start/Pause to begin cooking.
9. Serve warm.

Serving Suggestion: Serve the fish with lemon slices and fried rice.
Variation Tip: Use white pepper for seasoning for a change of flavor.
Nutritional Information Per Serving:
Calories 438 | Fat 21g | Sodium 146mg | Carbs 7.1g | Fiber 0.1g | Sugar 0.4g | Protein 23g

Blackened Fish Tacos

Preparation Time: 10 minutes
Cooking Time: 10 minutes
Servings: 4
Ingredients:
- 1 pound mahi mahi fillets
- ¾ teaspoon salt
- 1 tablespoon paprika
- 1 teaspoon oregano
- ¾ teaspoon cayenne
- ½ teaspoon garlic powder
- ½ teaspoon onion powder
- ½ teaspoon black pepper
- 1 teaspoon brown sugar

For the tacos:
- 8 corn tortillas
- Mango salsa

Preparation:
1. Take a shallow mixing bowl, and combine the paprika, garlic powder, oregano, brown sugar, cayenne, and black pepper.
2. Pat the fish fillets dry with paper towels, then drizzle over some olive oil.
3. Sprinkle one side of the fish fillets with the spice mix, and gently pat to stick the spices to the fish.
4. Flip the fillets and brush the other side with oil and sprinkle on the remaining spices. Again press gently to stick the spices to the fish.
5. Select the AIR FRY function, 360°F, for 9 minutes. Allow the oven to preheat. Place the fish in the air fryer basket and spray with some cooking oil.
6. While the fish is cooking, warm the tortillas to your liking. When the fillets are done, add one fillet to each tortilla. Top with 2 tablespoons of mango salsa, and it's done.

Serving Suggestion: Add some cut-up fruit or greens on top before serving.
Variation Tip: You can skip brown sugar for a low-carb meal. And feel free to use any other white fish.
Nutritional Information Per Serving:
Calories: 247 | Fat: 3g | Sodium: 707mg | Carbs: 32g | Fiber: 5g | Sugar: 7g | Protein: 25g

Air Fryer Tuna Patties

Preparation Time: 15 minutes
Cooking Time: 10 minutes
Servings: 2 to 3
Ingredients:
- 1-pound fresh tuna
- 2 to 3 large eggs
- Zest of 1 medium lemon
- 1 tablespoon lemon juice
- ½ cup breadcrumbs
- 3 tablespoons parmesan cheese, grated
- 1 celery stalk, finely chopped
- 3 tablespoons onion, minced
- ½ teaspoon garlic powder
- ½ teaspoon dried herbs
- ¼ teaspoon kosher salt
- Fresh cracked black pepper, to taste

Preparation:
1. Take a medium bowl, and combine the fresh tuna, lemon juice, lemon zest, eggs, garlic powder, celery, parmesan cheese, onion, dried herbs, salt, breadcrumbs and pepper. Stir and combine well.
2. Prepare the air fryer basket with perforated air fryer baking paper and lightly spray the sheet.
3. Scoop up ¼ cup of the mixture and shape it into patties. Try to keep the patties the same size. Chill them for about 1 hour.
4. Select the AIR FRY function. Place the patties in the prepared air fryer basket (you may need to cook in batches), spray with some cooking oil, and cook them for about 10 minutes at 360°F, flipping halfway through. Respray the tops after flipping them.

Serving Suggestion: Serve with tartar sauce and some lemon slices.
Variation Tip: You can try adding any combo of dried herbs like oregano, dill, basil, or thyme.
Nutritional Information Per Serving:
Calories: 85k | Fat: 3g | Sodium: 282mg | Carbs: 1g | Fiber: 1g | Sugar: 1g | Protein: 13g

Air Fryer White Fish with Garlic and Lemon

Preparation Time: 5 minutes
Cooking Time: 12 minutes
Servings: 2
Ingredients:
- 12 ounces tilapia fillets
- ½ teaspoon garlic powder
- ½ teaspoon onion powder
- ½ teaspoon lemon pepper seasoning
- Kosher salt or sea salt, to taste
- Fresh cracked black pepper, to taste
- 1 tablespoon fresh parsley, chopped for serving
- 1 lemon, cut into wedges

Preparation:
1. Select the AIR FRY function, 360°F, for 12 minutes. While the oven is preheating, prepare the ingredients.
2. Rinse and pat dry the fish fillets and spray with olive oil. Then season both sides with the garlic powder, onion powder, salt, and pepper.
3. Prepare the air fryer basket with perforated baking paper and lightly spray the paper with cooking oil. Lay the fish on the paper and place a few lemon wedges next to the fish.
4. Cook the fish for about 6 to 12 minutes.

Serving Suggestion: Sprinkle with the chopped parsley and serve with lemon wedges.
Variation Tip: You can use other white fish. You can also add ½ teaspoon of onion powder.
Nutritional Information Per Serving:
Calories: 169 | Fat: 3g | Sodium: 89mg | Carbs: 1g | Fiber: 1g | Sugar: 1g | Protein: 34g

Air Fryer Shrimp Caesar Salad

Preparation Time: 15 minutes
Cooking Time: 5 minutes/batch
Servings: 4
Ingredients:
- 2 romaine hearts, coarsely chopped
- 1 cup cherry tomatoes
- ¼ cup parmesan cheese, shredded
- ½ cup all-purpose flour
- ¾ teaspoon salt
- ½ teaspoon pepper
- 1-pound uncooked shrimp
- Cooking spray
- ½ cup creamy Caesar salad dressing

Preparation:
1. Select the AIR FRY function, 375°F, for 15 minutes. While the oven is preheating, prepare the ingredients. You'll be cooking the shrimp in batches.
2. Take a large bowl, combine the tomatoes, romaine, and cheese, and put it in the refrigerator.
3. Take a shallow bowl, and mix the salt, pepper, and flour. Then add the shrimp, a few pieces at a time, and toss to coat.
4. Lay the shrimp in the greased air fryer basket in a single layer. Spray with cooking spray and cook for about 2 to 3 minutes. Flip and spray with cooking spray and cook for another 2 to 3 minutes.
5. Repeat the same for the next batches.
6. Drizzle the dressing over the romaine mixture, toss to coat, and place the shrimp on top. It's ready to eat!

Serving Suggestion: Sprinkle with cheese and pepper before serving.
Variation Tip: You can try Asiago cheese instead of parmesan.
Nutritional Information Per Serving:
Calories: 313k | Fat: 21g | Sodium: 680mg | Carbs: 8g | Fiber: 2g | Sugar: 2g | Protein: 23g

Spiced Chicken Breasts

Preparation Time: 10 minutes
Cooking Time: 35 minutes
Servings: 4
Ingredients:
- 1½ tablespoons smoked paprika
- 1 teaspoon ground cumin
- Salt and ground black pepper, as required
- 2 (12-ounce) chicken breasts
- 1 tablespoon olive oil

Preparation:
1. In a small bowl, mix together the paprika, cumin, salt and black pepper.
2. Coat the chicken breasts with oil evenly and then season with the spice mixture generously.
3. Press "Power" button of Ninja Foodi Digital Air Fry Oven and turn the dial to select "Air Fry" mode.
4. Press TIME/SLICE button and again turn the dial to set the cooking time to 35 minutes.
5. Now push TEMP/DARKNESS button and rotate the dial to set the temperature at 375 degrees F.
6. Press "Start/Pause" button to start.
7. When the unit beeps to show that it is preheated, open the oven door.
8. Arrange the peanuts into the air fry basket and insert in the oven.
9. When the cooking time is completed, open the oven door and place the chicken breasts onto a cutting board for about 5 minutes.
10. Cut each breast in 2 equal-sized pieces and serve.
Serving Suggestions: Serve with sautéed kale.
Variation Tip: Fat of chicken breasts should always be white or deep yellow and never pale or gray.
Nutritional Information per Serving:
Calories: 363 | Fat: 16.6g | Sat Fat: 4g | Carbohydrates: 1.7g | Fiber: 1g | Sugar: 0.3g | Protein: 49.7g

Herbed Chicken Thighs

Preparation Time: 10 minutes
Cooking Time: 20 minutes
Servings: 4
Ingredients:
- ½ tablespoon fresh rosemary, minced
- ½ tablespoon fresh thyme, minced
- Salt and ground black pepper, as required
- 4 (5-ounce) chicken thighs
- 2 tablespoons olive oil

Preparation:
1. In a large bowl, add the herbs, salt and black pepper and mix well.
2. Coat the chicken thighs with oil and then, rub with herb mixture.
3. Arrange the chicken thighs onto the greased sheet pan.
4. Press "Power" button of Ninja Foodi Digital Air Fry Oven and turn the dial to select "Air Fry" mode.
5. Press TIME/SLICE button and again turn the dial to set the cooking time to 20 minutes.

6. Now push TEMP/DARKNESS button and rotate the dial to set the temperature at 400 degrees F.
7. Press "Start/Pause" button to start.
8. When the unit beeps to show that it is preheated, open the oven door and insert the sheet pan in oven.
9. Flip the chicken thighs once halfway through.
10. When the cooking time is completed, open the oven door and serve hot.
Serving Suggestions: Serve with couscous salad.
Variation Tip: Cook the chicken thighs until it reaches an internal temperature of 165° F.
Nutritional Information per Serving:
Calories: 332 | Fat: 17.6g | Sat Fat: 2.9g | Carbohydrates: 0.5g | Fiber: 0.3g | Sugar: 0g | Protein: 41.1g

Chinese Chicken Drumsticks

Preparation Time: 10 minutes
Cooking Time: 20 minutes
Servings: 4
Ingredients:
- 1 tablespoon oyster sauce
- 1 teaspoon light soy sauce
- ½ teaspoon sesame oil
- 1 teaspoon Chinese five-spice powder
- Salt and ground white pepper, as required
- 4 (6-ounce) chicken drumsticks
- 1 cup cornflour

Preparation:
1. In a bowl, mix together the sauces, oil, five-spice powder, salt, and black pepper.
2. Add the chicken drumsticks and generously coat with the marinade.
3. Refrigerate for at least 30-40 minutes.
4. In a shallow dish, place the Cornflour.
5. Remove the chicken from marinade and lightly coat with cornflour.
6. Press "Power" button of Ninja Foodi Digital Air Fry Oven and turn the dial to select "Air Fry" mode.
7. Press TIME/SLICE button and again turn the dial to set the cooking time to 20 minutes.
8. Now push TEMP/DARKNESS button and rotate the dial to set the temperature at 390 degrees F.
9. Press "Start/Pause" button to start.
10. When the unit beeps to show that it is preheated, open the oven door and grease the air fry basket.
11. Place the chicken drumsticks into the prepared air fry basket and insert in the oven.
12. When cooking time is completed, open the oven door and serve hot.
Serving Suggestions: Serve with fresh greens.
Variation Tip: Use best quality sauces.
Nutritional Information per Serving:
Calories: 287 | Fat: 13.8g | Sat Fat: 7.1g | Carbohydrates: 1.6g | Fiber: 0.2g | Sugar: 0.1g | Protein: 38.3g

Cheesy Chicken Cutlets

Preparation Time: 10 minutes
Cooking Time: 30 minutes
Servings: 2
Ingredients:
- 1 large egg
- 6 tablespoons flour
- ¾ cup panko breadcrumbs
- 2 tablespoons parmesan cheese, grated
- 2 chicken cutlets, skinless and boneless
- ½ tablespoon mustard powder
- Salt and black pepper, to taste

Preparation:
1. Take a shallow bowl, add the flour.
2. In a second bowl, crack the egg and beat well.
3. Take a third bowl and mix together breadcrumbs, cheeses, mustard powder, salt and black pepper.
4. Season the chicken with salt and black pepper.
5. Coat the chicken with flour, then dip into beaten egg and then finally coat with the breadcrumbs mixture.
6. Turn on your Ninja Foodi Digital Air Fry Oven and rotate the knob to select "Air Fry".
7. Select the timer for about 30 minutes and temperature for 355 degrees F.
8. Grease the air fry basket and place the chicken cutlets into the prepared basket.
9. Remove from the oven and serve on a platter.
10. Serve hot and enjoy!

Serving Suggestions: Serve with a topping of lemon slices.
Variation Tip: You can also use mozzarella cheese instead.
Nutritional Information per Serving:
Calories: 510 | Fat: 16.3g | Sat Fat: 7.5g | Carbohydrates: 26.2g | Fiber: 1.2g | Sugar: 0.5g | Protein: 41.4g

Bacon-Wrapped Chicken Breasts

Preparation Time: 10 minutes
Cooking Time: 35 minutes
Servings: 2
Ingredients:
- 2 (5- to 6-ounce) boneless, skinless chicken breasts
- ½ teaspoon smoked paprika
- ½ teaspoon garlic powder
- Salt and ground black pepper, as required
- 4 thin bacon slices

Preparation:
1. With a meat mallet, pound each chicken breast into ¾-inch thickness.
2. In a bowl, mix together the paprika, garlic powder, salt and black pepper.
3. Rub the chicken breasts with spice mixture evenly.
4. Wrap each chicken breast with bacon strips.
5. Press "Power" button of Ninja Foodi Digital Air Fry Oven and turn the dial to select "Air Fry" mode.
6. Press TIME/SLICE button and again turn the dial to set the cooking time to 35 minutes.
7. Now push TEMP/DARKNESS button and rotate the dial to set the temperature at 400 degrees F.
8. Press "Start/Pause" button to start.
9. When the unit beeps to show that it is preheated, open the oven door.
10. Arrange the chicken pieces into the greased air fry basket and insert in the oven.
11. When the cooking time is completed, open the oven door and serve hot.

Serving Suggestions: Serve with fresh baby greens.
Variation Tip: Secure the wrapping of bacon with toothpicks.
Nutritional Information per Serving:
Calories: 293 | Fat: 17.4g | Sat Fat: 5.4g | Carbohydrates: 0.8g | Fiber: 0.1g | Sugar: 0.1g | Protein: 31.3g

Molasses Glazed Duck Breast

Preparation Time: 15 minutes
Cooking Time: 44 minutes
Servings: 3
Ingredients:
- 2 cups fresh pomegranate juice
- 2 tablespoons fresh lemon juice
- 3 tablespoons brown sugar
- 1 pound boneless duck breast
- Salt and ground black pepper, as required

Preparation:
1. For pomegranate molasses: in a medium saucepan, add the pomegranate juice, lemon and brown sugar over medium heat and bring to a boil.
2. Reduce the heat to low and simmer for about 25 minutes until the mixture is thick.
3. Remove from the hat and set aside to cool slightly.
4. Meanwhile, with a knife, make the slit on the duck breast.
5. Season the duck breast with salt and black pepper generously.
6. Press "Power" button of Ninja Foodi Digital Air Fry Oven and turn the dial to select "Air Fry" mode.
7. Press TIME/SLICE button and again turn the dial to set the cooking time to 14 minutes.
8. Now push TEMP/DARKNESS button and rotate the dial to set the temperature at 400 degrees F.
9. Press "Start/Pause" button to start.
10. When the unit beeps to show that it is preheated, open the oven door.
11. Arrange the duck breast into the greased air fry basket, skin side up and insert in the oven.
12. After 6 minutes of cooking, flip the duck breast.
13. When the cooking time is completed, open the oven door and place the duck breast onto a platter for about 5 minutes before slicing.
14. With a sharp knife, cut the duck breast into desired sized slices and transfer onto a platter.
15. Drizzle with warm molasses and serve.

Serving Suggestions: Serve alongside the garlicky sweet potatoes.
Variation Tip: You can also use store-bought pomegranate molasses.
Nutritional Information per Serving:
Calories: 332 | Fat: 6.1g | Sat Fat: 0.1g | Carbohydrates: 337g | Fiber: 0g | Sugar: 31.6g | Protein: 34g

Spiced Turkey Breast

Preparation Time: 10 minutes
Cooking Time: 45 minutes
Servings: 8
Ingredients:
- 2 tablespoons fresh rosemary, chopped
- 1 teaspoon ground cumin
- 1 teaspoon ground cinnamon
- 1 teaspoon smoked paprika
- 1 teaspoon cayenne pepper
- Salt and ground black pepper, as required
- 1 (3-pound) turkey breast

Preparation:
1. In a bowl, mix together the rosemary, spices, salt and black pepper.
2. Rub the turkey breast with rosemary mixture evenly.
3. With kitchen twines, tie the turkey breast to keep it compact.
4. Press "Power" button of Ninja Foodi Digital Air Fry Oven and turn the dial to select "Air Fry" mode.
5. Press TIME/SLICE button and again turn the dial to set the cooking time to 45 minutes.
6. Now push TEMP/DARKNESS button and rotate the dial to set the temperature at 360 degrees F.
7. Press "Start/Pause" button to start.
8. When the unit beeps to show that it is preheated, open the oven door.
9. Arrange the turkey breast into the greased air fry basket and insert in oven.
10. When the cooking time is completed, open the oven door and place the turkey breast onto a platter for about 5-10 minutes before slicing.
11. With a sharp knife, cut the turkey breast into desired sized slices and serve.
Serving Suggestions: Serve alongside the cranberry sauce.
Variation Tip: Season the turkey breast generously.
Nutritional Information per Serving:
Calories: 190 | Fat: 0.9g | Sat Fat: 0.1g | Carbohydrates: 0.9g | Fiber: 0.5g | Sugar: 6g | Protein: 29.5g

Chicken Potato Bake

Preparation Time: 15 minutes.
Cooking Time: 25 minutes.
Servings: 4
Ingredients:
- 4 potatoes, diced
- 1 tablespoon garlic, minced
- 1.5 tablespoons olive oil
- ⅛ teaspoon salt
- ⅛ teaspoon pepper
- 1.5 pounds boneless skinless chicken
- ¾ cup mozzarella cheese, shredded
- Parsley, chopped

Preparation:
1. Toss chicken and potatoes with all the spices and oil in a sheet pan.
2. Drizzle the cheese on top of the chicken and potato.
3. Transfer the pan to the Ninja Foodi Digital Air Fry Oven and close the door.
4. Select "Bake" mode by rotating the dial.

5. Press the TIME/SLICE button and change the value to 25 minutes.
6. Press the TEMP/DARKNESS button and change the value to 375 degrees F.
7. Press Start/Pause to begin cooking.
8. Serve warm.
Serving Suggestion: Serve the chicken potato bake with avocado guacamole.
Variation Tip: Add sliced eggplant instead of potatoes for a change of taste.
Nutritional Information Per Serving:
Calories 462 | Fat 14g | Sodium 220mg | Carbs 16g | Fiber 0.2g | Sugar 1g | Protein 26g

Crispy Roasted Chicken

Preparation Time: 15 minutes
Cooking Time: 40 minutes
Servings: 8
Ingredients:
- 1 (3½-pound) whole chicken, cut into 8 pieces
- Salt and ground black pepper, as required
- 2 cups buttermilk
- 2 cups all-purpose flour
- 1 tablespoon ground mustard
- 1 tablespoon garlic powder
- 1 tablespoon onion powder
- 1 tablespoon paprika

Preparation:
1. Rub the chicken pieces with salt and black pepper.
2. In a large bowl, add the chicken pieces and buttermilk and refrigerate to marinate for at least 1 hour.
3. Meanwhile, in a large bowl, place the flour, mustard, spices, salt and black pepper and mix well.
4. Remove the chicken pieces from bowl and drip off the excess buttermilk.
5. Coat the chicken pieces with the flour mixture, shaking any excess off.
6. Press "Power" button of Ninja Foodi Digital Air Fry Oven and turn the dial to select "Air Fry" mode.
7. Press TIME/SLICE button and again turn the dial to set the cooking time to 20 minutes.
8. Now push TEMP/DARKNESS button and rotate the dial to set the temperature at 390 degrees F.
9. Press "Start/Pause" button to start.
10. When the unit beeps to show that it is preheated, open the oven door and grease air fry basket.
11. Arrange half of the chicken pieces into air fry basket and insert in the oven.
12. Repeat with the remaining chicken pieces.
13. When the cooking time is completed, open the oven door and serve immediately.
Serving Suggestions: Serve alongside the French fries.
Variation Tip: Adjust the ratio of spices according to your taste.
Nutritional Information per Serving:
Calories: 518 | Fat: 8.5g | Sat Fat: 2.4g | Carbohydrates: 33.4g | Fiber: 1.8 | Sugar: 4.3g | Protein: 72.6g

Marinated Ranch Broiled Chicken

Preparation Time: 5 minutes
Cooking Time: 15 minutes
Servings: 1
Ingredients:
- 1 tablespoon olive oil
- ½ tablespoon red wine vinegar
- 2 tablespoons dry Ranch-style dressing mix
- 1 chicken breast half, skinless and boneless

Preparation:
1. Take a bowl and mix together dressing mix, oil and vinegar.
2. Add chicken in it and toss to coat well.
3. Refrigerate for about an hour.
4. Turn on your Ninja Foodi Digital Air Fry Oven and rotate the knob to select "Air Broil".
5. Set timer for 15 minutes and temperature level to HI. Press Start/Pause button to begin preheating.
6. When the unit beeps to signify that it is preheated, place chicken onto the dish and broil for about 15 minutes until chicken is cooked through.
7. Serve warm and enjoy!

Serving Suggestions: Serve with some rice.
Variation Tip: You can use any type of vinegar.
Nutritional Information per Serving:
Calories: 372 | Fat: 28g | Sat Fat: 5.5g | Carbohydrates: 1.1g | Fiber: 0g | Sugar: 0g | Protein: 25g

Crispy Chicken Drumsticks

Preparation Time: 15 minutes
Cooking Time: 25 minutes
Servings: 4
Ingredients:
- 4 chicken drumsticks
- 1 tablespoon adobo seasoning
- Salt, as required
- 1 tablespoon onion powder
- 1 tablespoon garlic powder
- ½ tablespoon paprika
- Ground black pepper, as required
- 2 eggs
- 2 tablespoons milk
- 1 cup all-purpose flour
- ¼ cup cornstarch

Preparation:
1. Season chicken drumsticks with adobo seasoning and a pinch of salt.
2. Set aside for about 5minutes.
3. In a small bowl, add the spices, salt and black pepper and mix well.
4. In a shallow bowl, add the eggs, milk and 1 teaspoon of spice mixture and beat until well combined.
5. In another shallow bowl, add the flour, cornstarch and remaining spice mixture.
6. Coat the chicken drumsticks with flour mixture and tap off the excess.
7. Now, dip the chicken drumsticks in egg mixture.
8. Again coat the chicken drumsticks with flour mixture.
9. Arrange the chicken drumsticks onto a wire rack lined baking sheet and set aside for about 15 minutes.
10. Now, arrange the chicken drumsticks onto a sheet pan and spray the chicken with cooking spray lightly.
11. Press "Power" button of Ninja Foodi Digital Air Fry Oven and turn the dial to select "Air Fry" mode.
12. Press TIME/SLICE button and again turn the dial to set the cooking time to 25 minutes.
13. Now push TEMP/DARKNESS button and rotate the dial to set the temperature at 350 degrees F.
14. Press "Start/Pause" button to start.
15. When the unit beeps to show that it is preheated, open the oven door and grease the air fry basket.
16. Place the chicken drumsticks into the prepared air fry basket and insert in the oven.
17. When cooking time is completed, open the oven door and serve hot.

Serving Suggestions: Serve with French fries.
Variation Tip: Make sure to coat chicken pieces completely.
Nutritional Information per Serving:
Calories: 483 | Fat: 12.5g | Sat Fat: 3.4g | Carbohydrates: 35.1g | Fiber: 1.6g | Sugar: 1.8g | Protein: 53.7g

Deviled Chicken

Preparation Time: 15 minutes.
Cooking Time: 40 minutes.
Servings: 8
Ingredients:
- 2 tablespoons butter
- 2 cloves garlic, chopped
- 1 cup Dijon mustard
- ½ teaspoon cayenne pepper
- 1 ½ cups panko breadcrumbs
- ¾ cup Parmesan, freshly grated
- ¼ cup chives, chopped
- 2 teaspoons paprika
- 8 small bone-in chicken thighs, skin removed

Preparation:
1. Toss the chicken thighs with crumbs, cheese, chives, butter, and spices in a bowl and mix well to coat.
2. Transfer the chicken along with its spice mix to a sheet pan.
3. Transfer the pan to the Ninja Foodi Digital Air Fry Oven and close the door.
4. Select "Air Fry" mode by rotating the dial.
5. Press the TIME/SLICE button and change the value to 40 minutes.
6. Press the TEMP/DARKNESS button and change the value to 375 degrees F.
7. Press Start/Pause to begin cooking.
8. Serve warm.

Serving Suggestion: Serve the chicken fried rice or sautéed vegetable.
Variation Tip: Coat the chicken with crushed cornflakes for a crispy texture.
Nutritional Information Per Serving:
Calories 497 | Fat 14g | Sodium 364mg | Carbs 8g | Fiber 1g | Sugar 3g | Protein 32g

Herbed Whole Chicken

Preparation Time: 15 minutes
Cooking Time: 1 hour
Servings: 8
Ingredients:
- 1 tablespoon fresh basil, chopped
- 1 tablespoon fresh oregano, chopped
- 1 tablespoon fresh thyme, chopped
- Salt and ground black pepper, as required
- 1 (4½-pound) whole chicken, necks and giblets removed
- 3 tablespoons olive oil, divided

Preparation:
1. In a bowl, mix together the herbs, salt and black pepper.
2. Coat the chicken with 2 tablespoons of oil and then, rub inside, outside, and underneath the skin with half of the herb mixture generously.
3. Press "Power" button of Ninja Foodi Digital Air Fry Oven and turn the dial to select "Air Fry" mode.
4. Press TIME/SLICE button and again turn the dial to set the cooking time to 60 minutes.
5. Now push TEMP/DARKNESS button and rotate the dial to set the temperature at 360 degrees F.
6. Press "Start/Pause" button to start.
7. When the unit beeps to show that it is preheated, open the oven door.
8. Arrange the chicken into the greased air fry basket, breast-side down and insert in the oven.
9. After 30 minutes of cooking, arrange the chicken, breast-side up and coat with the remaining oil.
10. Then rub with the remaining herb mixture.
11. When the cooking time is completed, open the oven door and place the chicken onto a cutting board for about 10 minutes before carving.
12. With a sharp knife, cut the chicken into desired sized pieces and serve.

Serving Suggestions: Serve with roasted vegetables.
Variation Tip: Dried herbs can be used instead of fresh herbs.
Nutritional Information per Serving:
Calories: 533 | Fat: 24.3g | Sat Fat: 6g | Carbohydrates: 0.6g | Fiber: 0.4g | Sugar: 0g | Protein: 73.9g

Buttered Turkey Breast

Preparation Time: 15 minutes
Cooking Time: 1¼ hours
Servings: 10
Ingredients:
- ¼ cup butter
- 5 carrots, peeled and cut into chunks
- 1 (6-pound) boneless turkey breast
- Salt and ground black pepper, as required
- 1 cup chicken broth

Preparation:
1. In a pan, heat the oil over medium heat and the carrots for about 4-5 minutes.
2. Add the turkey breast and cook for about 10 minutes or until golden brown from both sides.
3. Remove from the heat and stir in salt, black pepper and broth.
4. Transfer the mixture into a baking dish.

5. Press "Power" button of Ninja Foodi Digital Air Fry Oven and turn the dial to select "Bake" mode.
6. Press TIME/SLICE button and again turn the dial to set the cooking time to 60 minutes.
7. Now push TEMP/DARKNESS button and rotate the dial to set the temperature at 375 degrees F.
8. Press "Start/Pause" button to start.
9. When the unit beeps to show that it is preheated, open the oven door.
10. Arrange the baking dish over the wire rack and insert in the oven.
11. When the cooking time is completed, open the oven door and with tongs, place the turkey onto a cutting board for about 5 minutes before slicing.
12. Cut into desired-sized slices and serve alongside carrots.

Serving Suggestions: Serve with fresh salad.
Variation Tip: You can also cook fennel and parsnip alongside the carrot in this recipe.
Nutritional Information per Serving:
Calories: 322 | Fat: 6g | Sat Fat: 3g | Carbohydrates: 3.1g | Fiber: 0.8g | Sugar: 1.6g | Protein: 6.2g

Parmesan Crusted Chicken Breasts

Preparation Time: 15 minutes
Cooking Time: 15 minutes
Servings: 4
Ingredients:
- 2 large chicken breasts
- 1 cup mayonnaise
- 1 cup Parmesan cheese, shredded
- 1 cup panko breadcrumbs

Preparation:
1. Cut each chicken breast in half and then with a meat mallet pound each into even thickness.
2. Spread the mayonnaise on both sides of each chicken piece evenly.
3. In a shallow bowl, mix together the Parmesan and breadcrumbs.
4. Coat the chicken piece Parmesan mixture evenly.
5. Press "Power" button of Ninja Foodi Digital Air Fry Oven and turn the dial to select "Air Fry" mode.
6. Press TIME/SLICE button and again turn the dial to set the cooking time to 15 minutes.
7. Now push TEMP/DARKNESS button and rotate the dial to set the temperature at 390 degrees F.
8. Press "Start/Pause" button to start.
9. When the unit beeps to show that it is preheated, open the oven door.
10. Arrange the chicken pieces into the greased air fry basket and insert in the oven.
11. After 10 minutes of cooking, flip the chicken pieces once.
12. When the cooking time is completed, open the oven door and serve hot.

Serving Suggestions: Serve with ranch dip.
Variation Tip: Use real mayonnaise.
Nutritional Information per Serving:
Calories: 625 | Fat: 35.4g | Sat Fat: 9.4g | Carbohydrates: 18.8g | Fiber: 0.1g | Sugar: 3.8g | Protein: 41.6g

Herbed Turkey Legs

Preparation Time: 15 minutes
Cooking Time: 30 minutes
Servings: 2
Ingredients:
- 1 tablespoon butter, melted
- 2 garlic cloves, minced
- ¼ teaspoon dried rosemary
- ¼ teaspoon dried thyme
- ¼ teaspoon dried oregano
- Salt and ground black pepper, as required
- 2 turkey legs

Preparation:
1. In a large bowl, mix together the butter, garlic, herbs, salt, and black pepper.
2. Add the turkey legs and coat with mixture generously.
3. Press "Power" button of Ninja Foodi Digital Air Fry Oven and turn the dial to select "Air Fry" mode.
4. Press TIME/SLICE button and again turn the dial to set the cooking time to 27 minutes.
5. Now push TEMP/DARKNESS button and rotate the dial to set the temperature at 350 degrees F.
6. Press "Start/Pause" button to start.
7. When the unit beeps to show that it is preheated, open the oven door.
8. Arrange the turkey wings into the greased air fry basket and insert in the oven.
9. When the cooking time is completed, open the oven door and serve hot.

Serving Suggestions: Serve with cabbage slaw.
Variation Tip: Use unsalted butter.
Nutritional Information per Serving:
Calories: 592 | Fat: 22g | Sat Fat: 8.7g | Carbohydrates: 1.3g | Fiber: 0.3g | Sugar: 0g | Protein: 91.6g

Parmesan Chicken Tenders

Preparation Time: 15 minutes
Cooking Time: 15 minutes
Servings: 4
Ingredients:
- ½ cup flour
- Salt and ground black pepper, as required
- 2 eggs, beaten
- ¾ cup panko breadcrumbs
- ¾ cup Parmesan cheese, grated finely
- 1 teaspoon Italian seasoning
- 8 chicken tenders

Preparation:
1. In a shallow dish, mix together the flour, salt and black pepper.
2. In a second shallow dish, place the beaten eggs.
3. In a third shallow dish, mix together the breadcrumbs, parmesan cheese and Italian seasoning.
4. Coat the chicken tenders with flour mixture, then dip into the beaten eggs and finally coat with breadcrumb mixture.
5. Arrange the tenders onto a greased sheet pan in a single layer.
6. Press "Power" button of Ninja Foodi Digital Air Fry Oven and turn the dial to select "Air Fry" mode.

7. Press TIME/SLICE button and again turn the dial to set the cooking time to 15 minutes.
8. Now push TEMP/DARKNESS button and rotate the dial to set the temperature at 360 degrees F.
9. Press "Start/Pause" button to start.
10. When the unit beeps to show that it is preheated, open the oven door and insert the sheet pan in oven.
11. When the cooking time is completed, open the oven door and serve hot.

Serving Suggestions: Serve with blue cheese dip.
Variation Tip: Use dry breadcrumbs.
Nutritional Information per Serving:
Calories: 435 | Fat: 16.1g | Sat Fat: 5.4g | Carbohydrates: 15.3g | Fiber: 0g | Sugar: 0.5g | Protein: 0.4g

Cajun Spiced Whole Chicken

Preparation Time: 15 minutes
Cooking Time: 1 hour 10 minutes
Servings: 6
Ingredients:
- ¼ cup butter, softened
- 2 teaspoons dried rosemary
- 2 teaspoons dried thyme
- 1 tablespoon Cajun seasoning
- 1 tablespoon onion powder
- 1 tablespoon garlic powder
- 1 tablespoon paprika
- 1 teaspoon cayenne pepper
- Salt, as required
- 1 (3-pound) whole chicken, neck and giblets removed

Preparation:
1. In a bowl, add the butter, herbs, spices, and salt and mix well.
2. Rub the chicken with spicy mixture generously.
3. With kitchen twine, tie off wings and legs.
4. Press "Power" button of Ninja Foodi Digital Air Fry Oven and turn the dial to select "Bake" mode.
5. Press TIME/SLICE button and again turn the dial to set the cooking time to 70 minutes.
6. Now push TEMP/DARKNESS button and rotate the dial to set the temperature at 380 degrees F.
7. Press "Start/Pause" button to start.
8. When the unit beeps to show that it is preheated, open the oven door.
9. Arrange the chicken over the wire rack and insert in the oven.
10. When cooking time is completed, open the oven door and place the chicken onto a platter for about 10 minutes before carving.
11. Cut into desired sized pieces and serve.

Serving Suggestions: Serve alongside a fresh green salad.
Variation Tip: You can adjust the ratio of spices according to your choice.
Nutritional Information per Serving:
Calories: 421 | Fat: 14.8g | Sat Fat: 6.9g | Carbohydrates: 2.3g | Fiber: 0.9g | Sugar: 0.5g | Protein: 66.3g

Crispy Chicken Thighs

Preparation Time: 15 minutes
Cooking Time: 25 minutes
Servings: 4
Ingredients:
- ½ cup all-purpose flour
- 1½ tablespoons Cajun seasoning
- 1 teaspoon seasoning salt
- 1 egg
- 4 (4-ounce) skin-on chicken thighs

Preparation:
1. In a shallow bowl, mix together the flour, Cajun seasoning, and salt.
2. In another bowl, crack the egg and beat well.
3. Coat each chicken thigh with the flour mixture, then dip into beaten egg and finally, coat with the flour mixture again.
4. Shake off the excess flour thoroughly.
5. Press "Power" button of Ninja Foodi Digital Air Fry Oven and turn the dial to select "Air Fry" mode.
6. Press TIME/SLICE button and again turn the dial to set the cooking time to 25 minutes.
7. Now push TEMP/DARKNESS button and rotate the dial to set the temperature at 390 degrees F.
8. Press "Start/Pause" button to start.
9. When the unit beeps to show that it is preheated, open the oven door and grease the air fry basket.
10. Place the chicken thighs into the prepared air fry basket and insert in the oven.
11. When cooking time is completed, open the oven door and serve hot.
Serving Suggestions: Serve with ketchup.
Variation Tip: Feel free to use seasoning of your choice.
Nutritional Information per Serving:
Calories: 288 | Fat: 9.6g | Sat Fat: 2.7g | Carbohydrates: 12g | Fiber: 0.4g | Sugar: 0.1g | Protein: 35.9g

Chicken Kabobs

Preparation Time: 15 minutes
Cooking Time: 9 minutes
Servings: 2
Ingredients:
- 1 (8-ounce) chicken breast, cut into medium-sized pieces
- 1 tablespoon fresh lemon juice
- 3 garlic cloves, grated
- 1 tablespoon fresh oregano, minced
- ½ teaspoon lemon zest, grated
- Salt and ground black pepper, as required
- 1 teaspoon plain Greek yogurt
- 1 teaspoon olive oil

Preparation:
1. In a large bowl, add the chicken, lemon juice, garlic, oregano, lemon zest, salt and black pepper and toss to coat well.
2. Cover the bowl and refrigerate overnight.
3. Remove the bowl from the refrigerator and stir in the yogurt and oil.
4. Thread the chicken pieces onto the metal skewers.
5. Press "Power" button of Ninja Foodi Digital Air Fry Oven and turn the dial to select "Air Fry" mode.
6. Press TIME/SLICE button and again turn the dial to set the cooking time to 9 minutes.
7. Now push TEMP/DARKNESS button and rotate the dial to set the temperature at 350 degrees F.
8. Press "Start/Pause" button to start.
9. When the unit beeps to show that it is preheated, open the oven door and grease the air fry basket.
10. Place the skewers into the prepared air fry basket and insert in the oven.
11. Flip the skewers once halfway through.
12. When cooking time is completed, open the oven door and serve hot.
Serving Suggestions: Serve alongside fresh salad.
Variation Tip: Make sure to tri the chicken pieces.
Nutritional Information per Serving:
Calories: 167 | Fat: 5.5g | Sat Fat: 0.5g | Carbohydrates: 3.4g | Fiber: 0.5g | Sugar: 1.1g | Protein: 24.8g

Buttery Chicken and Rice Casserole

Preparation Time: 15 minutes
Cooking Time: 1 hour 50 minutes
Servings: 4
Ingredients:
- Extra-virgin olive oil
- 2 cups white rice
- 1 large onion, chopped
- 2 cups low-sodium chicken broth
- 10½ ounces cream of mushroom soup
- Kosher salt, to taste
- Freshly ground black pepper, to taste
- 2 pounds large bone-in, skin-on chicken thighs
- 2 tablespoons butter, melted
- 2 teaspoons fresh thyme
- 1 clove garlic, minced

Preparation:
1. Select the BAKE function, 350°F, for 1 hour and 30 minutes. While the oven is preheating, grease the sheet pan and prepare the ingredients.
2. Add the onion, soup, broth, and rice to a bowl, then season with salt and pepper.
3. Put the chicken thighs in the rice mixture, skin side up. Brush with the butter. Sprinkle with thyme and garlic, then season with salt and pepper. Place the mixture in the sheet pan.
4. Cover with foil and bake for 1 hour. Uncover and bake for an additional 30 minutes.
5. Select the BROIL function on HI and broil it for about 3 to 5 minutes.
Serving Suggestion: Garnish with freshly chopped parsley before serving.
Variation Tip: You can try replacing the low-sodium chicken broth with vegetable stock.
Nutritional Information Per Serving:
Calories: 1025 | Fat: 50g | Sodium: 1340g | Carbs: 94g | Fiber: 3g | Sugar: 3g | Protein: 44g

Gingered Chicken Drumsticks

Preparation Time: 10 minutes
Cooking Time: 25 minutes
Servings: 3
Ingredients:
- ¼ cup full-fat coconut milk
- 2 teaspoons fresh ginger, minced
- 2 teaspoons galangal, minced
- 2 teaspoons ground turmeric
- Salt, as required
- 3 (6-ounce) chicken drumsticks

Preparation:
1. Place the coconut milk, galangal, ginger, and spices in a large bowl and mix well.
2. Add the chicken drumsticks and coat with the marinade generously.
3. Refrigerate to marinate for at least 6-8 hours.
4. Press "Power" button of Ninja Foodi Digital Air Fry Oven and turn the dial to select "Air Fry" mode.
5. Press TIME/SLICE button and again turn the dial to set the cooking time to 25 minutes.
6. Now push TEMP/DARKNESS button and rotate the dial to set the temperature at 375 degrees F.
7. Press "Start/Pause" button to start.
8. When the unit beeps to show that it is preheated, open the oven door and grease the air fry basket.
9. Place the chicken drumsticks into the prepared air fry basket and insert in the oven.
10. When cooking time is completed, open the oven door and serve hot.
Serving Suggestions: Serve alongside the lemony couscous.
Variation Tip: Coconut milk can be replaced with cream.
Nutritional Information per Serving:
Calories: 347 | Fat: 14.8g | Sat Fat: 6.9g | Carbohydrates: 3.8g | Fiber: 1.1g | Sugar: 0.8g | Protein: 47.6g

Sweet and Sour Chicken Thighs

Preparation Time: 10 minutes
Cooking Time: 20 minutes
Servings: 1
Ingredients:
- ¼ tablespoon soy sauce
- ¼ tablespoon rice vinegar
- ½ teaspoon sugar
- ½ garlic, minced
- ½ scallion, finely chopped
- ¼ cup corn flour
- 1 chicken thigh, skinless and boneless
- Salt and black pepper, to taste

Preparation:
1. Take a bowl and mix all the ingredients together except chicken and corn flour.
2. Add the chicken thigh to the bowl to coat well.
3. Take another bowl and add corn flour.
4. Remove the chicken thighs from marinade and lightly coat with corn flour.
5. Turn on your Ninja Foodi Digital Air Fry Oven and rotate the knob to select "Air Fry".
6. Select the timer for about 10 minutes and temperature for 390 degrees F.

7. Grease the air fry basket and place the chicken thighs into the prepared basket.
8. Air fry for about 10 minutes and then for another to 10 minutes at 355 degrees F.
9. Remove from the oven and serve on a platter.
10. Serve hot and enjoy!
Serving Suggestions: Serve with red chili sauce.
Variation Tip: You can add lemon juice on top.
Nutritional Information per Serving:
Calories: 262 | Fat: 5.2g | Sat Fat: 1.7g | Carbohydrates: 25.8g | Fiber: 2.4g | Sugar: 2.5g | Protein: 27.5g

Lemony Whole Chicken

Preparation Time: 15 minutes
Cooking Time: 1 hour 20 minutes
Servings: 8
Ingredients:
- 1 (5-pound) whole chicken, neck and giblets removed
- Salt and ground black pepper, as required
- 2 fresh rosemary sprigs
- 1 small onion, peeled and quartered
- 1 garlic clove, peeled and cut in half
- 4 lemon zest slices
- 1 tablespoon extra-virgin olive oil
- 1 tablespoon fresh lemon juice

Preparation:
1. Rub the inside and outside of chicken with salt and black pepper evenly.
2. Place the rosemary sprigs, onion quarters, garlic halves and lemon zest in the cavity of the chicken.
3. With kitchen twine, tie off wings and legs.
4. Arrange the chicken onto a greased sheet pan and drizzle with oil and lemon juice.
5. Press "Power" button of Ninja Foodi Digital Air Fry Oven and turn the dial to select "Bake" mode.
6. Press TIME/SLICE button and again turn the dial to set the cooking time to 20 minutes.
7. Now push TEMP/DARKNESS button and rotate the dial to set the temperature at 400 degrees F.
8. Press "Start/Pause" button to start.
9. When the unit beeps to show that it is preheated, open the oven door.
10. Arrange the pan over the wire rack and insert in the oven.
11. After 20 minutes of cooking, set the temperature to 375 degrees F for 60 minutes.
12. When cooking time is completed, open the oven door and place the chicken onto a platter for about 10 minutes before carving.
13. Cut into desired sized pieces and serve.
Serving Suggestions: Serve alongside the steamed veggies.
Variation Tip: Lemon can be replaced with lime.
Nutritional Information per Serving:
Calories: 448 | Fat: 10.4g | Sat Fat: 2.7g | Carbohydrates: 1g | Fiber: 0.4g | Sugar: 0.2g | Protein: 82g

Buttermilk Whole Chicken

Preparation Time: 15 minutes
Cooking Time: 50 minutes
Servings: 6
Ingredients:
- 2 cups buttermilk
- ¼ cup olive oil
- 1 teaspoon garlic powder
- Salt, as required
- 1 (3-pound) whole chicken, neck and giblets removed
- Ground black pepper, as required

Preparation:
1. In a large resealable bag, mix together the buttermilk, oil, garlic powder and 1 tablespoon of salt.
2. Add the whole chicken and seal the bag tightly.
3. Refrigerate to marinate for 24 hours up to 2 days.
4. Remove the chicken from bag and pat dry with paper towels.
5. Season the chicken with salt and black pepper.
6. With kitchen twine, tie off wings and legs.
7. Press "Power" button of Ninja Foodi Digital Air Fry Oven and turn the dial to select "Air Fry" mode.
8. Press TIME/SLICE button and again turn the dial to set the cooking time to 50 minutes.
9. Now push TEMP/DARKNESS button and rotate the dial to set the temperature at 380 degrees F.
10. Press "Start/Pause" button to start.
11. When the unit beeps to show that it is preheated, open the oven door.
12. Arrange the chicken into the greased air fry basket, breast-side down and insert in the oven.
13. When the cooking time is completed, open the oven door and place the chicken onto a cutting board for about 10 minutes before carving.
14. With a sharp knife, cut the chicken into desired sized pieces and serve.

Serving Suggestions: Serve with steamed veggies.
Variation Tip: Kitchen shears are very useful for trimming excess fat from the chicken's cavity.
Nutritional Information per Serving:
Calories: 449 | Fat: 16g | Sat Fat: 3.6g | Carbohydrates: 68.5g | Fiber: 4.3g | Sugar: 0.1g | Protein: 4g

Parmesan Chicken Meatballs

Preparation Time: 15 minutes.
Cooking Time: 12 minutes.
Servings: 4
Ingredients:
- 1 pound ground chicken
- 1 large egg, beaten
- ½ cup Parmesan cheese, grated
- ½ cup pork rinds, ground
- 1 teaspoon garlic powder
- 1 teaspoon paprika
- 1 teaspoon kosher salt
- ½ teaspoon pepper
- ½ cup ground pork rinds, for crust

Preparation:
1. Toss all the meatball ingredients in a bowl and mix well.
2. Make small meatballs out of this mixture and roll them in the pork rinds.
3. Place the coated meatballs in the air fry basket.
4. Transfer the basket to the Ninja Foodi Digital Air Fry Oven and close the door.
5. Select "Bake" mode by rotating the dial.
6. Press the TIME/SLICE button and change the value to 12 minutes.
7. Press the TEMP/DARKNESS button and change the value to 400 degrees F.
8. Press Start/Pause to begin cooking.
9. Once preheated, place the air fry basket inside and close its oven door.
10. Serve warm.

Serving Suggestion: Serve the meatballs with fresh herbs on top and a bowl of steamed rice.
Variation Tip: Use crushed oats to the meatballs for a crispy texture.
Nutritional Information Per Serving:
Calories 486 | Fat 13g | Sodium 611mg | Carbs 15g | Fiber 0g | Sugar g4 | Protein 26g

Twice Baked Potatoes with Bacon

Preparation Time: 15 minutes
Cooking Time: 1 hour 15 minutes
Servings: 8
Ingredients:
- 4 large baking potatoes
- 8 slices bacon
- 1 cup sour cream
- ½ cup milk
- 4 tablespoons butter
- ½ teaspoon salt
- ½ teaspoon pepper
- 1 cup cheddar cheese, shredded
- 8 green onions, sliced

Preparation:
1. Select the BAKE function, 350°F, for 1 hour and 15 minutes. Allow the oven to preheat.
2. Bake the potatoes for about 1 hour.
3. Meanwhile, take a large, deep skillet, place the bacon in it, and cook over medium-high heat. Drain, crumble, and keep it aside.
4. Once the potatoes are done, let them cool down. Slice the cooled potatoes in half lengthwise, scoop the flesh into a large bowl, and save the skins.
5. Add the milk, salt, pepper, sour cream, butter, ½ cup cheese, and ½ the green onions. Mix well and spoon the mixture into the potato skins.
6. Top them with the remaining cheese, bacon, and green onions.
7. Bake for about 15 minutes.

Serving Suggestion: Sprinkle some cheese and greens on top before serving.
Variation Tip: You can try mushrooms instead of bacon to give this a vegetarian twist.
Nutritional Information Per Serving:
Calories: 422 | Fat: 29.5g | Sodium: 537mg | Carbs: 29.3g | Fiber: 2g | Sugar: 3.26g | Protein: 11g

Brie Stuffed Chicken Breasts

Preparation Time: 15 minutes
Cooking Time: 15 minutes
Servings: 4
Ingredients:
- 2 (8-ounce) skinless, boneless chicken fillets
- Salt and ground black pepper, as required
- 4 brie cheese slices
- 1 tablespoon fresh chive, minced
- 4 bacon slices

Preparation:
1. Cut each chicken fillet in 2 equal-sized pieces.
2. Carefully, make a slit in each chicken piece horizontally about ¼-inch from the edge.
3. Open each chicken piece and season with salt and black pepper.
4. Place 1 cheese slice in the open area of each chicken piece and sprinkle with chives.
5. Close the chicken pieces and wrap each one with a bacon slice.
6. Secure with toothpicks.
7. Press "Power" button of Ninja Foodi Digital Air Fry Oven and turn the dial to select "Air Fry" mode.
8. Press TIME/SLICE button and again turn the dial to set the cooking time to 15 minutes.
9. Now push TEMP/DARKNESS button and rotate the dial to set the temperature at 355 degrees F.
10. Press "Start/Pause" button to start.
11. When the unit beeps to show that it is preheated, open the oven door and grease the air fry basket.
12. Place the chicken pieces into the prepared air fry basket and insert in the oven.
13. When cooking time is completed, open the oven door and place the rolled chicken breasts onto a cutting board.
14. Cut into desired-sized slices and serve.
Serving Suggestions: Serve with creamy mashed potatoes.
Variation Tip: Season the chicken breasts slightly.
Nutritional Information per Serving:
Calories: 394 | Fat: 24g | Sat Fat: 10.4g | Carbohydrates: 0.6g | Fiber: 0g | Sugar: 0.1g | Protein: 42g

Marinated Spicy Chicken Legs

Preparation Time: 10 minutes
Cooking Time: 20 minutes
Servings: 4
Ingredients:
- 4 chicken legs
- 3 tablespoons fresh lemon juice
- 3 teaspoons ginger paste
- 3 teaspoons garlic paste
- Salt, as required
- 4 tablespoons plain yogurt
- 2 teaspoons red chili powder
- 1 teaspoon ground cumin
- 1 teaspoon ground coriander
- 1 teaspoon ground turmeric
- Ground black pepper, as required

Preparation:
1. In a bowl, mix together the chicken legs, lemon juice, ginger, garlic and salt. Set aside for about 15 minutes.

2. Meanwhile, in another bowl, mix together the yogurt and spices.
3. Add the chicken legs and coat with the spice mixture generously.
4. Cover the bowl and refrigerate for at least 10-12 hours.
5. Press "Power" button of Ninja Foodi Digital Air Fry Oven and turn the dial to select "Air Fry" mode.
6. Press TIME/SLICE button and again turn the dial to set the cooking time to 20 minutes.
7. Now push TEMP/DARKNESS button and rotate the dial to set the temperature at 440 degrees F.
8. Press "Start/Pause" button to start.
9. When the unit beeps to show that it is preheated, open the oven door and grease the air fry basket.
10. Place the chicken legs into the prepared air fry basket and insert in the oven.
11. When cooking time is completed, open the oven door and serve hot.
Serving Suggestions: Serve with fresh greens.
Variation Tip: Lemon juice can be replaced with vinegar.
Nutritional Information per Serving:
Calories: 461 | Fat: 17.6g | Sat Fat: 5g | Carbohydrates: 4.3g | Fiber: 0.9g | Sugar: 1.5g | Protein: 67.1g

Simple Turkey Wings

Preparation Time: 10 minutes
Cooking Time: 26 minutes
Servings: 4
Ingredients:
- 2 pounds turkey wings
- 4 tablespoons chicken rub
- 3 tablespoons olive oil

Preparation:
1. In a large bowl, add the turkey wings, chicken rub and olive oil and toss to coat well.
2. Press "Power" button of Ninja Foodi Digital Air Fry Oven and turn the dial to select "Air Fry" mode.
3. Press TIME/SLICE button and again turn the dial to set the cooking time to 26 minutes.
4. Now push TEMP/DARKNESS button and rotate the dial to set the temperature at 380 degrees F.
5. Press "Start/Pause" button to start.
6. When the unit beeps to show that it is preheated, open the oven door.
7. Arrange the turkey wings into the greased air fry basket and insert in the oven.
8. Flip the turkey wings once halfway through.
9. When the cooking time is completed, open the oven door and serve hot.
Serving Suggestions: Serve alongside the yogurt sauce.
Variation Tip: You can use seasoning of your choice.
Nutritional Information per Serving:
Calories: 558 | Fat: 38.9g | Sat Fat: 1.5g | Carbohydrates: 3g | Fiber: 0g | Sugar: 0g | Protein: 46.6g

Oat Crusted Chicken Breasts

Preparation Time: 15 minutes
Cooking Time: 12 minutes
Servings: 2
Ingredients:
- 2 (6-ounce) chicken breasts
- Salt and ground black pepper, as required
- ¾ cup oats
- 2 tablespoons mustard powder
- 1 tablespoon fresh parsley
- 2 medium eggs

Preparation:
1. Place the chicken breasts onto a cutting board and with a meat mallet, flatten each into even thickness.
2. Then, cut each breast in half.
3. Sprinkle the chicken pieces with salt and black pepper and set aside.
4. In a blender, add the oats, mustard powder, parsley, salt and black pepper and pulse until a coarse breadcrumb-like mixture is formed.
5. Transfer the oat mixture into a shallow bowl.
6. In another bowl, crack the eggs and beat well.
7. Coat the chicken with oats mixture and then, dip into beaten eggs and again, coat with the oats mixture.
8. Press "Power" button of Ninja Foodi Digital Air Fry Oven and turn the dial to select "Air Fry" mode.
9. Press TIME/SLICE button and again turn the dial to set the cooking time to 12 minutes.
10. Now push TEMP/DARKNESS button and rotate the dial to set the temperature at 350 degrees F.
11. Press "Start/Pause" button to start.
12. When the unit beeps to show that it is preheated, open the oven door and grease the air fry basket.
13. Place the chicken breasts into the prepared air fry basket and insert in the oven.
14. Flip the chicken breasts once halfway through.
15. When cooking time is completed, open the oven door and serve hot.
Serving Suggestions: Serve with mashed potatoes.
Variation Tip: Check the meat "best by" date.
Nutritional Information per Serving:
Calories: 556 | Fat: 22.2g | Sat Fat: 5.3g | Carbohydrates: 25.1g | Fiber: 4.8g | Sugar: 1.4g | Protein: 61.6g

Primavera Chicken

Preparation Time: 15 minutes.
Cooking Time: 25 minutes.
Servings: 4
Ingredients:
- 4 chicken breasts, boneless
- 1 zucchini, sliced
- 3 medium tomatoes, sliced
- 2 yellow bell peppers, sliced
- ½ red onion, sliced
- 2 tablespoons olive oil
- 1 teaspoon Italian seasoning
- Kosher salt, to taste
- Freshly ground black pepper, to taste

- 1 cup shredded mozzarella
- Freshly chopped parsley for garnish

Preparation:
1. Carve one side slit in the chicken breasts and stuff them with all the veggies.
2. Place these stuffed chicken breasts in a casserole dish, then drizzle oil, Italian seasoning, black pepper, salt, and Mozzarella over the chicken.
3. Transfer the dish to the Ninja Foodi Digital Air Fry Oven and close the door.
4. Select "Bake" mode by rotating the dial.
5. Press the TIME/SLICE button and change the value to 25 minutes.
6. Press the TEMP/DARKNESS button and change the value to 370 degrees F.
7. Press Start/Pause to begin cooking.
8. Garnish with parsley and serve warm.
Serving Suggestion: Serve chicken with a kale salad on the side.
Variation Tip: Brush the chicken with pesto before baking.
Nutritional Information Per Serving:
Calories 445 | Fat 25g | Sodium 122mg | Carbs 13g | Fiber 0.4g | Sugar 1g | Protein 33g

Baked Duck

Preparation Time: 15 minutes.
Cooking Time: 2 hours 20 minutes.
Servings: 4
Ingredients:
- 1 ½ sprigs fresh rosemary
- ½ nutmeg
- Black pepper
- Juice from 1 orange
- 1 whole duck
- 4 cloves garlic, chopped
- 1 ½ red onions, chopped
- a few stalks celery
- 1 ½ carrot
- 2 cm piece fresh ginger
- 1 ½ bay leaves
- 2 pounds Piper potatoes
- 4 cups chicken stock

Preparation:
1. Place duck in a large cooking pot and add broth along with all the ingredients.
2. Cook this duck for 2 hours on a simmer, then transfer to the sheet pan.
3. Transfer the sheet pan to the Ninja Foodi Digital Air Fry Oven and close the door.
4. Select "Air Fry" mode by rotating the dial.
5. Press the TIME/SLICE button and change the value to 20 minutes.
6. Press the TEMP/DARKNESS button and change the value to 350 degrees F.
7. Press Start/Pause to begin cooking.
8. Serve warm.
Serving Suggestion: Serve the duck with a fresh crouton salad.
Variation Tip: Stuff the duck with the bread stuffing and cheese.
Nutritional Information Per Serving:
Calories 505 | Fat 7.9g | Sodium 581mg | Carbs 21.8g | Fiber 2.6g | Sugar 7g | Protein 37.2g

Crispy Chicken Cutlets

Preparation Time: 15 minutes
Cooking Time: 30 minutes
Servings: 4
Ingredients:
- ¾ cup flour
- 2 large eggs
- 1½ cups breadcrumbs
- ¼ cup Parmesan cheese, grated
- 1 tablespoon mustard powder
- Salt and ground black pepper, as required
- 4 (6-ounce) (¼-inch thick) skinless, boneless chicken cutlets

Preparation:
1. In a shallow bowl, add the flour.
2. In a second bowl, crack the eggs and beat well.
3. In a third bowl, mix together the breadcrumbs, cheese, mustard powder, salt, and black pepper.
4. Season the chicken with salt, and black pepper.
5. Coat the chicken with flour, then dip into beaten eggs and finally coat with the breadcrumbs mixture.
6. Press "Power" button of Ninja Foodi Digital Air Fry Oven and turn the dial to select "Air Fry" mode.
7. Press TIME/SLICE button and again turn the dial to set the cooking time to 30 minutes.
8. Now push TEMP/DARKNESS button and rotate the dial to set the temperature at 355 degrees F.
9. Press "Start/Pause" button to start.
10. When the unit beeps to show that it is preheated, open the oven door and grease the air fry basket.
11. Place the chicken cutlets into the prepared air fry basket and insert in the oven.
12. When cooking time is completed, open the oven door and serve hot.
Serving Suggestions: Serve with favorite greens.
Variation Tip: Parmesan cheese can be replaced with your favorite cheese.
Nutritional Information per Serving:
Calories: 526 | Fat: 13g | Sat Fat: 4.2g | Carbohydrates: 48.6g | Fiber: 3g | Sugar: 3g | Protein: 51.7g

Chicken Kebabs

Preparation Time: 15 minutes.
Cooking Time: 20 minutes.
Servings: 6
Ingredients:
- 16 ounces skinless chicken breasts, cubed
- 2 tablespoons soy sauce
- ½ zucchini sliced
- 1 tablespoon chicken seasoning
- 1 teaspoon BBQ seasoning
- salt and pepper to taste
- ½ green pepper sliced
- ½ red pepper sliced
- ½ yellow pepper sliced
- ¼ red onion sliced
- 4 cherry tomatoes
- cooking spray

Preparation:
1. Toss chicken and veggies with all the spices and seasoning in a bowl.
2. Alternatively, thread them on skewers and place these skewers in the air fry basket.
3. Transfer the basket to the Ninja Foodi Digital Air Fry Oven and close the door.
4. Select "Air Fry" mode by rotating the dial.
5. Press the TIME/SLICE button and change the value to 20 minutes.
6. Press the TEMP/DARKNESS button and change the value to 350 degrees F.
7. Press Start/Pause to begin cooking.
8. Flip the skewers when cooked halfway through, then resume cooking.
9. Serve warm.
Serving Suggestion: Serve the kebabs with roasted veggies on the side.
Variation Tip: Add mozzarella balls to the skewers.
Nutritional Information Per Serving:
Calories 434 | Fat 16g | Sodium 462mg | Carbs 13g | Fiber 0.4g | Sugar 3g | Protein 35.3g

Roasted Duck

Preparation Time: 15 minutes.
Cooking Time: 3 hours
Servings: 6
Ingredients:
- 6 pounds whole Pekin duck
- Salt, to taste
- 5 garlic cloves, chopped
- 1 lemon, chopped

Glaze
- ½ cup balsamic vinegar
- 1 lemon, juiced
- ¼ cup honey

Preparation:
1. Place the Pekin duck in a baking tray and add garlic, lemon, and salt on top.
2. Whisk honey, the juiced lemon, and vinegar in a bowl.
3. Brush this glaze over the duck liberally. Marinate overnight in the refrigerator.
4. Remove the duck from the marinade and move the duck to sheet pan.
5. Transfer the sheet pan to the Ninja Foodi Digital Air Fry Oven and close the door.
6. Select "Air Roast" mode by rotating the dial.
7. Press the TIME/SLICE button and change the value to 2 hours.
8. Press the TEMP/DARKNESS button and change the value to 350 degrees F.
9. Press Start/Pause to begin cooking.
10. When cooking completed, set the oven the temperature to 350 degrees F and time to 1 hour at Air Roast mode. Press Start/Pause to begin.
11. When it is cooked, serve warm.
Serving Suggestion: Serve the duck with roasted green beans and mashed potatoes.
Variation Tip: Stuff the duck with the bread stuffing before baking.
Nutritional Information Per Serving:
Calories 465 | Fat 5g | Sodium 422mg | Carbs 16g | Fiber 0g | Sugar 1g | Protein 25g

Chicken and Rice Casserole

Preparation Time: 15 minutes.
Cooking Time: 23 minutes.
Servings: 4
Ingredients:
- 2 pounds bone-in chicken thighs
- Salt and black pepper
- 1 teaspoon olive oil
- 5 cloves garlic, chopped
- 2 large onions, chopped
- 2 large red bell peppers, chopped
- 1 tablespoon sweet Hungarian paprika
- 1 teaspoon hot Hungarian paprika
- 2 tablespoons tomato paste
- 2 cups chicken broth
- 3 cups brown rice, thawed
- 2 tablespoons parsley, chopped
- 6 tablespoons sour cream

Preparation:
1. Season the chicken with salt, black pepper, and olive oil.
2. Sear the chicken in a skillet for 5 minutes per side, then transfer to a casserole dish.
3. Sauté onion in the same skillet until soft.
4. Toss in garlic, peppers, and paprika, then sauté for 3 minutes.
5. Stir in tomato paste, chicken broth, and rice.
6. Mix well and cook until rice is soft, then add sour cream and parsley.
7. Spread the mixture over the chicken in the casserole dish.
8. Transfer the dish to the Ninja Foodi Digital Air Fry Oven and close the door.
9. Transfer the sandwich to the Ninja Foodi Digital Air Fry Oven and close the door.
10. Select "Bake" mode by rotating the dial.
11. Press the TIME/SLICE button and change the value to 10 minutes.
12. Press the TEMP/DARKNESS button and change the value to 375 degrees F.
13. Press Start/Pause to begin cooking.
14. Serve warm.
Serving Suggestion: Serve the chicken casserole with toasted bread slices.
Variation Tip: Add corn kernels to the chicken casserole.
Nutritional Information Per Serving:
Calories 454 | Fat 25g | Sodium 412mg | Carbs 22g | Fiber 0.2g | Sugar 1g | Protein 28.3g

Creamy Chicken Casserole

Preparation Time: 15 minutes.
Cooking Time: 47 minutes.
Servings: 4
Ingredients:
Chicken Mushroom Casserole
- 2 ½ pounds chicken breasts, cut into strips
- 1 ½ teaspoons salt
- ¼ teaspoon black pepper
- 1 cup all-purpose flour
- 6 tablespoons olive oil
- 1 pound white mushrooms, sliced
- 1 medium onion, diced
- 3 garlic cloves, minced

Sauce
- 3 tablespoons unsalted butter
- 3 tablespoons all-purpose flour
- ½ cup milk, optional
- 1 cups chicken broth, optional
- 1 tablespoon lemon juice
- 1 cup half and half cream

Preparation:
1. Butter a casserole dish and toss in chicken with mushrooms and all the casserole ingredients.
2. Prepare the sauce in a suitable pan. Add butter and melt over moderate heat.
3. Stir in all-purpose flour and whisk well for 2 minutes, then pour in milk, chicken broth, lemon juice, and cream.
4. Mix well and pour this creamy white sauce over the chicken mix in the casserole dish.
5. Transfer the dish to the Ninja Foodi Digital Air Fry Oven and close the door.
6. Select "Bake" mode by rotating the dial.
7. Press the TIME/SLICE button and change the value to 45 minutes.
8. Press the TEMP/DARKNESS button and change the value to 350 degrees F.
9. Press Start/Pause to begin cooking.
10. Serve warm.
Serving Suggestion: Serve the creamy chicken casserole with steaming white rice.
Variation Tip: Drizzle breadcrumbs on top of the casserole before baking.
Nutritional Information Per Serving:
Calories 601 | Fat 16g | Sodium 189mg | Carbs 32g | Fiber 0.3g | Sugar 0.1g | Protein 28.2g

Lemon-Lime Chicken

Preparation Time: 10 minutes
Cooking Time: 20 minutes
Servings: 2
Ingredients:
- 2 tablespoons vegetable oil
- 2 tablespoons lime juice
- ¼ cup lemon juice
- 2 skinless, boneless chicken breast halves
- Italian seasoning to taste
- Salt to taste

Preparation:
1. Take a large bowl and add lemon juice, lime juice and oil.
2. Place the chicken in the mixture and refrigerate for at least an hour.
3. Turn on your Ninja Foodi Digital Air Fry Oven and rotate the knob to select "Air Broil".
4. Take a sheet pan with a greased wire rack.
5. Arrange the chicken on the sheet pan and season with Italian seasoning and salt.
6. Broil chicken for 10 minutes and set temperature level to LO.
7. Turn chicken, season again and broil for another 10 minutes.
8. Serve warm and enjoy!
Serving Suggestions: Serve with lemon wedges.
Variation Tip: You can also add honey.
Nutritional Information per Serving:
Calories: 279 | Fat: 18g | Sat Fat: 4.4g | Carbohydrates: 4.4g | Fiber: 0.3g | Sugar: 1.4g | Protein: 25.4g

Honey-Glazed Chicken Drumsticks

Preparation Time: 10 minutes
Cooking Time: 22 minutes
Servings: 2
Ingredients:
- ½ tablespoon fresh thyme, minced
- 2 tablespoons Dijon mustard
- ½ tablespoon honey
- 1 tablespoon olive oil
- 1 teaspoon fresh rosemary, minced
- 2 chicken drumsticks, boneless
- Salt and black pepper, to taste

Preparation:
1. Take a bowl and mix together mustard, honey, herbs, salt, oil and black pepper.
2. Add chicken drumsticks to the bowl and coat them well with the mixture.
3. Cover and refrigerate overnight.
4. Turn on your Ninja Foodi Digital Air Fry Oven and rotate the knob to select "Air Fry".
5. Select the timer for about 12 minutes and temperature for 320 degrees F.
6. Grease the air fry basket and place the drumsticks into the prepared basket.
7. Air fry for about 12 minutes and then for about 10 more minutes at 355 degrees F.
8. Remove from the oven and serve on a platter.
9. Serve hot and enjoy!

Serving Suggestions: Serve with red chili sauce.
Variation Tip: You can add lemon juice to enhance taste.
Nutritional Information per Serving:
Calories: 301 | Fat: 19.8g | Sat Fat: 4.4g | Carbohydrates: 6.1g | Fiber: 1g | Sugar: 4.5g | Protein: 23.8g

Duck a la Orange

Preparation Time: 15 minutes.
Cooking Time: 60 minutes.
Servings: 8
Ingredients:
- 1 tablespoon salt
- 1 teaspoon ground coriander
- ½ teaspoon ground cumin
- 1 teaspoon black pepper
- 1 (5- to 6-pound) duck, skinned
- 1 juice orange, halved
- 4 fresh thyme sprigs
- 4 fresh marjoram sprigs
- 2 parsley sprigs
- 1 small onion, cut into wedges
- ½ cup dry white wine
- ½ cup chicken broth
- ½ carrot
- ½ celery rib

Preparation:
1. Place the Pekin duck in a sheet pan and whisk orange juice and the rest of the ingredients in a bowl.
2. Pour the herb sauce over the duck and brush it liberally.
3. Transfer the duck to the Ninja Foodi Digital Air Fry Oven and close the door.
4. Select "Air Fry" mode by rotating the dial.
5. Press the TIME/SLICE button and change the value to 60 minutes.
6. Press the TEMP/DARKNESS button and change the value to 350 degrees F.
7. Press Start/Pause to begin cooking.
8. Continue basting the duck during baking.
9. Serve warm.

Serving Suggestion: Serve the duck with chili garlic sauce.
Variation Tip: Add asparagus sticks around the duck and roast.
Nutritional Information Per Serving:
Calories 531 | Fat 20g | Sodium 941mg | Carbs 30g | Fiber 0.9g | Sugar 1.4g | Protein 24.6g

Herbed Duck Breast

Preparation Time: 15 minutes
Cooking Time: 20 minutes
Servings: 2
Ingredients:
- 1 (10-ounce) duck breast
- Olive oil cooking spray
- ½ tablespoon fresh thyme, chopped
- ½ tablespoon fresh rosemary, chopped
- 1 cup chicken broth
- 1 tablespoon fresh lemon juice
- Salt and ground black pepper, as required

Preparation:
1. Spray the duck breast with cooking spray evenly.
2. In a bowl, mix well the remaining ingredients.
3. Add the duck breast and coat with the marinade generously.
4. Refrigerate, covered for about 4 hours.
5. With a piece of foil, cover the duck breast
6. Press "Power" button of Ninja Foodi Digital Air Fry Oven and turn the dial to select "Air Fry" mode.
7. Press TIME/SLICE button and again turn the dial to set the cooking time to 15 minutes.
8. Now push TEMP/DARKNESS button and rotate the dial to set the temperature at 390 degrees F.
9. Press "Start/Pause" button to start.
10. When the unit beeps to show that it is preheated, open the oven door and grease the air fry basket.
11. Place the duck breast into the prepared air fry basket and insert in the oven.
12. After 15 minutes of cooking, set the temperature to 355 degrees F for 5 minutes.
13. When cooking time is completed, open the oven door and serve hot.

Serving Suggestions: Serve with spiced potatoes.
Variation Tip: Don't undercook the duck meat.
Nutritional Information per Serving:
Calories: 209 | Fat: 6.6g | Sat Fat: 0.3g | Carbohydrates: 1.6g | Fiber: 0.6g | Sugar: 0.5g | Protein: 33.8g

Chicken Alfredo Bake

Preparation Time: 8 minutes
Cooking Time: 25 minutes
Servings: 2
Ingredients:
- ¼ cup heavy cream
- ½ cup milk
- 1 tablespoon flour, divided
- ½ clove garlic, minced
- 1 cup penne pasta
- ½ tablespoon butter
- ½ cup cubed rotisserie chicken
- ½ cup Parmigiano-Reggiano cheese, freshly grated
- ½ pinch ground nutmeg

Preparation:
1. Take a large pot of lightly salted water and bring it to a boil.
2. Add penne and cook for about 11 minutes.
3. Turn on your Ninja Foodi Digital Air Fry Oven and rotate the knob to select "Bake".
4. Set time to 10 to 12 minutes and temperature to 375 degrees F. Press Start/Pause to begin preheating.
5. In the meanwhile, take a sauce pan and melt butter over medium heat and cook garlic for about a minute.
6. Add in flour and whisk continuously until you have a paste.
7. Pour in milk and cream, whisking continuously.
8. Stir in cheese and nutmeg.
9. Now add drained penne pasta and cooked chicken.
10. Pour the mixture into an oven-safe dish.
11. Sprinkle cheese on top.
12. When the unit beeps to signify that it is preheated, add the dish on wire rack into the Ninja Foodi Digital Air Fry Oven.
13. Bake in the preheated Ninja Foodi Digital Air Fry Oven for about 10 to 12 minutes at 375 degrees F.
14. Serve and enjoy!
Serving Suggestions: Serve with garlic bread.
Variation Tip: Add salt and black pepper according to taste.
Nutritional Information per Serving:
Calories: 403 | Fat: 16.2g | Sat Fat: 8.3g | Carbohydrates: 43g | Fiber: 0.1g | Sugar: 3.1g | Protein: 22g

Sweet and Spicy Chicken Drumsticks

Preparation Time: 10 minutes
Cooking Time: 20 minutes
Servings: 2
Ingredients:
- 2 chicken drumsticks
- ½ garlic clove, crushed
- 1 teaspoon ginger, crushed
- 1 teaspoon brown sugar
- ½ tablespoon mustard
- ½ teaspoon red chili powder
- ½ teaspoon cayenne pepper
- ½ tablespoon vegetable oil
- Salt and black pepper, to taste
Preparation:

1. Take a bowl and mix together mustard, ginger, brown sugar, oil and spices.
2. Add chicken drumsticks to the bowl for well coating.
3. Refrigerate for at least 20 to 30 minutes.
4. Turn on your Ninja Foodi Digital Air Fry Oven and rotate the knob to select "Air Fry".
5. Select the timer for about 10 minutes and temperature for 390 degrees F.
6. Grease the air fry basket and place the drumsticks into the prepared basket.
7. Air fry for about 10 minutes and then 10 more minutes at 300 degrees F.
8. Remove from the oven and serve on a platter.
9. Serve hot and enjoy!
Serving Suggestions: Serve with red chili sauce.
Variation Tip: You can add lemon juice to enhance taste.
Nutritional Information per Serving:
Calories: 131 | Fat: 7g | Sat Fat: 1.4g | Carbohydrates: 3.3g | Fiber: 0.8g | Sugar: 1.8g | Protein: 13.5g

Spiced Roasted Chicken

Preparation Time: 10 minutes
Cooking Time: 1 hour
Servings: 3
Ingredients:
- 1 teaspoon paprika
- ½ teaspoon cayenne pepper
- ½ teaspoon ground white pepper
- ½ teaspoon garlic powder
- 1 teaspoon dried thyme
- ½ teaspoon onion powder
- Salt and black pepper, to taste
- 2 tablespoons oil
- ½ whole chicken, necks and giblets removed

Preparation:
1. Take a bowl and mix together the thyme and spices.
2. Coat the chicken with oil and rub it with the spice mixture.
3. Turn on your Ninja Foodi Digital Air Fry Oven and rotate the knob to select "Air Fry".
4. Select the timer for about 30 minutes and temperature for 350 degrees F.
5. Place the chicken in the air fry basket and air fry for 30 minutes.
6. After that, take out the chicken, flip it over and let it air fry for another 30 minutes.
7. When cooked, let it sit for 10 minutes on a large plate and then carve to desired pieces.
8. Serve and enjoy!
Serving Suggestions: Top with chopped celery leaves and hot sauce.
Variation Tip: You can also add shredded mozzarella cheese on top.
Nutritional Information per Serving:
Calories: 113 | Fat: 8.7g | Sat Fat: 1.4g | Carbohydrates: 1.9g | Fiber: 0.7g | Sugar: 0.4g | Protein: 7.1g

Tender Italian Baked Chicken

Preparation Time: 10 minutes
Cooking Time: 20 minutes
Servings: 4
Ingredients:
- ¾ cup mayonnaise
- ½ cup grated parmesan cheese
- ¾ teaspoon garlic powder
- ¾ cup Italian seasoned breadcrumbs
- 4 skinless, boneless chicken breast halves

Preparation:
1. Select the BAKE function, 425°F, for 20 minutes. While the oven is preheating, prepare the ingredients.
2. Take a bowl, and mix the parmesan cheese, mayonnaise, and garlic powder. In a separate bowl, place the breadcrumbs.
3. First, dip the chicken in the mayonnaise mixture and then coat it into the breadcrumbs. Arrange the chicken on the sheet pan.
4. Bake the coated chicken for about 20 minutes.

Serving Suggestion: Serve with a sauce of your choice or mustard.
Variation Tip: Try experimenting with different flavored breadcrumbs.
Nutritional Information Per Serving:
Calories: 553 | Fat: 39.6g | Sodium: 768.3 | Carbs: 17.1g | Fiber: 0.8g | Sugar: 1.3g | Protein: 3.6g

Spicy Chicken Legs

Preparation Time: 20 minutes
Cooking Time: 25 minutes
Servings: 6
Ingredients:
- 6 chicken legs
- 4 cups white flour
- 2 cups buttermilk
- 2 teaspoons onion powder
- 2 teaspoons garlic powder
- 2 teaspoons paprika
- 2 teaspoons ground cumin
- Salt and black pepper, to taste
- 2 tablespoons olive oil

Preparation:
1. Take a bowl, add chicken legs and buttermilk. Refrigerate for about 2 hours.
2. Take another bowl, mix together flour and spices.
3. Remove the chicken legs from buttermilk and coat them with the flour mixture.
4. Do it again until we have a fine coating.
5. Turn on your Ninja Foodi Digital Air Fry Oven and rotate the knob to select "Air Fry".
6. Select the timer for about 20 to 25 minutes and temperature for 360 degrees F.
7. Grease the air fry basket and arrange the chicken legs on it.
8. Take it out when chicken legs are brown enough and serve onto a serving platter.

Serving Suggestions: Add hot sauce on top.
Variation Tip: You can also add dried basil.
Nutritional Information per Serving:
Calories: 653 | Fat: 16.9g | Sat Fat: 4.1g | Carbohydrates: 69.5g | Fiber: 2.7g | Sugar: 4.7g | Protein: 52.3g

Herb Butter Chicken

Preparation Time: 10 minutes
Cooking Time: 15 minutes
Servings: 2
Ingredients:
- 1½ cloves garlic, minced
- ½ teaspoon dried parsley
- ⅛ teaspoon dried rosemary
- ⅛ teaspoon dried thyme
- 2 skinless, boneless chicken breast halves
- ¼ cup butter, softened

Preparation:
1. Turn on your Ninja Foodi Digital Air Fry Oven and rotate the knob to select "Air Broil".
2. Cover the sheet pan with aluminum foil and place chicken on it.
3. Take a small bowl and mix together parsley, rosemary, thyme, butter and garlic.
4. Spread the mixture on top of chicken.
5. Broil in the oven with the coating of butter and herbs for at least 30 minutes at LO.
6. Serve warm and enjoy!

Serving Suggestions: Top with some extra herbs before serving.
Variation Tip: You can also use chopped onions.
Nutritional Information per Serving:
Calories: 354 | Fat: 27.2g | Sat Fat: 16.1g | Carbohydrates: 2.6g | Fiber: 1.2g | Sugar: 0g | Protein: 25.3g

Breaded Chicken Tenderloins

Preparation Time: 10 minutes
Cooking Time: 15 minutes
Servings: 2
Ingredients:
- 4 chicken tenderloins, skinless and boneless
- ½ egg, beaten
- 1 tablespoon vegetable oil
- ¼ cup breadcrumbs

Preparation:
1. Take a shallow dish and add the beaten egg.
2. Take another dish and mix together oil and breadcrumbs until you have a crumbly mixture.
3. Dip the chicken tenderloins into the beaten egg and then coat with the breadcrumbs mixture.
4. Shake off the excess coating.
5. Turn on your Ninja Foodi Digital Air Fry Oven and rotate the knob to select "Air Fry".
6. Select the timer for about 15 minutes and temperature for 355 degrees F.
7. Grease the air fry basket and place the chicken tenderloins into the prepared basket.
8. Remove from the oven and serve on a platter.
9. Serve hot and enjoy!

Serving Suggestions: Serve with red chili sauce or ketchup.
Variation Tip: You can use foil to cover the chicken.
Nutritional Information per Serving:
Calories: 409 | Fat: 16.6g | Sat Fat: 4.8g | Carbohydrates: 9.8g | Fiber: 0.6g | Sugar: 0.9g | Protein: 53.2g

Mushroom, Broccoli, and Cheese Stuffed Chicken

Preparation Time: 10 minutes
Cooking Time: 40 minutes
Servings: 4
Ingredients:
- 2 cups broccoli florets, chopped
- 2 tablespoons water
- ½ cup pepper jack cheese
- ¼ cup mayonnaise
- 4 small button mushrooms
- 1 teaspoon garlic powder
- 4 large skinless, boneless chicken breasts
- 1 teaspoon paprika
- Salt and ground black pepper, to taste

Preparation:
1. Select the BAKE function, 400°F, for 35 minutes. While the oven is preheating, prepare the ingredients.
2. Take a microwave-safe bowl and mix the broccoli with the water. Cook for 2 minutes in the microwave on high power. Drain.
3. Combine the pepper jack cheese, mushrooms, broccoli, mayonnaise, and garlic powder in a large bowl.
4. Then, season the chicken breasts with salt, paprika, and pepper. Cut a slice through the middle of each with a sharp knife, creating a deep pocket. Make sure you don't cut all the way through.
5. Stuff the chicken breasts with the broccoli mixture and lay them on the sheet pan.
6. Bake the chicken for about 35 minutes.

Serving Suggestion: Serve the chicken on a bed of rice along with some greens.
Variation Tip: You are free to experiment with different combinations of veggies.
Nutritional Information Per Serving:
Calories: 579 | Fat: 36.6g | Sodium: 650mg | Carbs: 18.8g | Fiber: 2g | Sugar: 1.3g | Protein: 43.2g

Baked Honey Mustard Chicken

Preparation Time: 15 minutes
Cooking Time: 45 minutes
Servings: 6
Ingredients:
- 6 skinless, boneless chicken breast halves
- Salt and pepper, to taste
- ½ cup honey
- ½ cup mustard
- 1 teaspoon dried basil
- 1 teaspoon paprika
- ½ teaspoon dried parsley

Preparation:
1. Select the BAKE function, 350°F, for 45 minutes. Prepare a greased baking dish. While the oven is preheating, prepare the ingredients.
2. Season the chicken with salt and pepper and place it in the baking dish.
3. Take a small bowl, and combine the mustard, paprika, honey, parsley, and basil. Mix well. Pour half of the honey-mustard mixture over the chicken, then brush to cover.
4. Bake the chicken for about 30 minutes, turn over, brush with the remaining honey-mustard mixture, and bake for 10 to 15 more minutes.

5. Let the chicken cool for 10 minutes before serving.
Serving Suggestion: You can serve it on a bed of rice alongside some veggies.
Variation Tip: You can try using almond cream instead of mustard.
Nutritional Information Per Serving:
Calories: 232 | Fat: 3.7g | Sodium: 296mg | Carbs: 24.8g | Fiber: 1g | Sugar: 23.4g | Protein: 25.6g

Lasagna Stuffed Chicken

Preparation Time: 10 minutes
Cooking Time: 35 minutes
Servings: 3
Ingredients:
- 3 large boneless, skinless chicken breasts
- 1 tablespoon olive oil
- 1½ teaspoons Italian seasoning
- 1 teaspoon garlic powder
- 1 teaspoon salt
- 1 cup ricotta cheese
- 1½ cups mozzarella, grated
- 2 teaspoons parsley, for serving
- ½ cup marinara sauce

Preparation:
1. Select the BAKE function, 375°F, for 35 minutes. While the oven is preheating, prepare a baking dish with non-stick spray and get the rest of the ingredients ready.
2. Using a sharp knife, cut a deep slit into the side of each chicken breast.
3. Drizzle the chicken breasts with olive oil and season with the garlic powder, ½ teaspoon Italian seasoning, and ½ teaspoon of salt.
4. In a mixing bowl, combine ½ cup of the mozzarella, the ricotta, ½ teaspoon of parsley, 1 teaspoon of Italian seasoning, and ½ teaspoon salt.
5. Stuff the ricotta mixture into the chicken breasts. Then place them in the prepared dish.
6. Spoon the marinara over the chicken breasts.
7. Bake them for about 30 minutes, sprinkle 1 cup of mozzarella over the top, and bake for another 5 minutes.

Serving Suggestion: Sprinkle with the rest of the parsley before serving.
Variation Tip: You can use oregano instead of Italian seasoning.
Nutritional Information Per Serving:
Calories: 374 | Fat: 18g | Sodium: 987mg | Carbs: 5g | Fiber: 1g | Sugar: 3g | Protein: 50g

Sesame Crusted Baked Chicken Tenders

Preparation Time: 5 minutes
Cooking Time: 15 minutes
Servings: 4
Ingredients:
- 18 ounces chicken tenderloins
- ¾ teaspoon kosher salt
- Black pepper, to taste
- 2 teaspoons sesame oil
- 2 teaspoons low-sodium soy sauce
- 6 tablespoons toasted sesame seeds
- ½ teaspoon kosher salt
- ¼ cup panko
- Olive oil spray

Preparation:
1. Select the BAKE function, 425°F, for 15 minutes. Grease the sheet pan with non-stick spray.
2. In a mixing bowl, combine the soy sauce with the sesame oil. In another bowl, mix the salt, sesame seeds, and panko.
3. First, dip the chicken into the sauce mixture and then in the sesame seed mixture. Coat well.
4. Place the chicken on the sheet pan, then spray with the olive oil spray.
5. Bake for about 4 to 5 minutes, turn the chicken over and cook for 4 to 5 more minutes.

Serving Suggestion: Serve the chicken on a bed of rice with some soy sauce.
Variation Tip: If you don't want to use soy sauce, you can try miso paste or tamari.
Nutritional Information Per Serving:
Calories: 197 | Fat: 9g | Sodium: 400mg | Carbs: 5.5g | Fiber: 1.7g | Sugar: 1.5g | Protein: 23g

Air Fryer Nashville Hot Chicken

Preparation Time: 30 minutes
Cooking Time: 10 minutes/batch
Servings: 6
Ingredients:
- 2 tablespoons dill pickle juice, divided
- 2 tablespoons hot pepper sauce, divided
- 1 teaspoon salt, divided
- 2 pounds chicken tenderloins
- 1 cup all-purpose flour
- ½ teaspoon pepper
- 1 large egg
- ½ cup buttermilk
- Cooking spray
- ½ cup olive oil
- 2 tablespoons cayenne pepper
- 2 tablespoons dark brown sugar
- 1 teaspoon paprika
- 1 teaspoon chili powder
- ½ teaspoon garlic powder
- Dill pickle slices, for serving

Preparation:
1. Mix 1 tablespoon hot sauce, 1 tablespoon pickle juice, and ½ teaspoon salt. Add the chicken and coat it in the mixture. Cover and refrigerate for 1 hour.
2. Select the AIR FRY function, 375°F, for 20 minutes. Prepare the rest of the ingredients while the oven is preheating.

3. Mix the remaining salt and pepper in a shallow bowl. Whisk the buttermilk, egg, 1 tablespoon pickle juice, and 1 tablespoon hot sauce in another shallow bowl. Put the flour in a third bowl.
4. First, dip the chicken in the flour to coat, dip in the egg mixture, then again in the flour mixture.
5. Lay the chicken in a single layer in the air fryer basket and place it on the sheet pan. Spray the chicken with cooking spray. You'll need to cook in batches.
6. Cook the chicken for about 5 to 6 minutes, turn, spray with cooking spray, and cook for another 5 to 6 minutes.
7. Whisk together the brown sugar, oil, seasoning, and cayenne pepper. Pour the mixture over the chicken, and serve.

Serving Suggestion: Serve the chicken with pickles.
Variation Tip: You can try adding cottage cheese to the recipe.
Nutritional Information Per Serving:
Calories: 413 | Fat: 21g | Sodium: 170 | Carbs: 20g | Fiber: 1g | Sugar: 5g | Protein: 39g

Air Fryer Chicken Taco Pockets

Preparation Time: 5 minutes
Cooking Time: 25 minutes
Servings: 8
Ingredients:
- 2 8-ounce tubes of crescent rolls
- ½ cup salsa
- ½ cup sour cream
- 2 tablespoons taco seasoning
- 1 cup rotisserie chicken, shredded
- 1 cup cheddar cheese, shredded

Preparation:
1. Select the AIR FRY function, 375°F, for 15 minutes. While the oven is preheating, prepare the ingredients.
2. Unroll 1 tube of crescent roll, separate it into 2 rectangles, and press the perforation to seal. Repeat for the other tube.
3. Take a bowl, and combine the sour cream, salsa, and taco seasoning. Place some shredded chicken on the left sides of the rectangles and top them with the salsa mixture. Sprinkle with the cheese and fold the dough over the filling, then pinch the edges to seal.
4. Transfer the pockets to the air fryer basket and cook for about 13 to 15 minutes. Cut in half and serve.

Serving Suggestion: Serve with salsa and a topping of your choice.
Variation Tip: You can add shredded lettuce and guacamole to the recipe.
Nutritional Information Per Serving:
Calories: 393 | Fat: 24g | Sodium: 896 | Carbs: 29g | Fiber: 0g | Sugar: 7g | Protein: 16g

Oven-Baked Jambalaya

Preparation Time: 45 minutes
Cooking Time: 2 hours
Servings: 8
Ingredients:
- ½ cup butter
- 1 large onion, diced
- 1 large green bell pepper, chopped
- 4 celery stalks, chopped
- 4 cloves garlic, minced
- 6 ounces tomato paste
- 3 bay leaves
- 3 tablespoons Creole seasoning blend
- 4 teaspoons Worcestershire sauce
- 28 ounces whole tomatoes, peeled
- 7 cups chicken stock
- 3 cups cooked ham, chopped
- 3 cups cooked andouille sausage
- 3 cups cooked chicken
- 3 cups frozen cooked shrimp
- 4 cups uncooked long-grain white rice

Preparation:
1. Select the BAKE function, 350°F, for 1 hour and 30 minutes. While the oven is preheating, prepare the ingredients.
2. Take a large stockpot and melt the butter in it. Add the green pepper, garlic, onion, and celery; sauté until tender. Add the tomato paste and continue to cook. Stir in the Creole seasoning blend, bay leaves, and Worcestershire sauce.
3. Pour the mixture into a large roasting pan. Squeeze the tomatoes and then add to the pan. Stir in the chicken stock, ham, chicken, shrimp, sausage, and rice. Mix well and cover with aluminum foil.
4. Baking time is about 1½ hours. Stir once halfway through cooking time. Remove the bay leaves before serving.

Serving Suggestion: Serve the meal on a bed of rice with some greens on top.
Variation Tip: You can try using Old Bay seasoning instead of Creole seasoning blend.
Nutritional Information Per Serving:
Calories: 540 | Fat: 26g | Sodium: 1857 | Carbs: 47.6g | Fiber: 2.6g | Sugar: 5.3g | Protein: 28.5g

Oven-Baked Peri-Peri Chicken

Preparation Time: 5 minutes
Cooking Time: 45 minutes
Marinate Time: 1 hour
Servings: 4
Ingredients:
- 3 cloves garlic
- Juice and zest of 1 lemon
- Juice of 1 orange
- ¼ cup olive oil
- 2 teaspoons sweet paprika
- ¼ teaspoon black pepper
- ½ teaspoon red pepper flakes
- 1 teaspoon dried oregano
- 2.2 pounds skin-on chicken pieces
- ½ teaspoon salt

Preparation:
1. Select the BAKE function, 390°F, for 45 minutes.

2. Combine the lemon juice, orange juice, minced garlic, and olive oil in a large plastic bowl.
3. Add the sweet paprika, chili flakes, lemon zest, and oregano and combine well.
4. Add the chicken pieces and leave them to marinate for about 1 hour in the refrigerator.
5. Place the chicken pieces on a baking dish. Sprinkle them with salt, and cook for about 45 minutes.
6. Pour the pan juices carefully over the chicken before serving.

Serving Suggestion: Add fresh chopped parsley before serving. Serve alongside garlic rice.
Variation Tip: Add more chili flakes to make it spicier, and you can also try Italian seasoning.
Nutritional Information Per Serving:
Calories: 638 | Fat: 41g | Sodium: 1037mg | Carbs: 6g | Fiber: 2g | Sugar: 2g | Protein: 61g

Oven-Roasted Chicken Shawarma

Preparation Time: 20 minutes
Cooking Time: 45 minutes
Servings: 4 to 6
Ingredients:
- Juice of 2 lemons
- ½ cup plus 1 tablespoon olive oil
- 6 garlic cloves, smashed and minced
- 1 teaspoon kosher salt
- 2 teaspoons freshly ground black pepper
- 2 teaspoons ground cumin
- 2 teaspoons paprika
- ½ teaspoon turmeric
- Pinch of ground cinnamon
- Red pepper flakes, to taste
- 2 pounds boneless, skinless chicken thighs
- 1 large red onion, quartered
- 2 tablespoons fresh parsley, chopped for serving

Preparation:
1. Take a large bowl, and mix ½ cup of olive oil, cumin, cinnamon, garlic, lemon juice, salt, pepper, paprika, and red pepper flakes. Add the chicken thighs and toss to coat. Cover and refrigerate for at least 1 hour.
2. Select the AIR ROAST function, 425°F, for 40 minutes. Allow the oven to preheat.
3. Prepare a rimmed sheet pan with the remaining olive oil. Add the onion to the chicken, marinade, and toss to combine. Remove the chicken and onion and spread them on the prepared pan evenly.
4. Let the chicken roast for about 30 to 40 minutes. Take it out and leave it to rest for 2 minutes to cool down, then slice it.

Serving Suggestion: Sprinkle with the fresh parsley and serve with cucumbers, pita, and yogurt sauce.
Variation Tip: Try adding red wine vinegar.
Nutritional Information Per Serving:
Calories: 390 | Fat: 27g | Sodium: 453mg | Carbs: 7g | Fiber: 2g | Sugar: 2g | Protein: 31g

Air Fryer Chicken Pesto Stuffed Peppers

Preparation Time: 10 minutes
Cooking Time: 25 minutes
Servings: 4
Ingredients:
- 4 medium sweet peppers
- 1½ cups rotisserie chicken, shredded
- 1½ cups brown rice, cooked
- 1 cup pesto
- ½ cup Havarti cheese, shredded

Preparation:
1. Select the AIR FRY function, 400°F, for 25 minutes. While the oven is preheating, prepare the ingredients.
2. Cut the peppers in half, lengthwise. Remove the seeds and stems.
3. Place the peppers in the air fry basket in a single layer.
4. Cook for about 10 to 15 minutes, then turn the temperature down to 350°F.
5. Meanwhile, take a large bowl, and combine the rice, chicken, and pesto. Use the chicken mixture to fill the peppers.
6. Cook for about 5 minutes. Sprinkle with the cheese and cook for another 3 to 5 minutes.

Serving Suggestion: Sprinkle with fresh basil leaves and serve.
Variation Tip: You can try cheddar or Gouda instead of Havarti cheese.
Nutritional Information Per Serving:
Calories: 521 | Fat: 31g | Sodium: 865mg | Carbs: 33g | Fiber: 5g | Sugar: 7g | Protein: 25g

Pepper Chicken Bake

Preparation Time: 5 minutes
Cooking Time: 25 minutes
Servings: 4
Ingredients:
- 2 pounds boneless, skinless chicken breast
- 1 green bell pepper, thinly sliced
- 1 red bell pepper, thinly sliced
- 1 onion, diced
- ½ cup low-sodium chicken stock
- 3 tablespoons soy sauce
- ¼ teaspoon ground ginger
- ¼ teaspoon garlic powder
- ¼ teaspoon cracked black pepper
- 2 tablespoons unsalted butter

Preparation:
1. Select the BAKE function, 400°F, for 30 minutes. While the oven is preheating, prepare the ingredients.
2. Chop the chicken breasts into small pieces and place them into an air fryer-safe baking dish.
3. Take a small bowl, and combine the soy sauce, half of the garlic powder, chicken stock, cracked black pepper, and ginger.

4. Put the diced onions and sliced peppers over the chicken pieces and sprinkle with the remaining garlic powder.
5. Pour the sauce mixture over the chicken and stir to mix evenly. Place the butter on top of the chicken.
6. Bake for 25 to 30 minutes.

Serving Suggestion: Garnish with lemon slices and basil.
Variation Tip: You can try using Worcestershire sauce or coconut aminos instead of soy sauce.
Nutritional Information Per Serving:
Calories: 492 | Fat: 27.43g | Sodium: 661mg | Carbs: 7g | Fiber: 0.64g | Sugar: 0.8g | Protein: 53.21g

Chicken Chardon

Preparation Time: 10 minutes
Cooking Time: 45 minutes
Servings: 8
Ingredients:
- 8 skinless, boneless chicken breast halves
- 1 egg
- Salt and pepper, to taste
- 2 teaspoons garlic powder
- 1 cup breadcrumbs
- ½ cup parmesan cheese, grated
- 1 pound mushrooms, sliced
- ¼ cup butter, melted
- 1 tablespoon lemon juice
- 1 teaspoon fresh parsley, chopped

Preparation:
1. Select the BAKE function, 375°F, for 45 minutes. While the oven is preheating, prepare the ingredients.
2. Beat the egg in a shallow bowl with pepper, salt, and 1 teaspoon garlic powder.
3. Mix the parmesan cheese, breadcrumbs, and remaining garlic powder in another dish. Set it aside.
4. Mix the lemon juice and melted butter. Pour about ⅔ of this mixture into a baking dish, coating the bottom. Lay the mushrooms in the dish in an even layer.
5. First, dip the chicken breasts into the egg mixture and then into the breadcrumb mixture. Place the breasts on top of the mushrooms.
6. Drizzle with the remaining butter mixture and sprinkle with the parsley.
7. Bake the chicken for about 45 minutes.

Serving Suggestion: Serve with rice and veggies.
Variation Tip: Try using Romano cheese instead of parmesan.
Nutritional Information Per Serving:
Calories: 280 | Fat: 11.6g | Sodium: 334mg | Carbs: 13g | Fiber: 1.3g | Sugar: 1.8g | Protein: 30.3g

Lamb Chops with Carrots

Preparation Time: 15 minutes
Cooking Time: 10 minutes
Servings: 4
Ingredients:
- 2 tablespoons fresh rosemary, minced
- 2 tablespoons fresh mint leaves, minced
- 1 garlic clove, minced
- 3 tablespoons olive oil
- Salt and ground black pepper, as required
- 4 (6-ounce) lamb chops
- 2 large carrots, peeled and cubed

Preparation:
1. In a large bowl, mix together the herbs, garlic, oil, salt, and black pepper.
2. Add the chops and generously coat with mixture.
3. Refrigerate to marinate for about 3 hours.
4. In a large pan of water, soak the carrots for about 15 minutes.
5. Drain the carrots completely.
6. Press "Power" button of Ninja Foodi Digital Air Fry Oven and turn the dial to select "Air Fry" mode.
7. Press TIME/SLICE button and again turn the dial to set the cooking time to 10 minutes.
8. Now push TEMP/DARKNESS button and rotate the dial to set the temperature at 390 degrees F.
9. Press "Start/Pause" button to start.
10. When the unit beeps to show that it is preheated, open the oven door.
11. Arrange chops into the greased air fry basket in a single layer and insert in the oven.
12. After 2 minutes of cooking, arrange carrots into the air fry basket and top with the chops in a single layer.
13. Insert the basket in oven.
14. When the cooking time is completed, open the oven door and transfer the chops and carrots onto serving plates.
15. Serve hot.
Serving Suggestions: Serve with fresh greens.
Variation Tip: You can use herbs of your choice.
Nutritional Information per Serving:
Calories: 429 | Fat: 23.2g | Sat Fat: 6.1g | Carbohydrates: 5.1g | Fiber: 1.8g | Sugar: 1.8g | Protein: 48.3g

BBQ Pork Chops

Preparation Time: 10 minutes
Cooking Time: 16 minutes
Servings: 6
Ingredients:
- 6 (8-ounce) pork loin chops
- Salt and ground black pepper, as required
- ½ cup BBQ sauce

Preparation:
1. With a meat tenderizer, tenderize the chops completely.
2. Sprinkle the chops with a little salt and black pepper.
3. In a large bowl, add the BBQ sauce and chops and mix well.

4. Refrigerate, covered for about 6-8 hours.
5. Press "Power" button of Ninja Foodi Digital Air Fry Oven and turn the dial to select "Air Fry" mode.
6. Press TIME/SLICE button and again turn the dial to set the cooking time to 16 minutes.
7. Now push TEMP/DARKNESS button and rotate the dial to set the temperature at 355 degrees F.
8. Press "Start/Pause" button to start.
9. When the unit beeps to show that it is preheated, open the oven door.
10. Arrange the pork chops into the greased air fry basket and insert in the oven.
11. Flip the chops once halfway through.
12. When the cooking time is completed, open the oven door and serve hot.
Serving Suggestions: Serve with roasted veggies.
Variation Tip: Make sure to use good quality BBQ sauce.
Nutritional Information per Serving:
Calories: 757 | Fat: 56.4g | Sat Fat: 21.1g | Carbohydrates: 7.6g | Fiber: 0.1g | Sugar: 5.4g | Protein: 51g

Mustard Lamb Loin Chops

Preparation Time: 10 minutes
Cooking Time: 15 minutes
Servings: 2
Ingredients:
- 1 tablespoon Dijon mustard
- ½ tablespoon white wine vinegar
- 1 teaspoon olive oil
- ½ teaspoon dried tarragon
- Salt and ground black pepper, as required
- 4 (4-ounce) lamb loin chops

Preparation:
1. In a large bowl, mix together the mustard, vinegar, oil, tarragon, salt, and black pepper.
2. Add the chops and coat with the mixture generously.
3. Arrange the chops onto the greased sheet pan.
4. Press "Power" button of Ninja Foodi Digital Air Fry Oven and turn the dial to select "Bake" mode.
5. Press TIME/SLICE button and again turn the dial to set the cooking time to 15 minutes.
6. Now push TEMP/DARKNESS button and rotate the dial to set the temperature at 390 degrees F.
7. Press "Start/Pause" button to start.
8. When the unit beeps to show that it is preheated, open the oven door and insert the sheet pan in the oven.
9. When the cooking time is completed, open the oven door and serve hot.
Serving Suggestions: Serve alongside the feta spinach.
Variation Tip: Remember to bring the chops to room temperature.
Nutritional Information per Serving:
Calories: 44 | Fat: 19.3g | Sat Fat: 6.3g | Carbohydrates: 0.5g | Fiber: 0.3g | Sugar: 0.1g | Protein: 64.1g

Balsamic Beef Top Roast

Preparation Time: 10 minutes
Cooking Time: 45 minutes
Servings: 10
Ingredients:

- 1 tablespoon butter, melted
- 1 tablespoon balsamic vinegar
- ½ teaspoon ground cumin
- ½ teaspoon smoked paprika
- ½ teaspoon red pepper flakes, crushed
- Salt and ground black pepper, as required
- 3 pounds beef top roast

Preparation:
1. In a bowl, add butter, vinegar, spices, salt and black pepper and mix well.
2. Coat the roast with spice mixture generously.
3. With kitchen twines, tie the roast to keep it compact.
4. Arrange the roast onto the greased sheet pan.
5. Press "Power" button of Ninja Foodi Digital Air Fry Oven and turn the dial to select "Air Fry" mode.
6. Press TIME/SLICE button and again turn the dial to set the cooking time to 45 minutes.
7. Now push TEMP/DARKNESS button and rotate the dial to set the temperature at 360 degrees F.
8. Press "Start/Pause" button to start.
9. When the unit beeps to show that it is preheated, open the oven door and insert the sheet pan in the oven.
10. When the cooking time is completed, open the oven door and place the roast onto a cutting board for about 10 minutes before slicing.
11. With a sharp knife, cut the roast into desired sized slices and serve.
Serving Suggestions: Serve alongside the buttered green beans.
Variation Tip: Use unsalted butter.
Nutritional Information per Serving:
Calories: 305 | Fat: 17.1g | Sat Fat: 6.1g | Carbohydrates: 0.1g | Fiber: 0.1g | Sugar: 0g | Protein: 35.1g

Rosemary Lamb Chops

Preparation Time: 10 minutes
Cooking Time: 6 minutes
Servings: 2
Ingredients:

- 1 tablespoon olive oil, divided
- 2 garlic cloves, minced
- 1 tablespoon fresh rosemary, chopped
- Salt and ground black pepper, as required
- 4 (4-ounce) lamb chops

Preparation:
1. In a large bowl, mix together the oil, garlic, rosemary, salt and black pepper.
2. Coat the chops with half of the garlic mixture.
3. Press "Power" button of Ninja Foodi Digital Air Fry Oven and turn the dial to select "Air Fry" mode.
4. Press TIME/SLICE button and again turn the dial to set the cooking time to 6 minutes.
5. Now push TEMP/DARKNESS button and rotate the dial to set the temperature at 390 degrees F.

6. Press "Start/Pause" button to start.
7. When the unit beeps to show that it is preheated, open the oven door and grease the air fry basket.
8. Place the lamb chops into the prepared air fry basket and insert in the oven.
9. Flip the chops once halfway through.
10. When cooking time is completed, open the oven door and serve hot with the topping of the remaining garlic mixture.
Serving Suggestions: Serve with yogurt sauce.
Variation Tip: Lamb chops that has dried out edges and does not smell fresh should not be purchased.
Nutritional Information per Serving:
Calories: 492 | Fat: 23.9g | Sat Fat: 7.1g | Carbohydrates: 2.1g | Fiber: 0.8g | Sugar: 0g | Protein: 64g

Steak with Bell Peppers

Preparation Time: 15 minutes
Cooking Time: 11 minutes
Servings: 4
Ingredients:

- 1 teaspoon dried oregano, crushed
- 1 teaspoon onion powder
- 1 teaspoon garlic powder
- 1 teaspoon red chili powder
- 1 teaspoon paprika
- Salt, as required
- 1¼ pounds flank steak, cut into thin strips
- 3 green bell peppers, seeded and cubed
- 1 red onion, sliced
- 2 tablespoons olive oil
- 3-4 tablespoons feta cheese, crumbled

Preparation:
1. In a large bowl, mix together the oregano and spices.
2. Add the steak strips, bell peppers, onion, and oil and mix until well combined.
3. Press "Power" button of Ninja Foodi Digital Air Fry Oven and turn the dial to select "Air Fry" mode.
4. Press TIME/SLICE button and again turn the dial to set the cooking time to 11 minutes.
5. Now push TEMP/DARKNESS button and rotate the dial to set the temperature at 390 degrees F.
6. Press "Start/Pause" button to start.
7. When the unit beeps to show that it is preheated, open the oven door and grease the air fry basket.
8. Place the steak mixture into the prepared air fry basket and insert in the oven.
9. When cooking time is completed, open the oven door and transfer the steak mixture onto serving plates.
10. Serve immediately with the topping of feta.
Serving Suggestions: Serve with plain rice.
Variation Tip: Adjust the ratio of spices according to your taste.
Nutritional Information per Serving:
Calories: 732 | Fat: 35g | Sat Fat: 12.9g | Carbohydrates: 11.5g | Fiber: 2.5g | Sugar: 6.5g | Protein: 89.3g

Citrus Pork Chops

Preparation Time: 15 minutes
Cooking Time: 15 minutes
Servings: 6
Ingredients:
- ½ cup olive oil
- 1 teaspoon fresh orange zest, grated
- 3 tablespoons fresh orange juice
- 1 teaspoon fresh lime zest, grated
- 3 tablespoons fresh lime juice
- 8 garlic cloves, minced
- 1 cup fresh cilantro, chopped finely
- ¼ cup fresh mint leaves, chopped finely
- 1 teaspoon dried oregano, crushed
- 1 teaspoon ground cumin
- Salt and ground black pepper, as required
- 6 thick-cut pork chops

Preparation:
1. In a bowl, place the oil, orange zest, orange juice, lime zest, lime juice, garlic, fresh herbs, oregano, cumin, salt and black pepper and beat until well combined.
2. In a small bowl, reserve ¼ cup of the marinade.
3. In a large zip lock bag, place the remaining marinade and pork chops.
4. Seal the bag and shake to coat well.
5. Refrigerate to marinate overnight.
6. Remove the pork chops from the bag and shake off to remove the excess marinade.
7. Press "Power" button of Ninja Foodi Digital Air Fry Oven and turn the dial to select the "Air Broil" mode.
8. Press the TEMP/DARKNESS button and use the dial to select HI. To set the temperature, press the TEMP/DARKNESS button again.
9. Press TIME/SLICE button and again turn the dial to set the cooking time to 15 minutes.
10. Press "Start/Pause" button to start.
11. When the unit beeps to show that it is preheated, open the oven door.
12. Place the pork chops over the wire rack and insert in oven.
13. After 8 minutes of cooking, flip the chops once.
14. When the cooking time is completed, open the oven door and serve hot.

Serving Suggestions: Serve with steamed broccoli.
Variation Tip: Use fresh orange juice and zest.
Nutritional Information per Serving:
Calories: 700 | Fat: 59.3g | Sat Fat: 18.3g | Carbohydrates: 2.1g | Fiber: 0.4g | Sugar: 0.3g | Protein: 38.7g

Herbed Leg of Lamb

Preparation Time: 10 minutes
Cooking Time: 1¼ hours
Servings: 6
Ingredients:
- 2¼ pounds boneless leg of lamb
- 2 tablespoons olive oil
- Salt and ground black pepper, as required
- 2 fresh rosemary sprigs
- 2 fresh thyme sprigs

Preparation:
1. Coat the leg of lamb with oil and sprinkle with salt and black pepper.
2. Wrap the leg of lamb with herb sprigs.
3. Press "Power" button of Ninja Foodi Digital Air Fry Oven and turn the dial to select "Air Fry" mode.
4. Press TIME/SLICE button and again turn the dial to set the cooking time to 75 minutes.
5. Now push TEMP/DARKNESS button and rotate the dial to set the temperature at 300 degrees F.
6. Press "Start/Pause" button to start.
7. When the unit beeps to show that it is preheated, open the oven door.
8. Arrange the leg of lamb into the greased air fry basket and insert in the oven.
9. Immediately set the temperature at 355 degrees F.
10. When the cooking time is completed, open the oven door and place the leg of lamb onto a cutting board for about 10 minutes.
11. Cut the leg of lamb into desired-sized pieces and serve.

Serving Suggestions: Serve alongside the roasted Brussels sprout.
Variation Tip: Always slice the meat against the grain.
Nutritional Information per Serving:
Calories: 360 | Fat: 17.3g | Sat Fat: 5.2g | Carbohydrates: 0.7g | Fiber: 0.5g | Sugar: 0g | Protein: 47.8g

Tarragon Beef Shanks

Preparation Time: 15 minutes.
Cooking Time: 15 minutes.
Servings: 4
Ingredients:
- 2 tablespoons olive oil
- 2 pounds beef shank
- Salt and black pepper to taste
- 1 onion, diced
- 2 stalks celery, diced
- 1 cup Marsala wine
- 2 tablespoons dried tarragon

Preparation:
1. Place the beef shanks in a baking pan.
2. Whisk the rest of the ingredients in a bowl and pour over the shanks.
3. Place these shanks in the air fry basket.
4. Transfer the basket to the Ninja Foodi Digital Air Fry Oven and close the door.
5. Select "Air Fry" mode by rotating the dial.
6. Press the TIME/SLICE button and change the value to 15 minutes.
7. Press the TEMP/DARKNESS button and change the value to 375 degrees F.
8. Press Start/Pause to begin cooking.
9. Serve warm.

Serving Suggestion: Serve the beef shanks with sweet potato casserole.
Variation Tip: Cook the beef shanks with the mushrooms sauce.
Nutritional Information Per Serving:
Calories 425 | Fat 15g | Sodium 345mg | Carbs 12.3g | Fiber 1.4g | Sugar 3g | Protein 23.3g

Simple Beef Tenderloin

Preparation Time: 10 minutes
Cooking Time: 50 minutes
Servings: 10
Ingredients:
- 1 (3½-pound) beef tenderloin, trimmed
- 2 tablespoons olive oil
- Salt and ground black pepper, as required

Preparation:
1. With kitchen twine, tie the tenderloin.
2. Rub the tenderloin with oil and season with salt and black pepper.
3. Place the tenderloin into the greased sheet pan.
4. Press "Power" button of Ninja Foodi Digital Air Fry Oven and turn the dial to select the "Air Roast" mode.
5. Press TIME/SLICE button and again turn the dial to set the cooking time to 50 minutes.
6. Now push TEMP/DARKNESS button and rotate the dial to set the temperature at 400 degrees F.
7. Press "Start/Pause" button to start.
8. When the unit beeps to show that it is preheated, open the oven door and insert the sheet pan in the oven.
9. When cooking time is completed, open the oven door and place the tenderloin onto a platter for about 10 minutes before slicing.
10. With a sharp knife, cut the tenderloin into desired sized slices and serve.

Serving Suggestions: Serve with lemony herbed couscous.
Variation Tip: Make sure to trim the meat before cooking.
Nutritional Information per Serving:
Calories: 351 | Fat: 17.3g | Sat Fat: 5.9g | Carbohydrates: 0g | Fiber: 0g | Sugar: 0g | Protein: .46g

Herbed Chuck Roast

Preparation Time: 10 minutes
Cooking Time: 45 minutes
Servings: 6
Ingredients:
- 1 (2-pound) beef chuck roast
- 1 tablespoon olive oil
- 1 teaspoon dried rosemary, crushed
- 1 teaspoon dried thyme, crushed
- Salt, as required

Preparation:
1. In a bowl, add the oil, herbs and salt and mix well.
2. Coat the beef roast with herb mixture generously.
3. Arrange the beef roast onto the greased sheet pan.
4. Press "Power" button of Ninja Foodi Digital Air Fry Oven and turn the dial to select "Air Fry" mode.
5. Press TIME/SLICE button and again turn the dial to set the cooking time to 45 minutes.
6. Now push TEMP/DARKNESS button and rotate the dial to set the temperature at 360 degrees F.
7. Press "Start/Pause" button to start.
8. When the unit beeps to show that it is preheated, open the oven door and insert the sheet pan in the oven.
9. When cooking time is completed, open the oven door and place the roast onto a cutting board.
10. With a piece of foil, cover the beef roast for about 20 minutes before slicing.
11. With a sharp knife, cut the beef roast into desired size slices and serve.

Serving Suggestions: Serve with roasted Brussels sprouts.
Variation Tip: Dried herbs can be replaced with fresh herbs.
Nutritional Information per Serving:
Calories: 304 | Fat: 14g | Sat Fat: 4.5g | Carbohydrates: 0.2g | Fiber: 0.2g | Sugar: 0g | Protein: 41.5g

Pork Stuffed Bell Peppers

Preparation Time: 20 minutes
Cooking Time: 1 hour 10 minutes
Servings: 4
Ingredients:
- 4 medium green bell peppers
- ⅔ pound ground pork
- 2 cups cooked white rice
- 1½ cups marinara sauce, divided
- 1 teaspoon Worcestershire sauce
- 1 teaspoon Italian seasoning
- Salt and ground black pepper, as required
- ½ cup mozzarella cheese, shredded

Preparation:
1. Cut the tops from bell peppers and then carefully remove the seeds.
2. Heat a large skillet over medium heat and cook the pork for about 6-8 minutes. Mince the pork.
3. Add the rice, ¾ cup of marinara sauce, Worcestershire sauce, Italian seasoning, salt and black pepper and stir to combine.
4. Remove from the heat.
5. Arrange the bell peppers into the greased sheet pan.
6. Carefully, stuff each bell pepper with the pork mixture and top each with the remaining sauce.
7. Press "Power" button of Ninja Foodi Digital Air Fry Oven and turn the dial to select the "Bake" mode.
8. Press TIME/SLICE button and again turn the dial to set the cooking time to 60 minutes.
9. Now push TEMP/DARKNESS button and rotate the dial to set the temperature at 350 degrees F.
10. Press "Start/Pause" button to start.
11. When the unit beeps to show that it is preheated, open the oven door.
12. Insert the sheet pan in oven.
13. After 50 minute of cooking, top each bell pepper with cheese.
14. When cooking time is completed, open the oven door and transfer the bell peppers onto a platter.
15. Serve warm.

Serving Suggestions: Serve with baby greens.
Variation Tip: Use best quality ground pork.
Nutritional Information per Serving:
Calories: 580 | Fat: 7.1g | Sat Fat: 2.2g | Carbohydrates: 96.4g | Fiber: 5.2g | Sugar: 14.8g | Protein: 30.3g

Bacon-Wrapped Pork Tenderloin

Preparation Time: 15 minutes
Cooking Time: 30 minutes
Servings: 4
Ingredients:
- 1 (1½-pound) pork tenderloin
- 2 tablespoons Dijon mustard
- 1 tablespoon honey
- 4 bacon strips

Preparation:
1. Coat the tenderloin with mustard and honey.
2. Wrap the pork tenderloin with bacon strips.
3. Press "Power" button of Ninja Foodi Digital Air Fry Oven and turn the dial to select "Air Fry" mode.
4. Press TIME/SLICE button and again turn the dial to set the cooking time to 30 minutes.
5. Now push TEMP/DARKNESS button and rotate the dial to set the temperature at 360 degrees F.
6. Press "Start/Pause" button to start.
7. When the unit beeps to show that it is preheated, open the oven door and grease the air fry basket.
8. Place the pork tenderloin into the prepared air fry basket and insert in the oven.
9. Flip the pork tenderloin once halfway through.
10. When cooking time is completed, open the oven door and place the pork loin onto a cutting board for about 10 minutes before slicing.
11. With a sharp knife, cut the tenderloin into desired sized slices and serve.
Serving Suggestions: Enjoy with mashed potatoes.
Variation Tip: Make sure to remove the silver skin from the tenderloin.
Nutritional Information per Serving:
Calories: 386 | Fat: 16.1g | Sat Fat: 5.7g | Carbohydrates: 4.8g | Fiber: 0.3g | Sugar: 4.4g | Protein: 52g

Herbs Crumbed Rack of Lamb

Preparation Time: 15 minutes
Cooking Time: 30 minutes
Servings: 5
Ingredients:
- 1 tablespoon butter, melted
- 1 garlic clove, finely chopped
- 1¾ pounds rack of lamb
- Salt and ground black pepper, as required
- 1 egg
- ½ cup panko breadcrumbs
- 1 tablespoon fresh thyme, minced
- 1 tablespoon fresh rosemary, minced

Preparation:
1. In a bowl, mix together the butter, garlic, salt, and black pepper.
2. Coat the rack of lamb evenly with garlic mixture.
3. In a shallow dish, beat the egg.
4. In another dish, mix together the breadcrumbs and herbs.
5. Dip the rack of lamb in beaten egg and then coat with breadcrumbs mixture.
6. Press "Power" button of Ninja Foodi Digital Air Fry Oven and turn the dial to select "Air Fry" mode.

7. Press TIME/SLICE button and again turn the dial to set the cooking time to 25 minutes.
8. Now push TEMP/DARKNESS button and rotate the dial to set the temperature at 250 degrees F.
9. Press "Start/Pause" button to start.
10. When the unit beeps to show that it is preheated, open the oven door and grease the air fry basket.
11. Place the rack of lamb into the prepared air fry basket and insert in the oven.
12. After 25 minutes of cooking,
13. When cooking time is completed, open the oven door and set the temperature at 390 degrees F for 5 minutes.
14. When cooking time is completed, open the oven door and place the rack of lamb onto a cutting board for about 5-10 minutes.
15. With a sharp knife, cut the rack of lamb into individual chops and serve.
Serving Suggestions: Serve with a drizzling of lemon juice.
Variation Tip: Make sure to rest the rack of lamb before cutting into chops.
Nutritional Information per Serving:
Calories: 331 | Fat: 17.2g | Sat Fat: 6.7g | Carbohydrates: 2.6g | Fiber: 0.5g | Sugar: 0g | Protein: 32.7g

Beef Zucchini Shashliks

Preparation Time: 15 minutes.
Cooking Time: 25 minutes.
Servings: 4
Ingredients:
- 1 pound beef, boned and diced
- 1 lime, juiced, and chopped
- 3 tablespoons olive oil
- 20 garlic cloves, chopped
- 1 handful rosemary, chopped
- 3 green peppers, cubed
- 2 zucchinis, cubed
- 2 red onions, cut into wedges

Preparation:
1. Toss the beef with the rest of the skewer's ingredients in a bowl.
2. Thread the beef, peppers, zucchini, and onion on the skewers.
3. Place these beef skewers in the air fry basket.
4. Transfer the basket to the Ninja Foodi Digital Air Fry Oven and close the door.
5. Select "Air Fry" mode by rotating the dial.
6. Press the TIME/SLICE button and change the value to 25 minutes.
7. Press the TEMP/DARKNESS button and change the value to 370 degrees F.
8. Press Start/Pause to begin cooking.
9. Flip the skewers when cooked halfway through, then resume cooking.
10. Serve warm.
Serving Suggestion: Serve the shashlik with crispy bacon and sautéed vegetables.
Variation Tip: Season the beef with yogurt and spice marinade.
Nutritional Information Per Serving:
Calories 416 | Fat 21g | Sodium 476mg | Carbs 22g | Fiber 3g | Sugar 4g | Protein 20g

Breaded Pork Chops

Preparation Time: 15 minutes
Cooking Time: 15 minutes
Servings: 3
Ingredients:
- 3 (6-ounce) pork chops
- Salt and ground black pepper, as required
- ¼ cup plain flour
- 1 egg
- 4 ounces seasoned breadcrumbs
- 1 tablespoon canola oil

Preparation:
1. Season each pork chop with salt and black pepper.
2. In a shallow bowl, place the flour.
3. In a second bowl, crack the egg and beat well.
4. In a third bowl, add the breadcrumbs and oil and mix until a crumbly mixture forms.
5. Coat the pork chop with flour, then dip into beaten egg and finally, coat with the breadcrumbs mixture.
6. Press "Power" button of Ninja Foodi Digital Air Fry Oven and turn the dial to select "Air Fry" mode.
7. Press TIME/SLICE button and again turn the dial to set the cooking time to 15 minutes.
8. Now push TEMP/DARKNESS button and rotate the dial to set the temperature at 400 degrees F.
9. Press "Start/Pause" button to start.
10. When the unit beeps to show that it is preheated, open the oven door and grease the air fry basket.
11. Place the lamb chops into the prepared air fry basket and insert in the oven.
12. Flip the chops once halfway through.
13. When cooking time is completed, open the oven door and serve hot.
Serving Suggestions: Serve with your favorite dipping sauce.
Variation Tip: Don't cook chops straight from the refrigerator
Nutritional Information per Serving:
Calories: 413 | Fat: 20.2g | Sat Fat: 4.4g | Carbohydrates: 31g | Fiber: 1.6g | Sugar: 0.1g | Protein: 28.3g

Crispy Sirloin Steaks

Preparation Time: 10 minutes
Cooking Time: 14 minutes
Servings: 2
Ingredients:
- ½ cup flour
- Salt and ground black pepper, as required
- 2 eggs
- ¾ cup breadcrumbs
- 3 (6-ounce) sirloin steaks, pounded

Preparation:
1. In a shallow bowl, place the flour, salt and black pepper and mix well.
2. In a second shallow bowl, beat the eggs.
3. In a third shallow bowl, place the breadcrumbs.
4. Coat the steak with flour, then dip into eggs, and finally coat with the panko mixture.
5. Press "Power" button of Ninja Foodi Digital Air Fry Oven and turn the dial to select "Air Fry" mode.
6. Press TIME/SLICE button and again turn the dial to set the cooking time to 14 minutes.
7. Now push TEMP/DARKNESS button and rotate the dial to set the temperature at 360 degrees F.
8. Press "Start/Pause" button to start.
9. When the unit beeps to show that it is preheated, open the oven door.
10. Arrange the steaks into the greased air fry basket and insert in the oven.
11. When the cooking time is completed, open the oven door and serve hot.
Serving Suggestions: Serve with your favorite dipping sauce.
Variation Tip: Feel free to use breadcrumbs of your choice.
Nutritional Information per Serving:
Calories: 540 | Fat: 15.2g | Sat Fat: 5.3g | Carbohydrates: 35.6g | Fiber: 1.8g | Sugar: 2g | Protein: 61g

Garlicky Lamb Steaks

Preparation Time: 15 minutes
Cooking Time: 15 minutes
Servings: 4
Ingredients:
- ½ onion, roughly chopped
- 5 garlic cloves, peeled
- 1 tablespoon fresh ginger, peeled
- 1 teaspoon ground fennel
- ½ teaspoon ground cumin
- ½ teaspoon ground cinnamon
- ½ teaspoon cayenne pepper
- Salt and ground black pepper, as required
- 1½ pounds boneless lamb sirloin steaks

Preparation:
1. In a blender, add the onion, garlic, ginger, and spices and pulse until smooth.
2. Transfer the mixture into a large bowl.
3. Add the lamb steaks and coat with the mixture generously.
4. Refrigerate to marinate for about 24 hours.
5. Press "Power" button of Ninja Foodi Digital Air Fry Oven and turn the dial to select "Air Fry" mode.
6. Press TIME/SLICE button and again turn the dial to set the cooking time to 15 minutes.
7. Now push TEMP/DARKNESS button and rotate the dial to set the temperature at 330 degrees F.
8. Press "Start/Pause" button to start.
9. When the unit beeps to show that it is preheated, open the oven door and grease the air fry basket.
10. Place the lamb steaks into the prepared air fry basket and insert in the oven.
11. Flip the steaks once halfway through.
12. When cooking time is completed, open the oven door and serve hot.
Serving Suggestions: Serve with your favorite greens.
Variation Tip: Allow the lamb steaks to reach room temperature before cooking.
Nutritional Information per Serving:
Calories: 336 | Fat: 12.8g | Sat Fat: 4.5g | Carbohydrates: 4.2g | Fiber: 1g | Sugar: 0.7g | Protein: 8.4g

Sauce Glazed Meatloaf

Preparation Time: 15 minutes.
Cooking Time: 60 minutes.
Servings: 6
Ingredients:
- 1 pound ground beef
- ½ onion chopped
- 1 egg
- 1 ½ garlic clove, minced
- 1 ½ tablespoons ketchup
- 1 ½ tablespoons fresh parsley, chopped
- ¼ cup breadcrumbs
- 2 tablespoons milk
- Salt to taste
- 1 ½ teaspoons herb seasoning
- ¼ teaspoon black pepper
- ½ teaspoon ground paprika

Glaze
- ¾ cup ketchup
- 1 ½ teaspoons white vinegar
- 2 ½ tablespoons brown sugar
- 1 teaspoon garlic powder
- ½ teaspoon onion powder
- ¼ teaspoon ground black pepper
- ¼ teaspoon salt

Preparation:
1. Thoroughly mix ground beef with egg, onion, garlic, crumbs, and all the ingredients in a bowl.
2. Grease a meatloaf pan with oil or butter and spread the minced beef in the pan.
3. Transfer the pan to the Ninja Foodi Digital Air Fry Oven and close the door.
4. Select "Air Fry" mode by rotating the dial.
5. Press the TIME/SLICE button and change the value to 40 minutes.
6. Press the TEMP/DARKNESS button and change the value to 375 degrees F.
7. Press Start/Pause to begin cooking.
8. Meanwhile, prepare the glaze by whisking its ingredients in a suitable saucepan.
9. Stir cook for 5 minutes until it thickens.
10. Brush this glaze over the meatloaf and bake it again for 15 minutes.
11. Slice and serve.
Serving Suggestion: Serve the meatloaf with mashed potatoes.
Variation Tip: Wrap the bacon over the meatloaf before baking.
Nutritional Information Per Serving:
Calories 435 | Fat 25g | Sodium 532mg | Carbs 23g | Fiber 0.4g | Sugar 2g | Protein 28.3g

Zucchini Beef Meatloaf

Preparation Time: 15 minutes.
Cooking Time: 40 minutes.
Servings: 4
Ingredients:
- 2 pounds ground beef
- 1 cup zucchini, shredded
- 2 eggs
- ½ cup onion,chopped
- 3 garlic cloves minced
- 3 tablespoons Worcestershire sauce
- 3 tablespoons fresh parsley, chopped
- ¾ cup Panko breadcrumbs
- ⅓ cup beef broth
- Salt to taste
- ¼ teaspoon ground black pepper
- ½ teaspoon ground paprika

Preparation:
1. Thoroughly mix ground beef with egg, zucchini, onion, garlic, crumbs,parsley, Worcertershire sauce,broth and all the seasoning ingredients in a bowl.
2. Grease a meatloaf pan with oil and spread the minced beef in the pan.
3. Transfer the pan to the Ninja Foodi Digital Air Fry Oven and close the door.
4. Select "Air Fry" mode by rotating the dial.
5. Press the TIME/SLICE button and change the value to 40 minutes.
6. Press the TEMP/DARKNESS button and change the value to 375 degrees F.
7. Press Start/Pause to begin cooking.
8. Slice and serve.
Serving Suggestion: Serve the meatloaf with toasted bread slices.
Variation Tip: Add crumbled bacon on top for a crispy texture.
Nutritional Information Per Serving:
Calories 325 | Fat 16g | Sodium 431mg | Carbs 22g | Fiber 1.2g | Sugar 4g | Protein 23g

Beef Short Ribs

Preparation Time: 15 minutes.
Cooking Time: 35 minutes.
Servings: 4
Ingredients:
- 1 ⅔ pounds short ribs
- Salt and black pepper, to taste
- 1 teaspoon grated garlic
- ½ teaspoon salt
- 1 teaspoon cumin seeds
- ¼ cup panko crumbs
- 1 teaspoon ground cumin
- 1 teaspoon avocado oil
- ½ teaspoon orange zest
- 1 egg, beaten

Preparation:
1. Place the beef ribs in a sheet pan and pour the whisked egg on top.
2. Whisk the rest of the crusting ingredients in a bowl and spread over the beef.
3. Transfer the pan to the Ninja Foodi Digital Air Fry Oven and close the door.
4. Select "Air Fry" mode by rotating the dial.
5. Press the TIME/SLICE button and change the value to 35 minutes.
6. Press the TEMP/DARKNESS button and change the value to 350 degrees F.
7. Press Start/Pause to begin cooking.
8. Serve warm.
Serving Suggestion: Serve the short ribs with white rice or warmed bread.
Variation Tip: Add orange juice to the marinade for a refreshing taste.
Nutritional Information Per Serving:
Calories 425 | Fat 14g | Sodium 411mg | Carbs 44g | Fiber 0.3g | Sugar 1g | Protein 23g

Garlic Braised Ribs

Preparation Time: 15 minutes.
Cooking Time: 20 minutes.
Servings: 8
Ingredients:
- 2 tablespoons vegetable oil
- 5 pounds bone-in short ribs
- Salt and black pepper, to taste
- 2 heads garlic, halved
- 1 medium onion, chopped
- 4 ribs celery, chopped
- 2 medium carrots, chopped
- 3 tablespoons tomato paste
- ¼ cup dry red wine
- ¼ cup beef stock
- 4 sprigs thyme
- 1 cup parsley, chopped
- ½ cup chives, chopped
- 1 tablespoon lemon zest, grated

Preparation:
1. Toss everything in a large bowl, then add short ribs.
2. Mix well to soak the ribs and marinate for 30 minutes.
3. Transfer the soaked ribs to the baking pan and add the marinade around them.
4. Transfer the pan to the Ninja Foodi Digital Air Fry Oven and close the door.
5. Select "Air Fry" mode by rotating the dial.
6. Press the TIME/SLICE button and change the value to 20 minutes.
7. Press the TEMP/DARKNESS button and change the value to 400 degrees F.
8. Press Start/Pause to begin cooking.
9. Serve warm.

Serving Suggestion: Serve the ribs with mashed potatoes.
Variation Tip: Add barbecue sauce to season the ribs.
Nutritional Information Per Serving:
Calories 441 | Fat 5g | Sodium 88mg | Carbs 13g | Fiber 0g | Sugar 0g | Protein 24g

Lamb Chops with Rosemary Sauce

Preparation Time: 15 minutes.
Cooking Time: 45 minutes.
Servings: 8
Ingredients:
- 8 lamb loin chops
- 1 small onion, peeled and chopped
- Salt and black pepper, to taste

For the sauce:
- 1 onion, peeled and chopped
- 1 tablespoon rosemary leaves
- 1 ounce butter
- 1 ounce plain flour
- 6 ounces milk
- 6 ounces vegetable stock
- 2 tablespoons cream, whipping
- Salt and black pepper, to taste

Preparation:
1. Place the lamb loin chops and onion in a sheet pan, then drizzle salt and black pepper on top.
2. Transfer the pan to the Ninja Foodi Digital Air Fry Oven and close the door.
3. Select "Air Fry" mode by rotating the dial.
4. Press the TIME/SLICE button and change the value to 45 minutes.
5. Press the TEMP/DARKNESS button and change the value to 350 degrees F.
6. Press Start/Pause to begin cooking.
7. Prepare the white sauce by melting butter in a suitable saucepan, then stir in onions.
8. Sauté for 5 minutes, then stir flour and stir cook for 2 minutes.
9. Stir in the rest of the ingredients and mix well.
10. Pour the sauce over baked chops and serve.

Serving Suggestion: Serve the chops with a fresh greens salad.
Variation Tip: Wrap the lamb chops with a foil sheet before baking for a rich taste.
Nutritional Information Per Serving:
Calories 450 | Fat 20g | Sodium 686mg | Carbs 3g | Fiber 1g | Sugar 1.2g | Protein 31g

Baked Beef Stew

Preparation Time: 15 minutes
Cooking Time: 2 hours
Servings: 4
Ingredients:
- 1 pound beef-stew, cut into cubes
- ½ cup water
- 2 tablespoons instant tapioca
- ½ can dried tomatoes with juice
- 1 teaspoon white sugar
- ½ tablespoon beef bouillon granules
- ¾ teaspoon salt
- ⅛ teaspoon ground black pepper
- 1 strip celery, cut into 3/4 inch pieces
- ½ onion, chopped
- 2 carrots, cut into 1-inch pieces
- ½ slice bread, cubed
- 2 potatoes, peeled and cubed

Preparation:
1. Turn on your Ninja Foodi Digital Air Fry Oven and rotate the knob to select "Bake".
2. Preheat by selecting the timer for 3 minutes and temperature for 375 degrees F.
3. Grease a sheet pan.
4. Take a large pan over medium heat and brown the stew meat.
5. Meanwhile, take a bowl and mix together tomatoes, water, tapioca, beef bouillon granules, sugar, salt and pepper.
6. Add prepared brown beef, celery, potatoes, carrots, onion and bread cubes.
7. Pour in the greased sheet pan.
8. Bake for about 2 hours in preheated Ninja Foodi Air Fryer at 375 degrees F.
9. Remove from oven and set aside for 2 minutes.
10. Serve warm and enjoy!

Serving Suggestions: Serve warm with rice.
Variation Tip: You can also add few tablespoons of cornstarch.
Nutritional Information per Serving:
Calories: 378 | Fat: 7.6g | Sat Fat: 2.7g | Carbohydrates: 30.1g | Fiber: 3.9g | Sugar: 5.6g | Protein: 44.8g

Garlicky Lamb Chops

Preparation Time: 15 minutes.
Cooking Time: 45 minutes.
Servings: 8
Ingredients:
- 8 medium lamb chops
- ¼ cup olive oil
- 3 thin lemon slices
- 2 garlic cloves, crushed
- 1 teaspoon dried oregano
- 1 teaspoon salt
- ½ teaspoon black pepper

Preparation:
1. Place the medium lamb chops in a sheet pan and rub them with olive oil.
2. Add lemon slices, garlic, oregano, salt, and black pepper on top of the lamb chops.
3. Transfer the tray to the Ninja Foodi Digital Air Fry Oven and close the door.
4. Select "Air Roast" mode by rotating the dial.
5. Press the TIME/SLICE button and change the value to 45 minutes.
6. Press the TEMP/DARKNESS button and change the value to 400 degrees F.
7. Press Start/Pause to begin cooking.
8. Serve warm.

Serving Suggestion: Serve the chops with boiled rice or cucumber salad.
Variation Tip: Cook the lamb chops with potatoes and asparagus
Nutritional Information Per Serving:
Calories 461 | Fat 16g | Sodium 515mg | Carbs 3g | Fiber 0.1g | Sugar 1.2g | Protein 21.3g

Lamb Kebabs

Preparation Time: 15 minutes.
Cooking Time: 20 minutes.
Servings: 4
Ingredients:
- 18 ounces lamb mince
- 1 teaspoon chili powder
- 1 teaspoon cumin powder
- 1 egg
- 2 ounces onion, chopped
- 2 teaspoons sesame oil

Preparation:
1. Whisk onion with egg, chili powder, oil, cumin powder, and salt in a bowl.
2. Add lamb to coat well, then thread it on the skewers.
3. Place these lamb skewers in the air fry basket.
4. Transfer the basket to the Ninja Foodi Digital Air Fry Oven and close the door.
5. Select "Air Fry" mode by rotating the dial.
6. Press the TIME/SLICE button and change the value to 20 minutes.
7. Press the TEMP/DARKNESS button and change the value to 395 degrees F.
8. Press Start/Pause to begin cooking.
9. Serve warm.

Serving Suggestion: Serve the lamb kebabs with garlic bread slices and fresh herbs on top.
Variation Tip: Add chopped green chilis to the meat mixture.
Nutritional Information Per Serving:
Calories 405 | Fat 22.7g | Sodium 227mg | Carbs 6.1g | Fiber 1.4g | Sugar 0.9g | Protein 45.2g

Seasoned Sirloin Steak

Preparation Time: 10 minutes
Cooking Time: 12 minutes
Servings: 2
Ingredients:
- 2 (7-ounce) top sirloin steaks
- 1 tablespoon steak seasoning
- Salt and ground black pepper, as required

Preparation:
1. Season each steak with steak seasoning, salt and black pepper.
2. Arrange the steaks onto the greased sheet pan.
3. Press "Power" button of Ninja Foodi Digital Air Fry Oven and turn the dial to select "Air Fry" mode.
4. Press TIME/SLICE button and again turn the dial to set the cooking time to 12 minutes.
5. Now push TEMP/DARKNESS button and rotate the dial to set the temperature at 400 degrees F.
6. Press "Start/Pause" button to start.
7. When the unit beeps to show that it is preheated, open the oven door and insert the sheet pan in the oven.
8. Flip the steaks once halfway through.
9. When cooking time is completed, open the oven door and serve hot.

Serving Suggestions: Serve with cheesy scalloped potatoes.
Variation Tip: The surface of the steak should be moist but not wet or sticky.
Nutritional Information per Serving:
Calories: 369 | Fat: 12.4g | Sat Fat: 4.7g | Carbohydrates: 0g | Fiber: 0g | Sugar: 0g | Protein: 60.2g

American Roast Beef

Preparation Time: 5 minutes
Cooking Time: 1 hour
Servings: 3
Ingredients:
- 1½ pounds beef eye of round roast
- ¼ teaspoon kosher salt
- ⅛ teaspoon black pepper, freshly ground
- ¼ teaspoon garlic powder

Preparation:
1. Turn on your Ninja Foodi Digital Air Fry Oven and rotate the knob to select "Air Roast".
2. Preheat by selecting the timer for 3 minutes and temperature for 375 degrees F.
3. Place beef in a sheet pan and season with salt, garlic powder and pepper.
4. Roast in oven for about an hour.
5. Remove from oven and set aside for 10 minutes before slicing.
6. Serve warm and enjoy!

Serving Suggestions: Serve it with mashed potatoes.
Variation Tip: You can add onions on top for a little flavoring.
Nutritional Information per Serving:
Calories: 382 | Fat: 11.1g | Sat Fat: 4g | Carbohydrates: 0.2g | Fiber: 0g | Sugar: 0.1g | Protein: 65.8g

Greek lamb Farfalle

Preparation Time: 15 minutes.
Cooking Time: 20 minutes.
Servings: 6
Ingredients:
- 1 tablespoon olive oil
- 1 onion, chopped
- 2 garlic cloves, chopped
- 2 teaspoons dried oregano
- 1 pound pack lamb mince
- ¾ pound tin tomatoes, chopped
- ¼ cup black olives pitted
- ½ cup frozen spinach, defrosted
- 2 tablespoons dill, removed and chopped
- 9 ounces farfalle paste, boiled
- 1 ball half-fat mozzarella, torn

Preparation:
1. Sauté onion and garlic with oil in a pan over moderate heat for 5 minutes.
2. Stir in tomatoes, spinach, dill, oregano, lamb, and olives, then stir cook for 5 minutes.
3. Spread the lamb in a casserole dish and toss in the boiled Farfalle pasta.
4. Top the pasta lamb mix with mozzarella cheese.
5. Transfer the dish to the Ninja Foodi Digital Air Fry Oven and close the door.
6. Select "Air Fry" mode by rotating the dial.
7. Press the TIME/SLICE button and change the value to 10 minutes.
8. Press the TEMP/DARKNESS button and change the value to 350 degrees F.
9. Press Start/Pause to begin cooking.
10. Serve warm.

Serving Suggestion: Serve the lamb farfalle with fresh green and mashed potatoes.
Variation Tip: Add shredded cheddar cheese to the meat mixture, then bake.
Nutritional Information Per Serving:
Calories 461 | Fat 5g | Sodium 340mg | Carbs 24.7g | Fiber 1.2g | Sugar 1.3g | Protein 15.3g

Herb and Pepper Crusted Rib of Beef

Preparation Time: 10 minutes
Cooking Time: 2 hours 30 minutes
Servings: 8
Ingredients:
- 1 tablespoon rock salt
- 2 tablespoons cracked black peppercorn
- 3 garlic cloves, crushed
- Small bunch rosemary, finely chopped
- Small bunch parsley, finely chopped
- 4 tablespoons olive oil
- 6.6 pounds rib of beef on the bone

For the gravy:
- 2 onions, sliced
- 1 cup red wine
- 1½ cups fresh beef stock

Preparation:
1. Select the AIR ROAST function, 430°F, for 2 hours and 30 minutes. While the oven is preheating, prepare the ingredients.
2. Mix the peppercorns, parsley, rock salt, rosemary, garlic, and olive oil in a mixing bowl. Rub the beef rub with the mixture and place it in a roasting tin.
3. Place the tin in the oven and cook for about 30 minutes. Reduce the heat to 320°F and cook for a further 1 hour and 20 minutes.
4. Take the tin out, cover it with tin foil, and leave the beef to rest for about 30 minutes.
5. Meanwhile, make the gravy. Retaining only 2 tablespoons, pour off all the fat from the roasting tin and reserve any juices.
6. Place a roasting tin over medium heat and fry the onions for about 10 minutes.
7. Then, add the stock, wine, and the reserved juices. Continue to cook for an additional 10 minutes to reduce the mixture to a thick sauce.
8. Transfer the gravy to a warm jug, carve the meat and serve it with the gravy

Serving Suggestion: Season the beef and serve alongside the sauce.
Variation Tip: Try using almond oil instead of olive oil.
Nutritional Information Per Serving:
Calories: 694 | Fat: 46g | Sodium: 572mg | Carbs: 4g | Fiber: 1g | Sugar: 2g | Protein: 63g

Pork Chops with Cashew Sauce

Preparation Time: 15 minutes.
Cooking Time: 52 minutes.
Servings: 8
Ingredients:
- 8 pork loin chops
- 1 small onion, peeled and chopped
- Salt and black pepper, to taste

For the Sauce:
- ¼ cup cashews, finely chopped
- 1 cup cashew butter
- 1 ounce wheat flour
- 6 fl. oz. milk
- 6 fl. oz. beef stock
- 2 tablespoons coconut cream, whipping
- Salt and black pepper, to taste

Preparation:
1. Place the pork loin chops and onion in a baking tray, then drizzle salt and black pepper on top.
2. Transfer the tray to the Ninja Foodi Digital Air Fry Oven and close the door.
3. Select "Bake" mode by rotating the dial.
4. Press the TIME/SLICE button and change the value to 45 minutes.
5. Press the TEMP/DARKNESS button and change the value to 375 degrees F.
6. Press Start/Pause to begin cooking.
7. Prepare the white sauce by first melting butter in a suitable saucepan, then stir in cashews.
8. Sauté for 5 minutes, then stir flour and stir cook for 2 minutes.
9. Stir in the rest of the sauce ingredients and mix well.
10. Pour the sauce over baked chops and serve.

Serving Suggestion: Serve the pork chops with sautéed vegetables and toasted bread slices.
Variation Tip: Add crushed cashews on top before baking.
Nutritional Information Per Serving:
Calories 309 | Fat 25g | Sodium 463mg | Carbs 9g | Fiber 0.3g | Sugar 0.3g | Protein 18g

Za'atar Chops

Preparation Time: 15 minutes.
Cooking Time: 20 minutes.
Servings: 8
Ingredients:
- 8 pork loin chops, bone-in
- 1 tablespoon Za'atar
- 3 garlic cloves, crushed
- 1 teaspoon avocado oil
- 2 tablespoons lemon juice
- 1 ¼ teaspoons salt
- Black pepper, to taste

Preparation:
1. Rub the pork chops with oil, za'atar, salt, lemon juice, garlic, and black pepper.
2. Place these chops in the air fry basket.
3. Transfer the basket to the Ninja Foodi Digital Air Fry Oven and close the door.
4. Select "Air Fry" mode by rotating the dial.
5. Press the TIME/SLICE button and change the value to 20 minutes.
6. Press the TEMP/DARKNESS button and change the value to 400 degrees F.
7. Press Start/Pause to begin cooking.
8. Flip the chops when cooked halfway through, then resume cooking.
9. Serve warm.

Serving Suggestion: Serve the chops with mashed potatoes.
Variation Tip: Add dried herbs to season the chops.
Nutritional Information Per Serving:
Calories 437 | Fat 20g | Sodium 719mg | Carbs 5.1g | Fiber 0.9g | Sugar 1.4g | Protein 37.8g

Herby Pork Bake

Preparation Time: 10 minutes
Cooking Time: 40 minutes
Servings: 2
Ingredients:
- 1 pork loin steak, cut into bite-sized pieces
- ½ red onion, cut into wedges
- 1 potato, halved
- ½ carrot, halved
- ½ tablespoon olive oil
- 1 tablespoon mixed dried herbs
- 4 tablespoons Cider Pour Over Sauce

Preparation:
1. Turn on your Ninja Foodi Digital Air Fry Oven and rotate the knob to select "Bake".
2. Preheat by selecting the timer for 3 minutes and temperature for 420 degrees F.
3. Take a dish and toss pork, onion, potatoes and carrots with herbs and olive oil.
4. Bake for about 25 minutes in preheated Ninja Foodi Digital Air Fry Oven at 420 degrees F.
5. Remove from the oven and add sauce on top.
6. Bake for 5 more minutes so that you have a bubbling sauce.
7. Serve and enjoy!

Serving Suggestions: Serve with garlic bread.
Variation Tip: You can also add tomatoes to your like.
Nutritional Information per Serving:
Calories: 269 | Fat: 9.6g | Sat Fat: 2.6g | Carbohydrates: 32g | Fiber: 3.3g | Sugar: 4g | Protein: 14.7g

Savory Pork Roast

Preparation Time: 10 minutes
Cooking Time: 1 hour
Servings: 3
Ingredients:
- ¼ teaspoon dried thyme
- 1 tablespoon fresh rosemary, divided
- 1 teaspoon garlic salt
- ⅛ teaspoon black pepper, freshly ground
- 1½ pounds pork loin roast, boneless

Preparation:
1. Turn on your Ninja Foodi Digital Air Fry Oven and rotate the knob to select "Air Roast".
2. Preheat by selecting the timer for 3 minutes and temperature for 350 degrees F.
3. Take a bowl mix well rosemary, garlic salt, thyme, and pepper together.
4. Now add pork to coat well.
5. Take a dish and place coated pork on it.
6. Roast pork for about an hour in preheated Ninja Foodi Digital Air Fry Oven at 350 degrees F.
7. Serve and enjoy!

Serving Suggestions: Serve with juice and salad.
Variation Tip: Use foil to avoid dryness.
Nutritional Information per Serving:
Calories: 331 | Fat: 8.2g | Sat Fat: 2.8g | Carbohydrates: 1.4g | Fiber: 0.6g | Sugar: 0.2g | Protein: 59.6g

Breaded Air Fryer Pork Chops

Preparation Time: 10 minutes
Cooking Time: 10 minutes
Servings: 4
Ingredients:
- 4 boneless and center-cut pork chops
- 1 teaspoon Cajun seasoning
- 1½ cups cheese and garlic-flavored croutons
- 2 eggs
- Cooking spray

Preparation:
1. Select the AIR FRY function, 390°F, for 10 minutes. While the oven is preheating, prepare the ingredients.
2. Use the Cajun seasoning to season both sides of the pork chops.
3. Blend the croutons in a small food processor and transfer them to a shallow dish.
4. Take a shallow dish and lightly beat the eggs in it. Dip the pork chops into the eggs and then coat them with the crouton breading. Spray them with the cooking spray.
5. Place the pork chops in the air fryer basket. Cook in batches if needed.
6. Cook the pork chops for about 5 minutes, flip, and mist with cooking spray, then cook for another 5 minutes.

Serving Suggestion: Garnish the pork chops with some lemon slices and serve alongside a sauce of your choice.
Variation Tip: You can try using Italian seasoning instead of Cajun seasoning.
Nutritional Information Per Serving:
Calories: 393 | Fat: 18g | Sodium: 428mg | Carbs: 10g | Fiber: 0.8g | Sugar: 1g | Protein: 44.7g

Roasted Pork Belly

Preparation Time: 10 minutes
Cooking Time: 1 hour and 30 minutes
Servings: 8
Ingredients:
- ¾ teaspoon dried oregano
- ¾ teaspoon ground cumin
- ¾ teaspoon ground black pepper
- ¾ teaspoon salt
- ¾ teaspoon paprika
- ¾ teaspoon onion powder
- ¾ teaspoon ground turmeric
- ¾ teaspoon garlic powder
- 2 pounds whole pork belly
- Cayenne pepper, to taste
- 1 tablespoon lemon juice

Preparation:
1. Take a bowl and add garlic powder, onion powder, turmeric, cayenne pepper, paprika, oregano, cumin, salt and pepper.
2. Rub the mixture onto pork belly.
3. Cover with a plastic wrap and refrigerate for at least 2 hours.
4. Turn on your Ninja Foodi Digital Air Fry Oven and rotate the knob to select "Air Roast".
5. Preheat by selecting the timer for 3 minutes and temperature for 450 degrees F.
6. Line a sheet pan with parchment paper.
7. Place pork belly onto the prepared dish, with shallow cuts.
8. Rub lemon juice on top.
9. Roast for about 40 minutes in preheated Ninja Foodi Digital Air Fry Oven at 350 degrees F until fat is crispy.
10. Remove from oven and set aside for 10 minutes before slicing.
11. Serve warm and enjoy!

Serving Suggestions: Serve it with slices of lemon and savor the taste.
Variation Tip: You can also add mushrooms.
Nutritional Information per Serving:
Calories: 602 | Fat: 61.8g | Sat Fat: 21.9g | Carbohydrates: 1g | Fiber: 0.3g | Sugar: 0.2g | Protein: 8.2g

Minced Lamb Casserole

Preparation Time: 15 minutes.
Cooking Time: 31 minutes.
Servings: 6
Ingredients:
- 2 tablespoons olive oil
- 1 medium onion, chopped
- ½ pound ground lamb
- 4 fresh mushrooms, sliced
- 1 cup small pasta shells, cooked
- 2 cups bottled marinara sauce
- 1 teaspoon butter
- 4 teaspoons flour
- 1 cup milk
- 1 egg, beaten
- 1 cup cheddar cheese, grated

Preparation:
1. Put a wok on moderate heat and add oil to heat.
2. Toss in onion and sauté until soft.
3. Stir in mushrooms and lamb, then cook until meat is brown.
4. Add marinara sauce and cook it to a simmer.
5. Stir in pasta, then spread this mixture in a casserole dish.
6. Prepare the sauce by melting butter in a suitable saucepan over moderate heat.
7. Stir in flour and whisk well, pour in the milk.
8. Mix well and whisk ¼ cup of sauce with egg, then return it to the saucepan.
9. Stir, cook for 1 minute, then pour this sauce over the lamb.
10. Drizzle cheese over the lamb casserole.
11. Transfer the dish to the Ninja Foodi Digital Air Fry Oven and close the door.
12. Select "Bake" mode by rotating the dial.
13. Press the TIME/SLICE button and change the value to 30 minutes.
14. Press the TEMP/DARKNESS button and change the value to 350 degrees F.
15. Press Start/Pause to begin cooking.
16. Serve warm.

Serving Suggestion: Serve the lamb casserole with quinoa salad.
Variation Tip: Add shredded cheese to the casserole for a cheesy taste.
Nutritional Information Per Serving:
Calories 448 | Fat 23g | Sodium 350mg | Carbs 18g | Fiber 6.3g | Sugar 1g | Protein 40.3g

Russian Baked Beef

Preparation Time: 10 minutes
Cooking Time: 1 hour
Servings: 3
Ingredients:
- ½ beef tenderloin
- 1 onion, sliced
- ¾ cup Cheddar cheese, grated
- ½ cup milk
- 1½ tablespoons mayonnaise
- Salt and black pepper, to taste

Preparation:
1. Turn on your Ninja Foodi Digital Air Fry Oven and rotate the knob to select "Bake".
2. Preheat by selecting the timer for 3 minutes and temperature for 350 degrees F.
3. Grease a sheet pan.
4. Cut the beef into thick slices and place in the sheet pan.
5. Season beef with salt and pepper and cover with onion slices. Also, spread cheese on top.
6. Take a bowl and stir together milk and mayonnaise and pour over cheese.
7. Bake for about an hour in preheated Ninja Foodi Digital Air Fry Oven at 350 degrees F.
8. Remove from oven and set aside for 2 minutes.
9. Serve warm and enjoy!

Serving Suggestions: Serve with roasted tomatoes.
Variation Tip: You can use any cheese instead of cheddar cheese.
Nutritional Information per Serving:
Calories: 207 | Fat: 14g | Sat Fat: 7.3g | Carbohydrates: 7.5g | Fiber: 0.8g | Sugar: 4g | Protein: 12.9g

Roast Beef and Yorkshire Pudding

Preparation Time: 20 minutes
Cooking Time: 1 hour 50 minutes
Servings: 2
Ingredients:
- 1 egg, beaten
- ½ cup milk
- ½ cup flour
- ⅛ teaspoon salt
- Salt, to taste
- Freshly ground pepper, to taste
- 1 pound rump roast
- Garlic powder, to taste

Preparation:
1. Turn on your Ninja Foodi Digital Air Fry Oven and rotate the knob to select "Air Roast".
2. Preheat by selecting the timer for 3 minutes and temperature for 375 degrees F.
3. Place beef in a sheet pan and season with salt, garlic powder and pepper.
4. Roast in oven for about 90 minutes until the thickest part of the beef is at 135 degrees F.
5. Remove from oven, reserving drippings.
6. Take a small bowl, beat egg until foamy.
7. Take another bowl, stir salt and flour. Pour in the beaten egg and add milk.
8. Now, preheat by selecting the timer for 3 minutes and temperature for 400 degrees F.
9. Pour the reserved drippings to a tin. Place in the preheated oven for about 3 minutes.
10. Remove from oven, add the flour mixture into the hot drippings.
11. Return to oven and set the timer for 20 minutes or until brown.
12. Serve warm and enjoy!

Serving Suggestions: Serve it with your favorite sauce.
Variation Tip: You can add an extra egg if you like.
Nutritional Information per Serving:
Calories: 582 | Fat: 17.4g | Sat Fat: 1.5g | Carbohydrates: 27.2g | Fiber: 0.9g | Sugar: 3g | Protein: 78.4g

Spiced Pork Shoulder

Preparation Time: 15 minutes
Cooking Time: 55 minutes
Servings: 4
Ingredients:
- 1 teaspoon ground cumin
- 1 teaspoon cayenne pepper
- ½ teaspoon garlic powder
- ½ teaspoon onion powder
- Salt and ground black pepper, as required
- 2 pounds skin-on pork shoulder

Preparation:
1. In a small bowl, place the spices, salt and black pepper and mix well.
2. Arrange the pork shoulder onto a cutting board, skin-side down.
3. Season the inner side of pork shoulder with salt and black pepper.
4. With kitchen twines, tie the pork shoulder into a long round cylinder shape.
5. Season the outer side of pork shoulder with spice mixture.
6. Press "Power" button of Ninja Foodi Digital Air Fry Oven and turn the dial to select the "Air Roast" mode.
7. Press TIME/SLICE button and again turn the dial to set the cooking time to 55 minutes.
8. Now push TEMP/DARKNESS button and rotate the dial to set the temperature at 350 degrees F.
9. Press "Start/Pause" button to start.
10. When the unit beeps to show that it is preheated, open the oven door and grease the air fry basket.
11. Arrange the pork shoulder into air fry basket and insert in the oven.
12. When cooking time is completed, open the oven door and place the pork shoulder onto a platter for about 10 minutes before slicing.
13. With a sharp knife, cut the pork shoulder into desired sized slices and serve.

Serving Suggestions: Serve with southern-style grits.
Variation Tip: Choose a pork shoulder with pinkish-red color.
Nutritional Information per Serving:
Calories: 445 | Fat: 32.5g | Sat Fat: 11.9g | Carbohydrates: 0.7g | Fiber: 0.2g | Sugar: 0.2g | Protein: 35.4g

Air Fryer Beef Taquitos

Preparation Time: 10 minutes
Cooking Time: 20 minutes
Servings: 4 to 6
Ingredients:
- 1 pound ground beef
- 14 medium-sized corn and flour blend tortillas
- 1½ cups Mexican blend cheese, shredded
- 1 teaspoon kosher salt
- 1 teaspoon oregano
- 1 teaspoon garlic powder
- ¾ teaspoon cumin
- ¼ teaspoon ground pepper
- Cooking oil spray

Preparation:
1. Select the AIR FRY function, 350°F, for 8 minutes.
2. Add the oregano, salt, pepper, garlic powder, and cumin seasoning to the ground beef in a large bowl. Mix well.
3. Add this beef filling to the tortillas, then add the cheese and roll tightly. Use toothpicks to secure the ends.
4. Spray the taquitos with the cooking oil spray on all sides.
5. Place the taquitos in the air fryer basket, toothpick side down, and cook for about 8 minutes.

Serving Suggestion: You can serve the taquitos with any dip or salsa of your choice.
Variation Tip: You can try using ricotta cheese instead of Mexican blend shredded cheese.
Nutritional Information Per Serving:
Calories: 217 | Fat: 12g | Sodium: 477mg | Carbs: 16g | Fiber: 1g | Sugar: 1g | Protein: 11g

Ground Beef Casserole

Preparation Time: 8 minutes
Cooking Time: 25 minutes
Servings: 3
Ingredients:
- ¼ medium onion, chopped
- ½ pound extra lean ground beef
- ½ pound penne
- ½ tablespoon olive oil
- ½ clove garlic, minced
- ½ cup marinara sauce
- 1 cup cheddar cheese, shredded
- Salt and pepper to taste

Preparation:
1. Turn on your Ninja Foodi Digital Air Fry Oven and rotate the knob to select "Bake".
2. Preheat by selecting the timer for 3 minutes and temperature for 400 degrees F.
3. Take a large pot with lightly salted water and bring it to a boil. Add penne and let it cook for about 10 minutes.
4. Take a pan and add oil, beef and onion.
5. Fry for about 10 minutes over medium-high heat and add garlic.
6. Stir in the marinara sauce and add salt and pepper according to taste.
7. Drain the pasta and pour into the sheet pan.
8. Add the beef-marinara mixture on top of the penne pasta. Lastly, add cheese with cheese.
9. Bake for about 10 minutes in preheated Ninja Foodi Digital Air Fry Oven until the cheese is nicely melted.
10. Serve immediately.

Serving Suggestions: Serve it with your favorite soda.
Variation Tip: You can add more marinara sauce if you want.
Nutritional Information per Serving:
Calories: 560 | Fat: 22.6g | Sat Fat: 11.1g | Carbohydrates: 48.6g | Fiber: 1.3g | Sugar: 4.3g | Protein: 38.7g

Italian Baked Meatballs

Preparation Time: 20 minutes
Cooking Time: 30 minutes
Servings: 6
Ingredients:
- 1 cup Italian-seasoned breadcrumbs
- ¼ cup Romano cheese, grated
- 2 tablespoons fresh parsley, chopped
- ½ teaspoon salt
- ½ teaspoon ground black pepper
- ½ teaspoon garlic powder
- ½ teaspoon onion powder
- ½ cup water
- 2 eggs
- 1½ pounds ground beef

Preparation:
1. Select the BAKE function, 350°F, for 30 minutes. While the oven is preheating, prepare the ingredients.
2. Mix the Romano cheese, salt, pepper, breadcrumbs, parsley, garlic powder, and onion powder. Then combine the mixture with the water and eggs.

3. Add the ground beef and mix well. Shape the mixture into balls and put them on the sheet pan greased with some non-stick cooking spray.
4. Bake the meatballs for about 30 minutes.
Serving Suggestion: Serve the meatballs with tomato sauce.
Variation Tip: Try using parmesan cheese instead of Romano cheese.
Nutritional Information Per Serving:
Calories: 343 | Fat: 20.4g | Sodium: 611mg | Carbs: 14g | Fiber: 0.8g | Sugar: 1g | Protein: 24.4g

Roast Sirloin of Beef and Port Gravy

Preparation Time: 10 minutes
Cooking Time: 2 hours 30 minutes
Servings: 6
Ingredients:
- 3 garlic cloves, finely chopped
- 2 tablespoons thyme leaves
- 2 tablespoons olive oil
- 4.8 pounds rolled sirloin of beef
For the gravy:
- 1 garlic clove
- 1 bay leaf
- Few thyme sprigs
- 5 tablespoons port
- 1½ cups red wine
- ¾ cup beef stock

Preparation:
1. Mix the thyme, olive oil, black pepper, and garlic in a bowl. Rub the beef with the mixture and leave for at least 1 hour.
2. Select the AIR ROAST function, 395°F, for 30 minutes. When the oven has preheated, season the beef with salt and pepper, then roast it for about 30 minutes.
3. Turn the heat down to 360°F and cook the beef for another 10 to 15 minutes.
4. Take the beef out when cooked and let it rest, loosely wrapped, for about 30 minutes.
5. Meanwhile, prepare the gravy. Take a roasting tin and place it on high heat. Add the garlic, bay leaves, and thyme. Then splash in the port, use a wooden spoon to stir, loosen any residue, and let it bubble until almost completely reduced.
6. Next, add the red wine and reduce it by three quarters. Put the stock in and bring it to a boil, then season to taste. Pour any remaining resting juices into the tin.
7. Transfer the gravy to a warm jug, carve the meat and serve it with the gravy.
Serving Suggestion: Serve with roasted potatoes and veggies.
Variation Tip: Double the quantity of stock if you want it to be alcohol-free.
Nutritional Information Per Serving:
Calories: 431 | Fat: 22g | Sodium: 128mg | Carbs: 2g | Fiber: 0g | Sugar: 2g | Protein: 52g

Lamb Chops

Preparation Time: 5 minutes
Cooking Time: 15 minutes
Servings: 4
Ingredients:
- 4 medium lamb chops
- 2 tablespoons olive oil
- 1 garlic clove, crushed
- 3 thin lemon slices
- ½ teaspoon dried oregano
- ¼ teaspoon black pepper, freshly ground
- ½ teaspoon kosher salt

Preparation:
1. Take a dish and mix together salt, pepper, olive oil, lemon slices, garlic, and oregano.
2. Add lamb in the dish and marinate for about 4 hours.
3. Turn on your Ninja Foodi Digital Air Fry Oven and rotate the knob to select "Bake".
4. Preheat by selecting the timer for 3 minutes and temperature for 400 degrees F.
5. Meanwhile, take a pan and add oil and heat over medium heat and cook each side of pork for 3 minutes until brown.
6. Bake for about 8 to 10 minutes in preheated Ninja Foodi Digital Air Fry Oven at 400 degrees F.
7. Remove from oven and set aside for 2 minutes.
8. Serve warm and enjoy!
Serving Suggestions: Serve with roasted carrots.
Variation Tip: You can also use foil.
Nutritional Information per Serving:
Calories: 302 | Fat: 18.5g | Sat Fat: 4.3g | Carbohydrates: 0.5g | Fiber: 0.1g | Sugar: 0g | Protein: 32.6g

Herby Baked Lamb in Tomato Sauce

Preparation Time: 5 minutes
Cooking Time: 4 hours 15 minutes
Servings: 4
Ingredients:
- 4.4 pounds shoulder of lamb
- 2 tablespoons olive oil
- 3 oregano sprigs
- 3 rosemary sprigs
- 3 garlic cloves, roughly chopped
- 2½ cups red wine
- 28 ounces tomatoes, chopped
- 1 tablespoon caster sugar

Preparation:
1. Select the AIR ROAST function, 430°F, for 20 minutes. While the oven is preheating, prepare the ingredients.
2. Put the lamb in a large baking dish.
3. Make a rough paste in a small food processor by combining the oil, oregano, garlic, and rosemary.
4. Rub the lamb with the paste and cook for about 20 minutes.
5. Reduce the temperature to 300°F and roast for about 3 hours, covered.
6. Take the lamb out and pour out all the fat, leaving the meat juices. Add the wine, tomatoes, and remaining herb sprigs. Cook for another 40 minutes, uncovered.
7. Spoon out the wine and tomato sauce to another pan, and skim off any fat rising to the surface. Cover then let it rest for about 30 minutes.
8. Meanwhile, prepare the sauce. Heat the tomato mixture until bubbling, and then let it simmer for about 10 to 15 minutes. Season with salt, sugar, and pepper, and then pour it around the lamb.
Serving Suggestion: Serve with rice along with the sauce.
Variation Tip: You can try using granulated sugar instead of caster sugar.
Nutritional Information Per Serving:
Calories: 595 | Fat: 40g | Sodium: 204mg | Carbs: 11g | Fiber: 1g | Sugar: 10g | Protein: 42g

Roast Lamb with Madeira Sauce

Preparation Time: 10 minutes
Cooking Time: 60 minutes
Servings: 4
Ingredients:
- 1 pound boneless rolled leg of lamb
- 1 to 2 tablespoons extra-virgin olive oil
- Fresh rosemary sprigs
- 1-pint chicken stock
- ¼ cup sweet wine
- Salt, to taste
- Freshly ground black pepper, to taste
- ¼ teaspoon butter

Preparation:
1. Select the AIR ROAST function, 450°F, for 45 minutes. While the oven is preheating, prepare the ingredients.
2. Generously rub the lamb with olive oil. Transfer the lamb leg to a roasting tin and sprinkle the rosemary on top.
3. Move the tin to the oven and roast for about 45 minutes.
4. Once done, leave the lamb to rest for at least 30 minutes, covered in foil.
5. Pour away the fat in the roasting tin and place it on high heat. Add sweet wine and reduce the mixture. Add the chicken stock and any juices. Reduce the mixture by two-thirds.
6. Add seasoning and whisk in ¼ teaspoon butter. Strain the mixture into a gravy boat using a fine sieve.
7. Once the lamb is well-rested, cut it into thick slices.
Serving Suggestion: Season well and serve with the sauce.
Variation Tip: You can use Pineau de Charentes or sherry instead of sweet wine.
Nutritional Information Per Serving:
Calories: 434 | Fat: 29g | Sodium: 538mg | Carbs: 5g | Fiber: 0g | Sugar: 2g | Protein: 35g

Glazed Pork Tenderloin

Preparation Time: 15 minutes
Cooking Time: 30 minutes
Servings: 6
Ingredients:
- 2 tablespoons olive oil
- 2 pork tenderloins
- ¼ teaspoon salt
- ¼ teaspoon freshly ground black pepper
- 1 cup peach, chopped
- 2 tablespoons balsamic vinegar
- 2 tablespoons Dijon mustard
- 2 tablespoons brown sugar

Preparation:
1. Select the AIR ROAST function, 350°F, for 30 minutes. While the oven is preheating, prepare the ingredients.
2. Take a large skillet and heat the olive oil in it over medium heat.
3. Trim the excess fat and silver skin from the pork, and then season with salt and pepper. Sear on all sides for about 6 to 8 minutes, and transfer to a baking pan.
4. Combine the remaining ingredients in a saucepan. Bring them to a simmer. Remove from the heat and keep it aside.
5. Cook the pork tenderloin for about 12 minutes in the oven. Take the glaze mixture and brush the pork generously with it. Continue to roast for another 5 to 10 minutes.
Serving Suggestion: Season with salt and pepper and serve it with the remaining glaze.
Variation Tip: You can use grill seasoning instead of salt and pepper to season the pork.
Nutritional Information Per Serving:
Calories: 357 | Fat: 9g | Sodium: 369mg | Carbs: 39g | Fiber: 0g | Sugar: 28g | Protein: 30g

Stuffed Pork Tenderloin

Preparation Time: 10 minutes
Cooking Time: 30 minutes
Servings: 6
Ingredients:
- 1 tablespoon extra-virgin olive oil
- 1 tablespoon yellow onion, finely chopped
- A dash of vinegar
- ⅓ cup breadcrumbs
- 3 tablespoons parsley, chopped
- 1 whole orange
- Orange zest, grated
- 2 tablespoons Dijon mustard
- 2 tablespoons honey
- A dash of black pepper
- 2 lean pork tenderloins

Preparation:
1. Butterfly the pork tenderloins by cutting them in half lengthwise but not all the way through.
2. Take a non-stick skillet to heat the olive oil over medium heat. Add the onions and sauté for about 20 minutes, stirring frequently. Stir in the vinegar, pepper, and salt, then cook for 5 minutes. Remove from the heat. Stir in the breadcrumbs, orange zest, and parsley. Set it aside.
3. Place the filling along the length of one tenderloin, then top it with another tenderloin

and tie it with string. Place it on the rack in the oven set over a foil-lined roasting pan.
4. Prepare the glaze: Take a small bowl, combine pepper, honey, and mustard, then brush over pork.
5. Select the AIR ROAST function and roast the pork at 375°F for about 40 minutes. Cover it and let it rest for about 10 minutes before carving it into slices.
Serving Suggestion: The pork slices can be served with mustard or cream.
Variation Tip: Horseradish sauce can be an excellent substitute for Dijon mustard.
Nutritional Information Per Serving:
Calories: 203 | Fat: 4.5g | Sodium: 218mg | Carbs: 15g | Fiber: 1.7g | Sugar: 7.7g | Protein: 26.7g

Lamb Rack with Lemon Crust

Preparation Time: 15 minutes.
Cooking Time: 25 minutes.
Servings: 3
Ingredients:
- 1 ⅔ pounds frenched rack of lamb
- Salt and black pepper, to taste
- ¼ pound dry breadcrumbs
- 1 teaspoon garlic, grated
- ½ teaspoon salt
- 1 teaspoon cumin seeds
- 1 teaspoon ground cumin
- 1 teaspoon oil
- ½ teaspoon grated lemon rind
- 1 egg, beaten

Preparation:
1. Place the lamb rack in a sheet pan and pour the whisked egg on top.
2. Whisk the rest of the crusting ingredients in a bowl and spread over the lamb.
3. Transfer the sheet pan to the Ninja Foodi Digital Air Fry Oven and close the door.
4. Select "Air Fry" mode by rotating the dial.
5. Press the TIME/SLICE button and change the value to 25 minutes.
6. Press the TEMP/DARKNESS button and change the value to 350 degrees F.
7. Press Start/Pause to begin cooking.
8. Serve warm.
Serving Suggestion: Serve the lamb rack with sautéed green beans and mashed potatoes.
Variation Tip: Drizzle parmesan cheese on top before cooking.
Nutritional Information Per Serving:
Calories 455 | Fat 9.5g | Sodium 655mg | Carbs 13.4g | Fiber 0.4g | Sugar 0.4g | Protein 28.3g

Japanese Air Fried Pork Tonkatsu

Preparation Time: 15 minutes
Cooking Time: 11 minutes
Servings: 8
Ingredients:
- 2 large eggs
- 1 teaspoon avocado oil
- Salt, to taste
- 2 cups panko breadcrumbs
- 2 pounds pork sirloin chops
- Avocado oil cooking spray
- 2 cups savoy cabbage, shredded for serving

Preparation:
1. Select the AIR FRY, 400°F, for 30 minutes. While the oven is preheating, prepare the ingredients.
2. Take a small bowl and mix the eggs, salt, and avocado oil in it. Place the panko crumbs on a separate plate.
3. Place parchment paper on a large plate or chopping board.
4. Dip the pork chops into the egg mixture and then in the panko crumbs, lightly pressing to make sure they stick. Place the pork chops on the prepared plate.
5. Spray all sides of the pork chops with cooking spray and place them into the air fryer basket. Cook in batches if needed.
6. Cook for 6 minutes, flip the pork chops and cook for another 5 minutes.

Serving Suggestion: Serve with rice, the shredded savoy cabbage, and tonkatsu sauce.
Variation Tip: Try vegetable oil instead of avocado oil.
Nutritional Information Per Serving:
Calories: 331 | Fat: 10.5g | Sodium: 341mg | Carbs: 44.7g | Fiber: 1g | Sugar: 0.8g | Protein: 19.3g

Herbed Lamb Loin Chops

Preparation Time: 10 minutes
Cooking Time: 12 minutes
Servings: 2
Ingredients:
- 4 (4-ounce) (½-inch thick) lamb loin chops
- 1 teaspoon fresh thyme, minced
- 1 teaspoon fresh rosemary, minced
- 1 teaspoon fresh oregano, minced
- 2 garlic cloves, crushed
- Salt and ground black pepper, as required

Preparation:
1. In a large bowl, place all ingredients and mix well.
2. Refrigerate to marinate overnight.
3. Arrange the chops onto the greased sheet pan.
4. Press "Power" button of Ninja Foodi Digital Air Fry Oven and turn the dial to select "Bake" mode.
5. Press TIME/SLICE button and again turn the dial to set the cooking time to 12 minutes.
6. Now push TEMP/DARKNESS button and rotate the dial to set the temperature at 400 degrees F.
7. Press "Start/Pause" button to start.

8. When the unit beeps to show that it is preheated, open the oven door and insert the sheet pan in the oven.
9. Flip the chops once halfway through.
10. When the cooking time is completed, open the oven door and serve hot.
Serving Suggestions: Serve with steamed cauliflower.
Variation Tip: Season the chops nicely.
Nutritional Information per Serving:
Calories: 432 | Fat: 16.9g | Sat Fat: 6g | Carbohydrates: 2.2g | Fiber: 0.8g | Sugar: 0.1g | Protein: 64g

Juicy Air Fryer Lamb Chops

Preparation Time: 10 minutes
Cooking Time: 8 minutes
Servings: 4
Ingredients:
- 4 lamb chops
- 2 tablespoons olive oil
- 1½ tablespoons minced rosemary
- 2 garlic cloves, minced
- ½ teaspoon ground oregano
- Salt and pepper, to taste

For the chimichurri sauce:
- ½ cup parsley
- 4 garlic cloves, minced
- 2 tablespoon oregano
- ¼ cup olive oil
- 2 tablespoons vinegar
- ¼ teaspoon salt
- ⅛ teaspoon pepper
- ½ teaspoon red pepper flakes

Preparation:
1. Select the AIR FRY function, 400°F, for 8 minutes. While the oven is preheating, prepare the ingredients.
2. Firstly, combine the olive oil with the spices in a bowl. Brush the mixture onto both sides of the lamb chops.
3. Place the lamb chops in the air fryer basket and cook for 8 minutes. Cook in batches if needed.
4. Meanwhile, mix all the ingredients of the chimichurri sauce in a mixing bowl.
Serving Suggestion: Serve with the chimichurri sauce.
Variation Tip: Try experimenting with different seasonings. You can also use dried rosemary.
Nutritional Information Per Serving:
Calories: 326 | Fat: 28g | Sodium: 0mg | Carbs: 1g | Fiber: 0g | Sugar: 0g | Protein: 17g

Buttered Strip Steak

Preparation Time: 10 minutes
Cooking Time: 15 minutes
Servings: 4
Ingredients:
- 2 (14-ounce) New York strip steaks
- 2 tablespoons butter, melted
- Salt and ground black pepper, as required

Preparation:
1. Brush each steak with the melted butter evenly and then season with salt and black pepper.
2. Press "Power" button of Ninja Foodi Digital Air Fry Oven and turn the dial to select the "Air Broil" mode.
3. Press the TEMP/DARKNESS button and use the dial to select HI. To set the temperature, press the TEMP/DARKNESS button again.
4. Press TIME/SLICE button and again turn the dial to set the cooking time to 15 minutes.
5. Press "Start/Pause" button to start.
6. When the unit beeps to show that it is preheated, open the oven door.
7. Place the steaks over the wire rack and insert in oven.
8. When cooking time is completed, open the oven door and place the steaks onto a cutting board for about 5 minutes before slicing.
9. Cut each steak into 2 portions and serve.
Serving Suggestions: Serve alongside the spiced potatoes.
Variation Tip: Use freshly ground black pepper.
Nutritional Information per Serving:
Calories: 296 | Fat: 12.7g | Sat Fat: 6.6g | Carbohydrates: 0g | Fiber: 0g | Sugar: 0g | Protein: 44.5g

Lamb Burgers

Preparation Time: 10 minutes
Cooking Time: 8 minutes
Servings: 6
Ingredients:
- 2 pounds ground lamb
- ½ tablespoon onion powder
- ½ tablespoon garlic powder
- ¼ teaspoon ground cumin
- Salt and ground black pepper, as required

Preparation:
1. In a bowl, add all the ingredients and mix well.
2. Make 6 equal-sized patties from the mixture.
3. Arrange the patties onto the greased sheet pan in a single layer.
4. Press "Power" button of Ninja Foodi Digital Air Fry Oven and turn the dial to select "Air Fry" mode.
5. Press TIME/SLICE button and again turn the dial to set the cooking time to 8 minutes.
6. Now push TEMP/DARKNESS button and rotate the dial to set the temperature at 360 degrees F.
7. Press "Start/Pause" button to start.
8. When the unit beeps to show that it is preheated, open the oven door.
9. Insert the sheet pan in oven.
10. Flip the burgers once halfway through.
11. When cooking time is completed, open the oven door and serve hot.
Serving Suggestions: Serve with fresh salad.
Variation Tip: For the best result, grind your meat at home.
Nutritional Information per Serving:
Calories: 286 | Fat: 11.1g | Sat Fat: 4g | Carbohydrates: 1g | Fiber: 0.1g | Sugar: 0.4g | Protein: 42.7g

Air Fryer Low-Carb Taco Casserole

Preparation Time: 15 minutes
Cooking Time: 25 minutes
Servings: 4
Ingredients:
- 1 pound 95% lean ground beef
- 2 tablespoons taco seasoning
- ¼ cup of water
- 10 ounces canned diced tomatoes
- 2 green chilies, seeded and chopped
- ¼ cup reduced-fat cheddar cheese, shredded
- 4 large eggs
- ¼ cup light sour cream
- ⅓ cup heavy cream

Preparation:
1. Prepare a baking dish by lightly spraying it with a non-stick cooking spray. Set it aside.
2. Take a medium skillet and place it over medium heat. Add the ground beef and cook it in the skillet for about 5 to 6 minutes. Drain the grease.
3. Then, add the taco seasoning, diced tomatoes, water, and green chilies to the skillet and simmer for about 5 minutes.
4. Transfer the beef mixture to the prepared dish.
5. Take a bowl, and whisk together the sour cream, eggs, and heavy cream. Pour it over to the beef mixture, and top with shredded cheese. Transfer the dish to the air fryer basket.
6. Select the AIR FRY function, 300°F, for 20 minutes. Allow the oven to preheat before cooking the casserole.
Serving Suggestion: Serve with some greens.
Variation Tip: Colby cheese can be a great substitute for cheddar cheese.
Nutritional Information Per Serving:
Calories: 441 | Fat: 24g | Sodium: 593mg | Carbs: 8g | Fiber: 1g | Sugar: 5g | Protein: 47g

Garlic and Herb Lamb

Preparation Time: 5 minutes
Cooking Time: 2 hours 30 minutes
Servings: 10
Ingredients:
- 5-pound leg of lamb
- 3 cloves garlic, cut into slivers
- 3 teaspoons dried dill weed
- 1½ teaspoons salt
- 1 teaspoon dried rosemary
- ½ teaspoon ground black pepper

Preparation:
1. Select the AIR ROAST function, 325°F, for 2 hours and 30 minutes.
2. Using a sharp knife, puncture the lamb far enough to insert the slivers of garlic.
3. Mix the dill, rosemary, garlic, pepper and salt, then rub the leg of the lamb with the mixture. Lay the lamb, fatty side up, on a shallow roasting pan.
4. Roast the lamb for about 2 to 2½ hours.
5. When it's done, tent the lamb with aluminum foil and let it sit for 15 to 20 minutes before serving.

Serving Suggestion: It's best to serve it with gravy and some veggies.
Variation Tip: Try using tarragon instead of dried dill weed.
Nutritional Information Per Serving:
Calories: 234 | Fat: 14g | Sodium: 393g | Carbs: 1.8g | Fiber: 0g | Sugar: 0g | Protein: 25.3g

Simple New York Strip Steak

Preparation Time: 5 minutes
Cooking Time: 8 minutes
Servings: 1
Ingredients:
- ½ teaspoon olive oil
- ½ New York strip steak
- Kosher salt and ground black pepper, to taste

Preparation:
1. Coat the steak with oil and then, generously season with salt and black pepper.
2. Grease an air fry basket.
3. Place steak into the prepared air fry basket.
4. Turn on your Ninja Foodi Digital Air Fry Oven and rotate the knob to select "Air Fry".
5. Select the timer for about 7 to 8 minutes and temperature for 400 degrees F.
6. Remove from the oven and place the steak onto a cutting board for about 10 minutes before slicing.
7. Cut the steak into desired-size slices and transfer onto serving plates.
8. Serve immediately.

Serving Suggestions: Add your favorite sauce or mushroom sauce on top.
Variation Tip: You can also add chopped rosemary.
Nutritional Information per Serving:
Calories: 245 | Fat: 16.3g | Sat Fat: 5.8g | Carbohydrates: 0g | Fiber: 0g | Sugar: 0g | Protein: 25g

Lamb and Potato Bake

Preparation Time: 8 minutes
Cooking Time: 55 minutes
Servings: 2
Ingredients:
- 2 potatoes
- ¾ lean lamb mince
- ½ teaspoon cinnamon
- ½ tablespoon olive oil
- 4 cups tomato pasta sauce
- 1 cup cheese sauce

Preparation:
1. Boil the potatoes for 12 minutes or until half cooked.
2. Meanwhile, take a pan and heat oil over medium heat.
3. Add lamb mince in to brown. Use a spoon to break up lumps.
4. Add cinnamon and fry for about a minute.
5. Pour in the tomato sauce and leave for about 5 minutes.
6. Once the potatoes are done, thinly slice them.
7. Turn on your Ninja Foodi Digital Air Fry Oven and rotate the knob to select "Bake".
8. Select the timer for 35 minutes and temperature for 390 degrees F.
9. Place everything on a sheet pan and spread cheeses on top.
10. Bake until well cooked.
11. Serve and enjoy!

Serving Suggestions: Top the peppers with the cheese.
Variation Tip: You can also use green peppers instead.
Nutritional Information per Serving:
Calories: 823 | Fat: 41.4g | Sat Fat: 20.8g | Carbohydrates: 78.1g | Fiber: 13.3g | Sugar: 27.3g | Protein: 34g

Chapter 7 Dessert Recipes

Brownie Muffins

Preparation Time: 10 minutes
Cooking Time: 10 minutes
Servings: 12
Ingredients:
- 1 package Betty Crocker fudge brownie mix
- ¼ cup walnuts, chopped
- 1 egg
- ⅓ cup vegetable oil
- 2 teaspoons water

Preparation:
1. Grease 12 muffin molds. Set aside.
2. In a bowl, mix together all the ingredients.
3. Place the mixture into the prepared muffin molds.
4. Press "Power" button of Ninja Foodi Digital Air Fry Oven and turn the dial to select "Air Fry" mode.
5. Press TIME/SLICE button and again turn the dial to set the cooking time to 10 minutes.
6. Now push TEMP/DARKNESS button and rotate the dial to set the temperature at 300 degrees F.
7. Press "Start/Pause" button to start.
8. When the unit beeps to show that it is preheated, open the oven door.
9. Arrange the muffin molds into the air fry basket and insert in the oven.
10. When cooking time is completed, open the oven door and place the muffin molds onto a wire rack to cool for about 10 minutes.
11. Carefully invert the muffins onto the wire rack to completely cool before serving.
Serving Suggestions: Serve with the topping of coconut.
Variation Tip: You can use oil of your choice.
Nutritional Information per Serving:
Calories: 168 | Fat: 8.9g | Sat Fat: 1.4g | Carbohydrates: 20.8g | Fiber: 1.1g | Sugar: 14g | Protein: 2g

Walnut Brownies

Preparation Time: 15 minutes
Cooking Time: 22 minutes
Servings: 4
Ingredients:
- ½ cup chocolate, roughly chopped
- ⅓ cup butter
- 5 tablespoons sugar
- 1 egg, beaten
- 1 teaspoon vanilla extract
- Pinch of salt
- 5 tablespoons self-rising flour
- ¼ cup walnuts, chopped

Preparation:
1. In a microwave-safe bowl, add the chocolate and butter. Microwave on high heat for about 2 minutes, stirring after every 30 seconds.
2. Remove from microwave and set aside to cool.
3. In another bowl, add the sugar, egg, vanilla extract, and salt and whisk until creamy and light.

4. Add the chocolate mixture and whisk until well combined.
5. Add the flour, and walnuts and mix until well combined.
6. Line a baking pan with a greased parchment paper.
7. Place mixture into the prepared pan and with the back of spatula, smooth the top surface.
8. Press "Power" button of Ninja Foodi Digital Air Fry Oven and turn the dial to select "Air Fry" mode.
9. Press TIME/SLICE button and again turn the dial to set the cooking time to 20 minutes.
10. Now push TEMP/DARKNESS button and rotate the dial to set the temperature at 355 degrees F.
11. Press "Start/Pause" button to start.
12. When the unit beeps to show that it is preheated, open the oven door.
13. Arrange the pan into the air fry basket and insert in the oven.
14. When cooking time is completed, open the oven door and place the baking pan onto a wire rack to cool completely.
15. Cut into 4 equal-sized squares and serve.
Serving Suggestions: Serve with the dusting of powdered sugar.
Variation Tip: You can also use almond extract n the recipe.
Nutritional Information per Serving:
Calories: 407 | Fat: 27.4g | Sat Fat: 14.7g | Carbohydrates: 35.9g | Fiber: 1.5g | Sugar: 26.2g | Protein: 6g

Roasted Bananas

Preparation Time: 5 minutes
Cooking Time: 7 minutes
Servings: 1
Ingredients:
- 1 banana, sliced
- Avocado oil cooking spray

Preparation:
1. Using parchment paper, line the air fry basket.
2. Place banana slices in the air fry basket, making sure they do not touch.
3. Mist banana slices with avocado oil.
4. Turn on Ninja Foodi Digital Air Fry Oven and rotate the knob to select "Air Roast".
5. Select the timer for 5 minutes and the temperature for 370 degrees F.
6. Remove the banana slices from the basket and carefully flip them.
7. Cook for another 3 minutes, or until the banana slices are browning and caramelized. Remove from the basket with care.
8. Allow cooling for two minutes before serving.
Serving Suggestions: Sprinkle vanilla sugar on top.
Variation Tip: You can also use brown sugar.
Nutritional Information per Serving:
Calories: 107 | Fat: 0.7g | Sat Fat: 0.1g | Carbohydrates: 27g | Fiber: 3.1g | Sugar: 14g | Protein: 1.3g

Raisin Bread Pudding

Preparation Time: 15 minutes
Cooking Time: 12 minutes
Servings: 3
Ingredients:
- 1 cup milk
- 1 egg
- 1 tablespoon brown sugar
- ½ teaspoon ground cinnamon
- ¼ teaspoon vanilla extract
- 2 tablespoons raisins, soaked in hot water for 15 minutes
- 2 bread slices, cut into small cubes
- 1 tablespoon sugar

Preparation:
1. In a bowl, mix together the milk, egg, brown sugar, cinnamon, and vanilla extract.
2. Stir in the raisins.
3. In a baking pan, spread the bread cubes and top evenly with the milk mixture.
4. Refrigerate for about 15-20 minutes.
5. Press "Power" button of Ninja Foodi Digital Air Fry Oven and turn the dial to select "Air Fry" mode.
6. Press TIME/SLICE button and again turn the dial to set the cooking time to 12 minutes.
7. Now push TEMP/DARKNESS button and rotate the dial to set the temperature at 375 degrees F.
8. Press "Start/Pause" button to start.
9. When the unit beeps to show that it is preheated, open the oven door.
10. Arrange the pan over the wire rack and insert in the oven.
11. When cooking time is completed, open the oven door and place the baking pan aside to cool slightly.
12. Serve warm.
Serving Suggestions: Serve with the drizzling of vanilla syrup.
Variation Tip: Use day-old bread.
Nutritional Information per Serving:
Calories: 143 | Fat: 4.4g | Sat Fat: 2.2g | Carbohydrates: 21.3g | Fiber: 6.7g | Sugar: 16.4g | Protein: 5.5g

Butter Cake

Preparation Time: 15 minutes
Cooking Time: 15 minutes
Servings: 6
Ingredients:
- 3 ounces butter, softened
- ½ cup caster sugar
- 1 egg
- 1⅓ cups plain flour, sifted
- Pinch of salt
- ½ cup milk
- 1 tablespoon icing sugar

Preparation:
1. In a bowl, add the butter and sugar and whisk until light and creamy.
2. Add the egg and whisk until smooth and fluffy.
3. Add the flour and salt and mix well alternately with the milk.
4. Grease a small Bundt cake pan.
5. Place mixture evenly into the prepared cake pan.
6. Press "Power" button of Ninja Foodi Digital Air Fry Oven and turn the dial to select "Air Fry" mode.
7. Press TIME/SLICE button and again turn the dial to set the cooking time to 15 minutes.
8. Now push TEMP/DARKNESS button and rotate the dial to set the temperature at 350 degrees F.
9. Press "Start/Pause" button to start.
10. When the unit beeps to show that it is preheated, open the oven door.
11. Arrange the pan into the air fry basket and insert in the oven.
12. When cooking time is completed, open the oven door and place the cake pan onto a wire rack to cool for about 10 minutes.
13. Carefully invert the cake onto the wire rack to completely cool before slicing.
14. Dust the cake with icing sugar and cut into desired size slices.
Serving Suggestions: Serve with the sprinkling of cocoa powder.
Variation Tip: Use unsalted butter.
Nutritional Information per Serving:
Calories: 291 | Fat: 12.9g | Sat Fat: 7.8g | Carbohydrates: 40.3g | Fiber: 0.8g | Sugar: 19g | Protein: 4.6g

Cookie Cake

Preparation Time: 10 minutes
Cooking Time: 10 minutes
Servings: 2
Ingredients:
- 1 stick butter, softened
- ½ cup brown sugar, packed
- ¼ cup sugar
- 1 egg
- 1 teaspoon vanilla extract
- 1½ cups all-purpose flour
- ½ teaspoon baking soda
- 1 cup semi-sweet chocolate chips

Preparation:
1. Mix the cream, butter, brown sugar, and sugar in a large mixing bowl.
2. Mix in the vanilla and eggs until everything is well mixed.
3. Slowly stir in the flour, baking soda, and salt until combined, then stir in the chocolate chips.
4. Spray a 6-inch pan with oil, pour half of the batter into the pan, and press it down to evenly fill it. Refrigerate the other half for later use.
5. Place inside the oven.
6. Turn on Ninja Foodi Digital Air Fry Oven and rotate the knob to select "Air Fry".
7. Select the timer for 5 minutes and the temperature for 370 degrees F.
8. Remove it from the oven and set it aside for 5 minutes to cool.
Serving Suggestions: Serve some vanilla ice cream.
Variation Tip: You can also use almond butter.
Nutritional Information per Serving:
Calories: 673 | Fat: 38g | Sat Fat: 23g | Carbohydrates: 82g | Fiber: 4g | Sugar: 2g | Protein: 8g

Strawberry Cupcakes

Preparation Time: 20 minutes
Cooking Time: 8 minutes
Servings: 10
Ingredients:
For Cupcakes:
- ½ cup caster sugar
- 7 tablespoons butter
- 2 eggs
- ½ teaspoon vanilla essence
- ⅞ cup self-rising flour

For Frosting:
- 1 cup icing sugar
- 3½ tablespoons butter
- 1 tablespoon whipped cream
- ¼ cup fresh strawberries, pureed
- ½ teaspoon pink food color

Preparation:
1. In a bowl, add the butter and sugar and beat until fluffy and light.
2. Add the eggs, one at a time and beat until well combined.
3. Stir in the vanilla extract.
4. Gradually, add the flour, beating continuously until well combined.
5. Place the mixture into 10 silicone cups.
6. Press "Power" button of Ninja Foodi Digital Air Fry Oven and turn the dial to select "Air Fry" mode.
7. Press TIME/SLICE button and again turn the dial to set the cooking time to 8 minutes.
8. Now push TEMP/DARKNESS button and rotate the dial to set the temperature at 340 degrees F.
9. Press "Start/Pause" button to start.
10. When the unit beeps to show that it is preheated, open the oven door.
11. Arrange the silicone cups into the air fry basket and insert in the oven.
12. When cooking time is completed, open the oven door and place the silicon cups onto a wire rack to cool for about 10 minutes.
13. Carefully invert the muffins onto the wire rack to completely cool before frosting.
14. For frosting: in a bowl, add the icing sugar and butter and whisk until fluffy and light.
15. Add the whipped cream, strawberry puree, and color. Mix until well combined.
16. Fill the pastry bag with frosting and decorate the cupcakes.
Serving Suggestions: Serve with the garnishing of fresh strawberries.
Variation Tip: Use room temperature eggs.
Nutritional Information per Serving:
Calories: 250 | Fat: 13.6g | Sat Fat: 8.2g | Carbohydrates: 30.7g | Fiber: 0.4g | Sugar: 22.1g | Protein: 2.4g

Honeyed Banana

Preparation Time: 10 minutes
Cooking Time: 10 minutes
Servings: 2
Ingredients:
- 1 ripe banana, peeled and sliced lengthwise
- ½ teaspoon fresh lemon juice
- 2 teaspoons honey
- ⅛ teaspoon ground cinnamon
Preparation:

1. Coat each banana half with lemon juice.
2. Arrange the banana halves onto the greased sheet pan cut sides up.
3. Drizzle the banana halves with honey and sprinkle with cinnamon.
4. Press "Power" button of Ninja Foodi Digital Air Fry Oven and turn the dial to select "Air Fry" mode.
5. Press TIME/SLICE button and again turn the dial to set the cooking time to 10 minutes.
6. Now push TEMP/DARKNESS button and rotate the dial to set the temperature at 350 degrees F.
7. Press "Start/Pause" button to start.
8. When the unit beeps to show that it is preheated, open the oven door.
9. Insert the sheet pan in oven.
10. When cooking time is completed, open the oven door and transfer the banana slices onto a platter.
11. Serve immediately.
Serving Suggestions: Serve with garnishing of almonds.
Variation Tip: Honey can be replaced with maple syrup.
Nutritional Information per Serving:
Calories: 74 | Fat: 0.2g | Sat Fat: 0.1g | Carbohydrates: 19.4g | Fiber: 1.6g | Sugar: 13g | Protein: 0.7g

Banana Pancakes Dippers

Preparation Time: 10 minutes
Cooking Time: 15 minutes
Servings: 2
Ingredients:
- 1½ cups all-purpose flour
- 3 bananas, halved and sliced lengthwise
- 1 tablespoon baking powder
- 1 tablespoon packed brown sugar
- 1 teaspoon salt
- ¾ cup whole milk
- ½ cup sour cream
- 2 large eggs
- 1 teaspoon vanilla extract
Preparation:
1. Combine flour, baking powder, brown sugar, and salt in bowl.
2. Mix the milk and sour cream in a separate bowl, then add the eggs one at a time. Pour in the vanilla extract.
3. Combine the wet and dry ingredients until just mixed.
4. Grease the sheet pan with cooking spray and line it with parchment paper.
5. Place bananas in a single layer on parchment paper after dipping them in pancake batter.
6. Turn on Ninja Foodi Digital Air Fry Oven and rotate the knob to select "Air Roast".
7. Select the timer for 16 minutes and the temperature to 375 degrees F.
8. Allow cooling for two minutes before serving.
Serving Suggestions: Serve with melted chocolate for dipping.
Variation Tip: You can also use almond milk.
Nutritional Information per Serving:
Calories: 670 | Fat: 18.6g | Sat Fat: 10g | Carbohydrates: 66g | Fiber: 5g | Sugar: 23g | Protein: 22g

Carrot Mug Cake

Preparation Time: 10 minutes
Cooking Time: 20 minutes
Servings: 1
Ingredients:
- ¼ cup whole-wheat pastry flour
- 1 tablespoon coconut sugar
- ¼ teaspoon baking powder
- ⅛ teaspoon ground cinnamon
- ⅛ teaspoon ground ginger
- Pinch of ground cloves
- Pinch of ground allspice
- Pinch of salt
- 2 tablespoons plus 2 teaspoons unsweetened almond milk
- 2 tablespoons carrot, peeled and grated
- 2 tablespoons walnuts, chopped
- 1 tablespoon raisins
- 2 teaspoons applesauce

Preparation:
1. In a bowl, mix together the flour, sugar, baking powder, spices and salt.
2. Add the remaining ingredients and mix until well combined.
3. Place the mixture into a lightly greased ramekin.
4. Press "Power" button of Ninja Foodi Digital Air Fry Oven and turn the dial to select the "Bake" mode.
5. Press TIME/SLICE button and again turn the dial to set the cooking time to 20 minutes.
6. Now push TEMP/DARKNESS button and rotate the dial to set the temperature at 350 degrees F.
7. Press "Start/Pause" button to start.
8. When the unit beeps to show that it is preheated, open the oven door.
9. Arrange the ramekin over the wire rack and insert in the oven.
10. When cooking time is completed, open the oven door and place the ramekin onto a wire rack to cool slightly before serving.
Serving Suggestions: Serve with the topping of whipped cream.
Variation Tip: Apple sauce can be replaced with honey.
Nutritional Information per Serving:
Calories: 301 | Fat: 10.1g | Sat Fat: 0.7g | Carbohydrates: 48.6g | Fiber: 3.2g | Sugar: 19.4g | Protein: 7.6g

Apple Pastries

Preparation Time: 15 minutes
Cooking Time: 10 minutes
Servings: 6
Ingredients:
- ½ of large apple, peeled, cored and chopped
- 1 teaspoon fresh orange zest, grated finely
- ½ tablespoon white sugar
- ½ teaspoon ground cinnamon
- 7.05 ounces prepared frozen puff pastry

Preparation:
1. In a bowl, mix together all ingredients except puff pastry.
2. Cut the pastry in 16 squares.
3. Place about a teaspoon of the apple mixture in the center of each square.

4. Fold each square into a triangle and press the edges slightly with wet fingers.
5. Then with a fork, press the edges firmly.
6. Press "Power" button of Ninja Foodi Digital Air Fry Oven and turn the dial to select "Air Fry" mode.
7. Press TIME/SLICE button and again turn the dial to set the cooking time to 10 minutes.
8. Now push TEMP/DARKNESS button and rotate the dial to set the temperature at 390 degrees F.
9. Press "Start/Pause" button to start.
10. When the unit beeps to show that it is preheated, open the oven door.
11. Arrange the pastries in the greased air fry basket and insert in the oven.
12. When cooking time is completed, open the oven door and transfer the pastries onto a platter.
13. Serve warm.
Serving Suggestions: Serve with a dusting of powdered sugar.
Variation Tip: Use sweet apple.
Nutritional Information per Serving:
Calories: 198 | Fat: 12.7g | Sat Fat: 3.2g | Carbohydrates: 18.8g | Fiber: 1.1g | Sugar: 3.2g | Protein: 2.5g

Blueberry Hand Pies

Preparation Time: 15 minutes
Cooking Time: 20 minutes
Servings: 8
Ingredients:
- 1 cup blueberries
- 2½ tablespoons caster sugar
- 1 teaspoon lemon juice
- 1 pinch salt
- 320g refrigerated pie crust
- Water

Preparation:
1. Combine the blueberries, sugar, lemon juice, and salt in a medium mixing bowl.
2. Roll out the piecrusts and cut out 6-8 separate circles (4 inches).
3. In the center of each circle, place roughly 1 spoonful of the blueberry filling.
4. Wet the edges of the dough and fold it over the filling to create a half-moon shape.
5. Gently crimp the piecrust's edges together with a fork. Then, on the top of the hand pies, cut three slits.
6. Spray cooking oil over the hand pies.
7. Place them onto the sheet pan.
8. Turn on Ninja Foodi Digital Air Fry Oven and rotate the knob to select "Bake".
9. Select the timer for 20 minutes and the temperature for 350 degrees F.
10. Allow cooling for two minutes before serving.
Serving Suggestions: Sprinkle vanilla sugar on top.
Variation Tip: You can also use brown sugar.
Nutritional Information per Serving:
Calories: 251 | Fat: 12 | Sat Fat: 4g | Carbohydrates: 30g | Fiber: 1g | Sugar: 5g | Protein: 3g

Brownie Bars

Preparation Time: 15 minutes.
Cooking Time: 28 minutes.
Servings: 8
Ingredients:
Brownie:
- ½ cup butter, cubed
- 1 ounce unsweetened chocolate
- 2 large eggs, beaten
- 1 teaspoon vanilla extract
- 1 cup sugar
- 1 cup all-purpose flour
- 1 teaspoon baking powder
- 1 cup walnuts, chopped

Filling
- 6 ounces cream cheese softened
- ½ cup sugar
- ¼ cup butter, softened
- 2 tablespoons all-purpose flour
- 1 large egg, beaten
- ½ teaspoon vanilla extract

Topping
- 1 cup (6 ounces) chocolate chips
- 1 cup walnuts, chopped
- 2 cups mini marshmallows

Frosting
- ¼ cup butter
- ¼ cup milk
- 2 ounces cream cheese
- 1 ounce unsweetened chocolate
- 3 cups confectioners' sugar
- 1 teaspoon vanilla extract

Preparation:
1. In a small bowl, add and whisk all the ingredients for filling until smooth.
2. Melt butter with chocolate in a large saucepan over medium heat.
3. Mix well, then remove the melted chocolate from the heat.
4. Now stir in vanilla, eggs, baking powder, flour, sugar, and nuts then mix well.
5. Spread this chocolate batter in the sheet pan.
6. Drizzle nuts, marshmallows, and chocolate chips over the batter.
7. Transfer the pan to the Ninja Foodi Digital Air Fry Oven and close the door.
8. Select "Air Fry" mode by rotating the dial.
9. Press the TIME/SLICE button and change the value to 28 minutes.
10. Press the TEMP/DARKNESS button and change the value to 350 degrees F.
11. Press Start/Pause to begin cooking.
12. Meanwhile, prepare the frosting by heating butter with cream cheese, chocolate and milk in a suitable saucepan over medium heat.
13. Mix well, then remove it from the heat.
14. Stir in vanilla and sugar, then mix well.
15. Pour this frosting over the brownie.
16. Allow the brownie to cool then slice into bars.
17. Serve.

Serving Suggestion: Serve the bars with whipped cream and chocolate syrup on top.
Variation Tip: Add crushed pecans or peanuts to the filling.
Nutritional Information Per Serving:
Calories 298 | Fat 14g | Sodium 272mg | Carbs 34g | Fiber 1g | Sugar 9.3g | Protein 13g

Vanilla Soufflé

Preparation Time: 15 minutes
Cooking Time: 23 minutes
Servings: 6
Ingredients:
- ¼ cup butter, softened
- ¼ cup all-purpose flour
- ½ cup plus 2 tablespoons sugar, divided
- 1 cup milk
- 3 teaspoons vanilla extract, divided
- 4 egg yolks
- 5 egg whites
- 1 teaspoon cream of tartar
- 2 tablespoons powdered sugar plus extra for dusting

Preparation:
1. In a bowl, add the butter, and flour and mix until a smooth paste forms.
2. In a medium pan, mix together ½ cup of sugar and milk over medium-low heat and cook for about 3 minutes or until the sugar is dissolved, stirring continuously.
3. Add the flour mixture, whisking continuously and simmer for about 3-4 minutes or until mixture becomes thick.
4. Remove from the heat and stir in 1 teaspoon of vanilla extract.
5. Set aside for about 10 minutes to cool.
6. In a bowl, add the egg yolks and 1 teaspoon of vanilla extract and mix well.
7. Add the egg yolk mixture into milk mixture and mix until well combined.
8. In another bowl, add the egg whites, cream of tartar, remaining sugar, and vanilla extract and with a wire whisk, beat until stiff peaks form.
9. Fold the egg white mixture into milk mixture.
10. Grease 6 ramekins and sprinkle each with a pinch of sugar.
11. Place mixture into the prepared ramekins and with the back of a spoon, smooth the top surface.
12. Press "Power" button of Ninja Foodi Digital Air Fry Oven and turn the dial to select "Air Fry" mode.
13. Press TIME/SLICE button and again turn the dial to set the cooking time to 16 minutes.
14. Now push TEMP/DARKNESS button and rotate the dial to set the temperature at 330 degrees F.
15. Press "Start/Pause" button to start.
16. When the unit beeps to show that it is preheated, open the oven door.
17. Arrange the ramekins in air fry basket and insert in the oven.
18. When cooking time is completed, open the oven door and place the ramekins onto a wire rack to cool slightly.
19. Sprinkle with the powdered sugar and serve warm.

Serving Suggestions: Serve with caramel sauce.
Variation Tip: Room temperature eggs will get the best results.
Nutritional Information per Serving:
Calories: 250 | Fat: 11.6g | Sat Fat: 6.5g | Carbohydrates: 29.8g | Fiber: 0.1g | Sugar: 25g | Protein: 6.8g

Blueberry Cobbler

Preparation Time: 15 minutes
Cooking Time: 20 minutes
Servings: 6
Ingredients:
For Filling:
- 2½ cups fresh blueberries
- 1 teaspoon vanilla extract
- 1 teaspoon fresh lemon juice
- 1 cup sugar
- 1 teaspoon flour
- 1 tablespoon butter, melted

For Topping:
- 1¾ cups all-purpose flour
- 6 tablespoons sugar
- 4 teaspoons baking powder
- 1 cup milk
- 5 tablespoons butter

For Sprinkling:
- 2 teaspoons sugar
- ¼ teaspoon ground cinnamon

Preparation:
1. For filling: in a bowl, add all the filling ingredients and mix until well combined.
2. For topping: in another large bowl, mix together the flour, baking powder, and sugar.
3. Add the milk and butter and mix until a crumply mixture forms.
4. For sprinkling: in a small bowl mix together the sugar and cinnamon.
5. In the bottom of a greased pan, place the blueberries mixture and top with the flour mixture evenly.
6. Sprinkle the cinnamon sugar on top evenly.
7. Press "Power" button of Ninja Foodi Digital Air Fry Oven and turn the dial to select "Air Fry" mode.
8. Press TIME/SLICE button and again turn the dial to set the cooking time to 20 minutes.
9. Now push TEMP/DARKNESS button and rotate the dial to set the temperature at 320 degrees F.
10. Press "Start/Pause" button to start.
11. When the unit beeps to show that it is preheated, open the oven door.
12. Arrange the pan in air fry basket and insert in the oven.
13. When cooking time is complete, open the oven door and place the pan onto a wire rack to cool for about 10 minutes before serving.
Serving Suggestions: Serve with the topping of vanilla ice cream.
Variation Tip: If You want to use frozen blueberries, then thaw them completely.
Nutritional Information per Serving:
Calories: 459 | Fat: 12.6g | Sat Fat: 7.8g | Carbohydrates: 84g | Fiber: 2.7g | Sugar: 53.6g | Protein: 5.5g

Chocolate Chip Cookie

Preparation Time: 15 minutes.
Cooking Time: 12 minutes.
Servings: 6
Ingredients:
- ½ cup butter, softened
- ½ cup sugar
- ½ cup brown sugar
- 1 egg
- 1 teaspoon vanilla
- ½ teaspoons baking soda
- ¼ teaspoons salt
- 1 ½ cups all-purpose flour
- 1 cup chocolate chips

Preparation:
1. Grease the sheet pan with cooking spray.
2. Beat butter with sugar and brown sugar in a mixing bowl.
3. Stir in vanilla, egg, salt, flour, and baking soda, then mix well.
4. Fold in chocolate chips, then knead this dough a bit.
5. Spread the prepared dough in the prepared sheet pan evenly.
6. Transfer the pan to the Ninja Foodi Digital Air Fry Oven and close the door.
7. Select "Bake" mode by rotating the dial.
8. Press the TIME/SLICE button and change the value to 12 minutes.
9. Press the TEMP/DARKNESS button and change the value to 400 degrees F.
10. Press Start/Pause to begin cooking.
11. Serve oven fresh.
Serving Suggestion: Serve the cookies with warm milk.
Variation Tip: Dip the cookies in chocolate syrup to coat well.
Nutritional Information Per Serving:
Calories 173 | Fat 12g | Sodium 79mg | Carbs 24.8g | Fiber 1.1g | Sugar 18g | Protein 15g

Air Fried Butter Cake

Preparation Time: 10 minutes
Cooking Time: 20 minutes
Servings: 4
Ingredients:
- Cooking spray
- 7 tablespoons butter
- ¼ cup plus 2 tablespoons white sugar
- 1 egg
- 1⅔ cups all-purpose flour
- 1 pinch salt
- 6 tablespoons milk

Preparation:
1. Select the AIR FRY function, 350°F, for 15 minutes. Prepare a small, air fryer-safe fluted tube pan with cooking spray.
2. Mix the sugar and the butter, then beat them together using an electric mixer. When it's light and creamy, add the egg and mix until the batter is fluffy and smooth.
3. Stir in the flour and salt, then add the milk and mix the batter thoroughly. Transfer the batter to the prepared pan and level the surface with the back of a spoon.
4. Place the pan in the air fryer. Bake it for about 15 minutes. Let the cake cool in the pan for about 5 minutes before removing it.
Serving Suggestion: Sprinkle with powdered sugar and serve with milk.
Variation Tip: You can experiment by using rice flour or almond flour instead of all-purpose flour.
Nutritional Information Per Serving:
Calories: 470 | Fat: 22.4g | Sodium: 208mg | Carbs: 59.7g | Fiber: 1.3g | Sugar: 20g | Protein: 7.7g

Shortbread Fingers

Preparation Time: 15 minutes
Cooking Time: 12 minutes
Servings: 10
Ingredients:
- ⅓ cup caster sugar
- 1⅔ cups plain flour
- ¾ cup butter

Preparation:
1. In a large bowl, mix together the sugar and flour.
2. Add the butter and mix until a smooth dough forms.
3. Cut the dough into 10 equal-sized fingers.
4. With a fork, lightly prick the fingers.
5. Place the fingers into the lightly greased sheet pan.
6. Press "Power" button of Ninja Foodi Digital Air Fry Oven and turn the dial to select "Air Fry" mode.
7. Press TIME/SLICE button and again turn the dial to set the cooking time to 12 minutes.
8. Now push TEMP/DARKNESS button and rotate the dial to set the temperature at 355 degrees F.
9. Press "Start/Pause" button to start.
10. When the unit beeps to show that it is preheated, open the oven door.
11. Arrange the pan in air fry basket and insert in the oven.
12. When cooking time is completed, open the oven door and place the baking pan onto a wire rack to cool for about 5-10 minutes.
13. Now, invert the shortbread fingers onto the wire rack to completely cool before serving.
Serving Suggestions: Serve with a dusting of powdered sugar.
Variation Tip: For best result, chill the dough in the refrigerator for 30 minutes before cooking.
Nutritional Information per Serving:
Calories: 223 | Fat: 14g | Sat Fat: 8.8g | Carbohydrates: 22.6g | Fiber: 0.6g | Sugar: 0.7g | Protein: 2.3g

Caramel Apple Pie

Preparation Time: 15 minutes.
Cooking Time: 48 minutes.
Servings: 6
Ingredients:
Topping
- ¼ cup all-purpose flour
- ⅓ cup packed brown sugar
- 2 tablespoons butter, softened
- ½ teaspoon ground cinnamon

Pie
- 6 cups sliced peeled tart apples
- 1 tablespoon lemon juice
- ½ cup sugar
- 3 tablespoons all-purpose flour
- ½ teaspoon ground cinnamon
- 1 unbaked pastry shell (9 inches)
- 28 caramels
- 1 can (5 ounces) evaporated milk

Preparation:
1. Mix flour with cinnamon, butter, and brown sugar.
2. Spread this mixture in an 8-inch baking pan.
3. Transfer the pan to the Ninja Foodi Digital Air Fry Oven and close the door.
4. Select "Bake" mode by rotating the dial.
5. Press the TIME/SLICE button and change the value to 8 minutes.
6. Press the TEMP/DARKNESS button and change the value to 350 degrees F.
7. Press Start/Pause to begin cooking.
8. Meanwhile, mix apple with lemon juice, cinnamon, flour, and sugar.
9. Spread the filling in the baked crust and return to the air fryer oven.
10. Bake again for 35 minutes in the oven.
11. Mix caramels with milk in a pan and cook until melted.
12. Spread the caramel on top of the pie and bake for 5 minutes.
13. Serve.
Serving Suggestion: Serve the pie with apple sauce on top.
Variation Tip: Crushed apple chips on top of the apple filling.
Nutritional Information Per Serving:
Calories 203 | Fat 8.9g | Sodium 340mg | Carbs 24.7g | Fiber 1.2g | Sugar 11.3g | Protein 5.3g

Peanut Brittle Bars

Preparation Time: 15 minutes.
Cooking Time: 28 minutes.
Servings: 6
Ingredients:
- 1-½ cups all-purpose flour
- ½ cup whole wheat flour
- 1 cup packed brown sugar
- 1 teaspoon baking soda
- ¼ teaspoon salt
- 1 cup butter

Topping
- 1 cup milk chocolate chips
- 2 cups salted peanuts
- 12 ¼ ounces caramel ice cream topping
- 3 tablespoons all-purpose flour

Preparation:
1. Mix flours with salt, baking soda, and brown sugar in a large bowl.
2. Spread the batter in a greased sheet pan.
3. Transfer the pan to the Ninja Foodi Digital Air Fry Oven and close the door.
4. Select "Bake" mode by rotating the dial.
5. Press the TIME/SLICE button and change the value to 12 minutes.
6. Press the TEMP/DARKNESS button and change the value to 350 degrees F.
7. Press Start/Pause to begin cooking.
8. Spread chocolate chips and peanuts on top.
9. Mix flour with caramels topping in a bowl and spread on top,
10. Bake again for 16 minutes.
11. Serve.
Serving Suggestion: Serve the bars with sweet cream cheese dip.
Variation Tip: Add crushed oats to bars for crumbly texture.
Nutritional Information Per Serving:
Calories 153 | Fat 1g | Sodium 8mg | Carbs 26g | Fiber 0.8g | Sugar 56g | Protein 11g

Chocolate Chip Cookies

Preparation Time: 10 minutes
Cooking Time: 45 minutes
Servings: 4
Ingredients:
- ½ cup butter, melted
- ¼ cup packed brown sugar
- ¼ cup granulated sugar
- 1 large egg
- 1 teaspoon pure vanilla extract
- 1½ cups all-purpose flour
- ½ teaspoon baking soda
- ½ teaspoon kosher salt
- ½ teaspoon chocolate chips

Preparation:
1. Whisk together melted butter and sugars in a medium mixing bowl. Whisk in the egg and vanilla extract until fully combined.
2. Combine the flour, baking soda, and salt.
3. Place sheet onto the air fry basket.
4. Scoop dough onto a sheet with a large cookie scoop (approximately 3 tablespoons), leaving 2 inches between each cookie, and press to flatten slightly.
5. Turn on Ninja Foodi Digital Air Fry Oven and rotate the knob to select "Air Fry".
6. Select the timer for 8 minutes and the temperature for 350 degrees F.
7. Allow cooling for two minutes before serving.

Serving Suggestions: Top some more chocolate chips.
Variation Tip: You can also add chopped walnuts.
Nutritional Information per Serving:
Calories: 319 | Fat: 16.6g | Sat Fat: 10.1g | Carbohydrates: 38.4g | Fiber: 0.9g | Sugar: 14.6g | Protein: 4.5g

Air Fryer Churros

Preparation Time: 5 minutes
Cooking Time: 20 minutes
Servings: 6
Ingredients:
- ¼ cup butter
- ½ cup milk
- 1 pinch salt
- ½ cup all-purpose flour
- 2 eggs
- ¼ cup white sugar
- ½ teaspoon ground cinnamon

Preparation:
1. Select the AIR FRY function, 340°F, for 5 minutes. While the oven is preheating, prepare the ingredients.
2. Take a saucepan and melt the butter over medium-high heat. Pour in the milk and add the salt. Turn the heat down to medium and bring the mixture to a boil, stirring constantly.
3. Add all the flour at once and keep stirring until the dough comes together.
4. Turn off the heat and let the mixture cool for 5 to 7 minutes. Add the eggs and mix with a wooden spoon. Spoon the dough into a plastic bag with a large star tip. With the help of the star tip, pipe the dough directly into the air fryer basket.

5. Cook the churros for about 5 minutes. You might need to cook in batches.
6. Meanwhile, in a small bowl, combine the cinnamon and sugar. Put it on a shallow plate.
7. Once the churros are done, roll them in the cinnamon-sugar mixture and serve.

Serving Suggestion: Drizzle with a little honey before serving.
Variation Tip: You can try nutmeg instead of cinnamon.
Nutritional Information Per Serving:
Calories: 172k | Fat: 9.8g | Sodium: 112mg | Carbs: 17.5g | Fiber: 0.4g | Sugar: 9.4 | Protein: 3.7g

Air Fried Doughnuts

Preparation Time: 15 minutes.
Cooking Time: 6 minutes.
Servings: 8
Ingredients:
- Cooking spray
- ½ cup milk
- ¼ cup/1 teaspoon granulated sugar
- 2 ¼ teaspoons active dry yeast
- 2 cups all-purpose flour
- ½ teaspoon kosher salt
- 4 tablespoons melted butter
- 1 large egg
- 1 teaspoon pure vanilla extract

Preparation:
1. Warm up the milk in a suitable saucepan, then add yeast and 1 teaspoon of sugar.
2. Mix well and leave this milk for 8 minutes.
3. Add flour, salt, butter, egg, vanilla, and ¼ cup of sugar to the warm milk.
4. Mix well and knead over a floured surface until smooth.
5. Place this dough in a lightly greased bowl and brush it with cooking oil.
6. Cover the prepared dough and leave it in a warm place for 1 hour.
7. Punch the raised dough, then roll into ½ inch thick rectangle.
8. Cut 3" circles out of this dough sheet using a biscuit cutter.
9. Now cut the rounds from the center to make a hole.
10. Place the doughnuts in the air fry basket.
11. Transfer the basket to the Ninja Foodi Digital Air Fry Oven and close the door.
12. Select "Air Fry" mode by rotating the dial.
13. Press the TIME/SLICE button and change the value to 6 minutes.
14. Press the TEMP/DARKNESS button and change the value to 375 degrees F.
15. Press Start/Pause to begin cooking.
16. Cook the doughnuts in batches to avoid overcrowding.
17. Serve fresh.

Serving Suggestion: Serve the doughnuts with strawberry jam.
Variation Tip: Roll the doughnuts in the powder sugar to coat.
Nutritional Information Per Serving:
Calories 128 | Fat 20g | Sodium 192mg | Carbs 27g | Fiber 0.9g | Sugar 19g | Protein 5.2g

Cherry Clafoutis

Preparation Time: 15 minutes
Cooking Time: 25 minutes
Servings: 4
Ingredients:
- 1½ cups fresh cherries, pitted
- 3 tablespoons vodka
- ¼ cup flour
- 2 tablespoons sugar
- Pinch of salt
- ½ cup sour cream
- 1 egg
- 1 tablespoon butter
- ¼ cup powdered sugar

Preparation:
1. In a bowl, mix together the cherries and vodka.
2. In another bowl, mix together the flour, sugar, and salt.
3. Add the sour cream, and egg and mix until a smooth dough forms.
4. Grease a cake pan.
5. Place flour mixture evenly into the prepared cake pan.
6. Spread cherry mixture over the dough.
7. Place butter on top in the form of dots.
8. Press "Power" button of Ninja Foodi Digital Air Fry Oven and turn the dial to select "Air Fry" mode.
9. Press TIME/SLICE button and again turn the dial to set the cooking time to 25 minutes.
10. Now push TEMP/DARKNESS button and rotate the dial to set the temperature at 355 degrees F.
11. Press "Start/Pause" button to start.
12. When the unit beeps to show that it is preheated, open the oven door.
13. Arrange the pan in air fry basket and insert in the oven.
14. When cooking time is completed, open the oven door and place the pan onto a wire rack to cool for about 10-15 minutes before serving.
15. Now, invert the Clafoutis onto a platter and sprinkle with powdered sugar.
16. Cut the Clafoutis into desired sized slices and serve warm.

Serving Suggestions: Serve with a topping of whipped cream.
Variation Tip: Replace vodka with kirsch.
Nutritional Information per Serving:
Calories: 241 | Fat: 10.1g | Sat Fat: 5.9g | Carbohydrates: 29g | Fiber: 1.3g | Sugar: 20.6g | Protein: 3.9g

Nutella Banana Muffins

Preparation Time: 15 minutes
Cooking Time: 25 minutes
Servings: 12
Ingredients:
- 1⅔ cups plain flour
- 1 teaspoon baking soda
- 1 teaspoon baking powder
- 1 teaspoon ground cinnamon
- ¼ teaspoon salt
- 4 ripe bananas, peeled and mashed
- 2 eggs
- ½ cup brown sugar
- 1 teaspoon vanilla essence
- 3 tablespoons milk
- 1 tablespoon Nutella
- ¼ cup walnuts

Preparation:
1. Grease 12 muffin molds. Set aside.
2. In a large bowl, put together the flour, baking soda, baking powder, cinnamon, and salt.
3. In another bowl, mix together the remaining ingredients except walnuts.
4. Add the banana mixture into flour mixture and mix until just combined.
5. Fold in the walnuts.
6. Place the mixture into the prepared muffin molds.
7. Press "Power" button of Ninja Foodi Digital Air Fry Oven and turn the dial to select "Air Fry" mode.
8. Press TIME/SLICE button and again turn the dial to set the cooking time to 25 minutes.
9. Now push TEMP/DARKNESS button and rotate the dial to set the temperature at 250 degrees F.
10. Press "Start/Pause" button to start.
11. When the unit beeps to show that it is preheated, open the oven door.
12. Arrange the muffin molds in air fry basket and insert in the oven.
13. When cooking time is completed, open the oven door and place the muffin molds onto a wire rack to cool for about 10 minutes.
14. Carefully, invert the muffins onto the wire rack to completely cool before serving.

Serving Suggestions: Enjoy with a glass of milk.
Variation Tip: Have all ingredients at room temperature before you start making the batter.
Nutritional Information per Serving:
Calories: 227 | Fat: 6.6g | Sat Fat: 1.5g | Carbohydrates: 38.1g | Fiber: 2.4g | Sugar: 15.8g | Protein: 5.2g

Air Fryer Fried Oreos

Preparation Time: 10 minutes
Cooking Time: 8 minutes
Servings: 3 to 4
Ingredients:
- 9 Oreo cookies
- 1 Crescent Dough Sheet

Preparation:
1. Select the AIR FRY function, 350°F, for 8 minutes. While the oven is preheating, prepare the ingredients.
2. Spread the sheet out. Line and cut it into 9 even squares with a knife.
3. Take the 9 cookies and wrap one in each square. Press the dough to seal. Spray each with some cooking oil.
4. Lay the parcels in the air fryer basket, cook them for 5 minutes, turn them over, spray with more oil, and cook for 3 more minutes or until golden brown.

Serving Suggestion: Sprinkle with powdered sugar or cinnamon before serving.
Variation Tip: Try drizzling with a bit of honey.
Nutritional Information Per Serving:
Calories: 67 | Fat: 3g | Sodium: 80mg | Carbs: 10g | Fiber: 1g | Sugar: 5g | Protein: 1g

Cinnamon Rolls

Preparation Time: 5 minutes
Cooking Time: 30 minutes
Servings: 6
Ingredients:
- 2 tablespoons butter, melted
- ⅓ cup packed brown sugar
- ½ teaspoon ground cinnamon
- Salt, to taste
- All-purpose flour for surface
- 1 tube refrigerated crescent rolls
- 56g cream cheese, softened
- ½ cup powdered sugar
- 1 tablespoon whole milk

Preparation:
1. Combine butter, brown sugar, cinnamon, and a large pinch of salt in a medium mixing bowl until smooth and fluffy.
2. Roll out crescent rolls in one piece on a lightly floured surface. Fold in half by pinching the seams together. Make a medium rectangle out of the dough.
3. Cover the dough with butter mixture, leaving a 1/4-inch border. Roll the dough, starting at one edge and cutting crosswise into 6 pieces.
4. Line bottom of basket with parchment paper and brush with butter.
5. Place the pieces cut-side up in the prepared air fry basket, equally spaced.
6. Turn on Ninja Foodi Digital Air Fry Oven and rotate the knob to select "Air Broil".
7. Select the timer for 15 minutes and the temperature for LO.
8. Allow cooling for two minutes before serving.
Serving Suggestions: Top with almond butter.
Variation Tip: You can also use almond milk.
Nutritional Information per Serving:
Calories: 183 | Fat: 8g | Sat Fat: 4g | Carbohydrates: 26g | Fiber: 0.4g | Sugar: 16g | Protein: 2.2g

Chocolate Oatmeal Cookies

Preparation Time: 15 minutes
Cooking Time: 10 minutes
Servings: 36
Ingredients:
- 3 cups quick-cooking oatmeal
- 1½ cups all-purpose flour
- ½ cup cream
- ¼ cup cocoa powder
- ¾ cup white sugar
- 1 package instant chocolate pudding mix
- 1 teaspoon baking soda
- 1 teaspoon salt
- 1 cup butter, softened
- ¾ cup brown sugar
- 2 eggs
- 1 teaspoon vanilla extract
- 2 cups chocolate chips
- Cooking spray

Preparation:
1. Using parchment paper, line the air fry basket.
2. Using nonstick cooking spray, coat the air fry basket.
3. Combine the oats, flour, cocoa powder, pudding mix, baking soda, and salt in a mixing dish. Set aside.
4. Mix cream, butter, brown sugar, and white sugar in a separate bowl using an electric mixer.
5. Combine the eggs and vanilla essence in a mixing bowl. Mix in the oatmeal mixture thoroughly. Mix the chocolate chips and walnuts in a bowl.
6. Using a large cookie scoop, drop dough into the air fry basket; level out and leave about 1 inch between each cookie.
7. Turn on Ninja Foodi Digital Air Fry Oven and rotate the knob to select "Air Fry".
8. Select the timer for 10 minutes and the temperature for 350 degrees F.
9. Before serving, cool on a wire rack.
Serving Suggestions: Sprinkle vanilla sugar on top.
Variation Tip: You can also add chopped walnuts.
Nutritional Information per Serving:
Calories: 199 | Fat: 10.7g | Sat Fat: 5g | Carbohydrates: 24g | Fiber: 1.9g | Sugar: 14g | Protein: 2g

Mini Crumb Cake Bites

Preparation Time: 30 minutes
Cooking Time: 15 minutes
Servings: 4 to 6
Ingredients:
- ¾ cup granulated sugar
- ⅓ cup vegetable oil
- 1 egg
- 1 teaspoon vanilla
- ½ cup milk
- 2 teaspoons baking powder
- ½ teaspoon plus a pinch of salt
- 1½ cups plus 2 tablespoons all-purpose flour
- 2 tablespoons butter, melted
- 2 teaspoons ground cinnamon
- ½ cup packed brown sugar

Preparation:
1. Select the BAKE function, 350°F, for 10 minutes. Prepare air fryer-safe mini muffin pans with non-stick cooking spray.
2. In a large bowl, mix the oil, vanilla, granulated sugar, and egg. Mix well and stir in the milk.
3. Take a medium bowl, and whisk ½ teaspoon salt, baking powder, and 1½ cups flour. Stir the dry ingredients into the wet ingredients, slowly. Fill each muffin cup with 1 tablespoon of the batter.
4. Mix the cinnamon, flour, brown sugar, and a pinch of salt. Top each muffin with ½ to ¾ teaspoon of this crumb topping.
5. Bake the muffins for about 9 to 10 minutes. Let them cool for a while before taking them out of the pans.
Serving Suggestion: Sprinkle with some sugar and serve with jam.
Variation Tip: You can also add chopped pecans or walnuts to the crumble.
Nutritional Information Per Serving:
Calories: 74 | Fat: 3g | Sodium: 42mg | Carbs: 12g | Fiber: 1g | Sugar: 7g | Protein: 1g

Brown Sugar Pecan Cookies

Preparation Time: 20 minutes
Cooking Time: 10 minutes
Servings: 6 to 8
Ingredients:
For the cookies:
- 1 cup butter
- ½ cup granulated sugar
- ½ cup packed brown sugar
- 1 large egg
- 1 teaspoon vanilla extract
- 2 cups all-purpose flour
- ½ teaspoon baking soda
- ¼ teaspoon salt
- ½ cup pecans, finely chopped

For the frosting:
- 1 cup packed brown sugar
- ½ cup milk
- 1 tablespoon butter
- 2 cups powdered sugar, sifted

Preparation:
1. First, make the cookie batter. Mix the butter and sugar in a bowl. Beat until it's light and fluffy using a stand mixer. Add in the egg and vanilla, then beat until combined.
2. Next, add in the baking soda, salt, and flour, then beat until combined. Stir in the chopped pecans. Cover and place it in the refrigerator for at least 30 minutes.
3. Select the BAKE function, 350°F, for 10 minutes. Prepare the cookies while the oven is preheating.
4. Shape the cookie batter into 1-inch balls and put them on the parchment-lined sheet pan. You may need to cook in batches. Bake for about 10 minutes, and then let the cookies cool for a while.
5. While the cookies are cooling down, prepare the frosting. In a small saucepan, combine the milk and brown sugar over medium heat. Bring the mixture to a boil, constantly stirring, for 3 to 4 minutes. Stir in the butter
6. Add 1½ cups of the powdered sugar and mix well. Top the cookies with this frosting.
Serving Suggestion: Top with chopped pecans and the rest of the powdered sugar.
Variation Tip: You can use margarine instead of butter, and cream can replace milk.
Nutritional Information Per Serving:
Calories: 166 | Fat: 7g | Sodium: 87mg | Carbs: 24g | Fiber: 0g | Sugar: 18g | Protein: 1g

Air Fryer Roasted Bananas

Preparation Time: 2 minutes
Cooking Time: 7 minutes
Servings: 1
Ingredients:
- 1 banana
- Avocado oil cooking spray

Preparation:
1. Select the AIR FRY function, 375°F, for 7 minutes. While the oven is preheating, prepare the banana.
2. Slice the banana into ⅛-inch thick diagonals. Line the air fryer basket with parchment paper.
3. Lay the banana slices on the air fryer basket and spray with avocado oil.
4. Cook for about 5 minutes, flip and cook for another 2 to 3 minutes.
Serving Suggestion: Serve the banana slices with vanilla ice cream.
Variation Tip: Try almond oil instead of avocado oil.
Nutritional Information Per Serving:
Calories: 107 | Fat: 0.8g | Sodium: 1.2mg | Carbs: 27g | Fiber: 3g | Sugar: 14.4g | Protein: 1.3g

Blueberry Muffins

Preparation Time: 15 minutes
Cooking Time: 12 minutes
Servings: 6
Ingredients:
- 1 egg, beaten
- 1 ripe banana, peeled and mashed
- 1¼ cups almond flour
- 2 tablespoons granulated sugar
- ½ teaspoon baking powder
- 1 tablespoon coconut oil, melted
- ⅛ cup maple syrup
- 1 teaspoon apple cider vinegar
- 1 teaspoon vanilla extract
- 1 teaspoon lemon zest, grated
- Pinch of ground cinnamon
- ½ cup fresh blueberries

Preparation:
1. In a large bowl, add all the ingredients except for blueberries and mix until well combined.
2. Gently fold in the blueberries.
3. Grease a 6-cup muffin pan.
4. Place the mixture into prepared muffin cups about ¾ full.
5. Press "Power" button of Ninja Foodi Digital Air Fry Oven and turn the dial to select "Bake" mode.
6. Press TIME/SLICE button and again turn the dial to set the cooking time to 12 minutes.
7. Now push TEMP/DARKNESS button and rotate the dial to set the temperature at 375 degrees F.
8. Press "Start/Pause" button to start.
9. When the unit beeps to show that it is preheated, open the oven door.
10. Arrange the muffin pan over the wire rack and insert in the oven.
11. When cooking time is completed, open the oven door and place the muffin molds onto a wire rack to cool for about 10 minutes.
12. Carefully invert the muffins onto the wire rack to completely cool before serving.
Serving Suggestions: Serve with a hot cup of coffee.
Variation Tip: Make sure to use ripened blueberries.
Nutritional Information per Serving:
Calories: 223 | Fat: 14.8g | Sat Fat: 3g | Carbohydrates: 20.1g | Fiber: 3.4g | Sugar: 12.5g | Protein: 6.2g

Fudgy Brownies

Preparation Time: 15 minutes
Cooking Time: 25 minutes
Servings: 9
Ingredients:
- 8 ounces semi-sweet chocolate
- 12 tablespoons butter, melted
- 1¼ cups sugar
- 2 eggs
- 2 teaspoons vanilla extract
- ¾ cup all-purpose flour
- ¼ cup cocoa powder
- 1 teaspoon salt

Preparation:
1. Select the BAKE function, 350°F, for 25 minutes. Line the sheet pan with parchment paper.
2. While the oven is preheating, chop the chocolate into chunks and melt half of the chocolate in the microwave.
3. Take a large bowl, and mix the sugar and butter using an electric hand mixer. Then, beat in the egg and vanilla until the mixture becomes fluffy, about 2 minutes.
4. Now, whisk in the melted chocolate and stir in the cocoa powder, flour, and salt. Fold gently to mix with the dry ingredients.
5. Fold in the remaining chocolate chunks and transfer to the prepared sheet pan.
6. Bake the brownies for about 20 to 25 minutes.
Serving Suggestion: Drizzle with a little honey or top with melted chocolate and serve with milk.
Variation Tip: Carob powder can be a great substitute for cocoa powder.
Nutritional Information Per Serving:
Calories: 404 | Fat: 27g | Sodium: 0g | Carbs: 39g | Fiber: 2g | Sugar: 25g | Protein: 5g

Fudge Brownies

Preparation Time: 15 minutes
Cooking Time: 20 minutes
Servings: 8
Ingredients:
- 1 cup sugar
- ½ cup butter, melted
- ½ cup flour
- ⅓ cup cocoa powder
- 1 teaspoon baking powder
- 2 eggs
- 1 teaspoon vanilla extract

Preparation:
1. Grease a baking pan.
2. In a large bowl, add the sugar and butter and whisk until light and fluffy.
3. Add the remaining ingredients and mix until well combined.
4. Place mixture into the prepared pan and with the back of a spatula, smooth the top surface.
5. Press "Power" button of Ninja Foodi Digital Air Fry Oven and turn the dial to select "Air Fry" mode.
6. Press TIME/SLICE button and again turn the dial to set the cooking time to 20 minutes.

7. Now push TEMP/DARKNESS button and rotate the dial to set the temperature at 350 degrees F.
8. Press "Start/Pause" button to start.
9. When the unit beeps to show that it is preheated, open the oven door.
10. Arrange the pan in air fry basket and insert in the oven.
11. When cooking time is completed, open the oven door and place the sheet pan onto a wire rack to cool completely.
12. Cut into 8 equal-sized squares and serve.
Serving Suggestions: Serve with a drizzling of melted chocolate.
Variation Tip: Choose good quality ingredients.
Nutritional Information per Serving:
Calories: 250 | Fat: 13.2g | Sat Fat: 7.9g | Carbohydrates: 33.4g | Fiber: 1.3g | Sugar: 25.2g | Protein: 3g

Chocolate Bites

Preparation Time: 15 minutes
Cooking Time: 13 minutes
Servings: 8
Ingredients:
- 2 cups plain flour
- 2 tablespoons cocoa powder
- ½ cup icing sugar
- Pinch of ground cinnamon
- 1 teaspoon vanilla extract
- ¾ cup chilled butter
- ¼ cup chocolate, chopped into 8 chunks

Preparation:
1. In a bowl, mix together the flour, icing sugar, cocoa powder, cinnamon and vanilla extract.
2. With a pastry cutter, cut the butter and mix till a smooth dough forms.
3. Divide the dough into 8 equal-sized balls.
4. Press 1 chocolate chunk in the center of each ball and cover with the dough completely.
5. Place the balls into the sheet pan.
6. Press "Power" button of Ninja Foodi Air Fry Digital Oven and turn the dial to select the "Air Fry" mode.
7. Press TIME/SLICE button and again turn the dial to set the cooking time to 8 minutes.
8. Now push TEMP/DARKNESS button and rotate the dial to set the temperature at 355 degrees F.
9. Press "Start/Pause" button to start.
10. When the unit beeps to show that it is preheated, open the oven door.
11. Arrange the pan in air fry basket and insert in the oven.
12. After 8 minutes of cooking, set the temperature at 320 degrees F for 5 minutes.
13. When cooking time is completed, open the oven door and place the sheet pan onto the wire rack to cool completely before serving.
Serving Suggestions: Serve with a sprinkling of coconut shreds.
Variation Tip: Use best quality cocoa powder.
Nutritional Information per Serving:
Calories: 328 | Fat: 19.3g | Sat Fat: 12.2g | Carbohydrates: 35.3g | Fiber: 1.4g | Sugar: 10.2g | Protein: 4.1g

Chocolate Soufflé

Preparation Time: 15 minutes
Cooking Time: 16 minutes
Servings: 2
Ingredients:
- 3 ounces semi-sweet chocolate, chopped
- ¼ cup butter
- 2 eggs, yolks and whites separated
- 3 tablespoons sugar
- ½ teaspoon pure vanilla extract
- 2 tablespoons all-purpose flour
- 1 teaspoon powdered sugar plus extra for dusting

Preparation:
1. In a microwave-safe bowl, place the butter and chocolate. Microwave on high heat for about 2 minutes or until melted completely, stirring after every 30 seconds.
2. Remove from the microwave and stir the mixture until smooth.
3. In another bowl, add the egg yolks and whisk well.
4. Add the sugar and vanilla extract and whisk well.
5. Add the chocolate mixture and mix until well combined.
6. Add the flour and mix well.
7. In a clean glass bowl, add the egg whites and whisk until soft peaks form.
8. Fold the whipped egg whites in 3 portions into the chocolate mixture.
9. Grease 2 ramekins and sprinkle each with a pinch of sugar.
10. Place mixture into the prepared ramekins and with the back of a spoon, smooth the top surface.
11. Press "Power" button of Ninja Foodi Digital Air Fry Oven and turn the dial to select "Air Fry" mode.
12. Press TIME/SLICE button and again turn the dial to set the cooking time to 14 minutes.
13. Now push TEMP/DARKNESS button and rotate the dial to set the temperature at 330 degrees F.
14. Press "Start/Pause" button to start.
15. When the unit beeps to show that it is preheated, open the oven door.
16. Arrange the ramekins into the air fry basket and insert in the oven.
17. When cooking time is completed, open the oven door and place the ramekins onto a wire rack to cool slightly.
18. Sprinkle with the powdered sugar and serve warm.

Serving Suggestions: Serve with the garnishing of berries.
Variation Tip: Use high-quality chocolate.
Nutritional Information per Serving:
Calories: 591 | Fat: 87.3g | Sat Fat: 23g | Carbohydrates: 52.6g | Fiber: 0.2g | Sugar: 41.1g | Protein: 9.4g

Cherry Jam tarts

Preparation Time: 15 minutes.
Cooking Time: 40 minutes.
Servings: 6
Ingredients:
- 2 sheets shortcrust pastry
For the frangipane
- 4 ounces butter softened
- 4 ounces golden caster sugar
- 1 egg
- 1 tablespoon plain flour
- 4 ounces ground almonds
- 3 ounces cherry jam
For the icing
- 1 cup icing sugar
- 12 glacé cherries

Preparation:
1. Grease the 12 cups of the muffin tray with butter.
2. Roll the puff pastry into a 10 cm sheet, then cut 12 rounds out of it.
3. Place these rounds into each muffin cup and press them into these cups.
4. Transfer the muffin tray to the refrigerator and leave it for 20 minutes.
5. Add dried beans or pulses into each tart crust to add weight.
6. Transfer the muffin tray to the Ninja Foodi Digital Air Fry Oven and close the door.
7. Select "Bake" mode by rotating the dial.
8. Press the TIME/SLICE button and change the value to 10 minutes.
9. Press the TEMP/DARKNESS button and change the value to 350 degrees F.
10. Press Start/Pause to begin cooking.
11. Now remove the dried beans from the crust and bake again for 10 minutes in the Ninja Foodi Digital Air Fry oven.
12. Meanwhile, prepare the filling beat, beat butter with sugar and egg until fluffy.
13. Stir in flour and almonds ground, then mix well.
14. Divide this filling in the baked crusts and top them with a tablespoon of cherry jam.
15. Now again, place the muffin tray in the Ninja Foodi Digital Air Fry oven.
16. Continue cooking on the "Bake" mode for 20 minutes at 350 degrees F.
17. Whisk the icing sugar with 2 tablespoons water and top the baked tarts with sugar mixture.
18. Serve.

Serving Suggestion: Serve the tarts with cherries on top.
Variation Tip: Add rum-soaked raisins to the tart filling.
Nutritional Information Per Serving:
Calories 193 | Fat 3g | Sodium 277mg | Carbs 21g | Fiber 1g | Sugar 9g | Protein 2g

Cranberry-Apple Pie

Preparation Time: 15 minutes.
Cooking Time: 45 minutes.
Servings: 8
Ingredients:
- 2 ½ cups all-purpose flour
- 1 tablespoon sugar
- ¾ teaspoon salt
- ½ cup cold unsalted butter, cubed
- ⅓ cup cold shortening
- 7 tablespoons ice water

Filling
- ½ cup dried currants or raisins
- 2 tablespoons dark rum
- 1 cup fresh cranberries, divided
- ¾ cup sugar, divided
- 6 baking apples, peeled and cut into slices
- 2 tablespoons tapioca
- 1 tablespoon lemon juice
- 2 teaspoons grated lemon zest
- ½ teaspoon ground cinnamon

Egg Wash
- 2 teaspoons sugar
- Dash ground cinnamon
- 1 large egg
- 1 tablespoon milk

Preparation:
1. Mix flour with butter, salt, and sugar in a bowl.
2. Stir in water and mix well until smooth.
3. Divide the prepared dough into two halves and spread each into a ⅛-inch-thick round.
4. Blend cranberries with sugar in a food processor.
5. Transfer to a bowl and stir in remaining filling ingredients.
6. Spread one dough round on a 9-inch pie plate.
7. Spread the prepared filling in the crust.
8. Slice the other dough round into strips and make a crisscross pattern on top.
9. Brush the pie with egg and milk mixture, then drizzle sugar and cinnamon top.
10. Transfer the pan to the Ninja Foodi Digital Air Fry Oven and close the door.
11. Select "Bake" mode by rotating the dial.
12. Press the TIME/SLICE button and change the value to 45 minutes.
13. Press the TEMP/DARKNESS button and change the value to 325 degrees F.
14. Press Start/Pause to begin cooking.
15. Cool on a wire rack for 30 minutes.
16. Serve.
Serving Suggestion: Serve the pie with whipped cream on top.
Variation Tip: Add a tablespoon of apple sauce to the filling for sweeter taste.
Nutritional Information Per Serving:
Calories 145 | Fat 3g | Sodium 355mg | Carbs 20g | Fiber 1g | Sugar 25g | Protein 1g

Cannoli

Preparation Time: 15 minutes.
Cooking Time: 12 minutes.
Servings: 4
Ingredients:
Filling
- 1 (16-ounce) container ricotta
- ½ cup mascarpone cheese
- ½ cup powdered sugar, divided
- ¾ cup heavy cream
- 1 teaspoon vanilla extract
- 1 teaspoon orange zest
- ¼ teaspoon kosher salt
- ½ cup mini chocolate chips, for garnish

Shells:
- 2 cups all-purpose flour
- ¼ cup granulated sugar
- 1 teaspoon kosher salt
- ½ teaspoon cinnamon
- 4 tablespoons cold butter, cut into cubes
- 6 tablespoons white wine
- 1 large egg
- 1 egg white for brushing
- Vegetable oil for frying

Preparation:
1. For the filling, beat all the ingredients in a mixer and fold in whipped cream.
2. Cover and refrigerate this filling for 1 hour.
3. Mix all the shell ingredients in a bowl until smooth.
4. Cover this dough and refrigerate for 1 hour.
5. Roll the prepared dough into a ⅛-inch-thick sheet.
6. Cut 4 small circles out of the prepared dough and wrap it around the cannoli molds.
7. Brush the prepared dough with egg whites to seal the edges.
8. Place the shells in the air fry basket.
9. Transfer the basket to the Ninja Foodi Digital Air Fry Oven and close the door.
10. Select "Air Fry" mode by rotating the dial.
11. Press the TIME/SLICE button and change the value to 12 minutes.
12. Press the TEMP/DARKNESS button and change the value to 350 degrees F.
13. Press Start/Pause to begin cooking.
14. Place filling in a pastry bag fitted with an open star tip. Pipe filling into shells, then dip ends in mini chocolate chips.
15. Transfer the prepared filling to a piping bag.
16. Pipe the filling into the cannoli shells.
17. Serve.
Serving Suggestion: Serve the cannoli with chocolate chips and chocolate syrup.
Variation Tip: Coat the cannoli shells with coconut shreds.
Nutritional Information Per Serving:
Calories 348 | Fat 16g | Sodium 95mg | Carbs 38.4g | Fiber 0.3g | Sugar 10g | Protein 14g

Air Fried Churros

Preparation Time: 15 minutes.
Cooking Time: 12 minutes.
Servings: 8
Ingredients:
- 1 cup water
- ⅓ cup butter, cut into cubes
- 2 tablespoons granulated sugar
- ¼ teaspoons salt
- 1 cup all-purpose flour
- 2 large eggs
- 1 teaspoon vanilla extract
- oil spray

Cinnamon Coating:
- ½ cup granulated sugar
- ¾ teaspoons ground cinnamon

Preparation:
1. Grease the sheet pan with cooking spray.
2. Warm water with butter, salt, and sugar in a suitable saucepan until it boils.
3. Now reduce its heat, then slowly stir in flour and mix well until smooth.
4. Remove the mixture from the heat and leave it for 4 minutes to cool.
5. Add vanilla extract and eggs, then beat the mixture until it comes together as a batter.
6. Transfer this churro mixture to a piping bag with star-shaped tips and pipe the batter on the prepared pan to get 4-inch churros using this batter.
7. Refrigerate these churros for 1 hour, then transfer them to the Air fry sheet.
8. Transfer the sheet to the Ninja Foodi Digital Air Fry Oven and close the door.
9. Select "Air Fry" mode by rotating the dial.
10. Press the TEMP/DARKNESS button and change the value to 375 degrees F.
11. Press the TIME/SLICE button and change the value to 12 minutes, then press Start/Pause to begin cooking.
12. Meanwhile, mix granulated sugar with cinnamon in a bowl.
13. Drizzle this mixture over the air fried churros.
14. Serve.

Serving Suggestion: Serve the churros with chocolate dip.
Variation Tip: Add powdered cinnamon to the churros batter.
Nutritional Information Per Serving:
Calories 278 | Fat 10g | Sodium 218mg | Carbs 26g | Fiber 10g | Sugar 30g | Protein 4g

Air Fryer Beignets

Preparation Time: 10 minutes
Cooking Time: 15 minutes
Servings: 7
Ingredients:
- Cooking spray
- ½ cup all-purpose flour
- ¼ cup white sugar
- ⅛ cup water
- 1 large egg
- 1½ teaspoons butter, melted
- ½ teaspoon baking powder
- ½ teaspoon vanilla extract
- 1 pinch salt
- 2 tablespoons powdered sugar

Preparation:
1. Select the AIR FRY function, 370°F, for 15 minutes. Prepare a silicone egg-bite mold with non-stick cooking spray. While the oven is preheating, prepare the ingredients.
2. Take a large bowl, and whisk the water, butter, sugar, baking powder, flour, vanilla extract, and salt.
3. Beat the egg in a small bowl with an electric hand mixer on medium speed.
4. Add the batter to the prepared mold using a small hinged ice cream scoop. Transfer the silicone mold to the air fryer basket.
5. Cook for about 10 minutes. When done, carefully flip them out onto parchment paper on a sheet pan.
6. Place the sheet pan in the oven and cook for another 4 minutes. Once done, take them out and dust them with the powdered sugar.

Serving Suggestion: Serve with jam.
Variation Tip: You can try using different flour like rice or almond flour.
Nutritional Information Per Serving:
Calories: 88 | Fat: 1.7g | Sodium: 73.5mg | Carbs: 16.2g | Fiber: 0.2g | Sugar: 9.3g | Protein: 1.8g

Conclusion

Ninja Foodi Digital Air Fry Oven is a great addition to any kitchen. It's powerful and straightforward to use and makes eating healthy effortless. With added functionalities like bake, air fry, broil, dehydrate, toast, and bagel, it can do the work of several appliances and much more efficiently. Saving on money, time, effort, yet providing delicious food, what else do you need? The recipes shared in this cookbook represent just the tip of the iceberg. With Ninja Foodi Digital Air Fry Oven, you can make many more exciting meals that are not just tasty but healthy. It's the smart way to cook your favorite food!

Appendix 1 Measurement Conversion Chart

WEIGHT EQUIVALENTS

US STANDARD	METRIC (APPROXIMATE)
1 ounce	28 g
2 ounces	57 g
5 ounces	142 g
10 ounces	284 g
15 ounces	425 g
16 ounces (1 pound)	455 g
1.5 pounds	680 g
2 pounds	907 g

VOLUME EQUIVALENTS (LIQUID)

US STANDARD	US STANDARD (OUNCES)	METRIC (APPROXIMATE)
2 tablespoons	1 fl.oz	30 mL
¼ cup	2 fl.oz	60 mL
½ cup	4 fl.oz	120 mL
1 cup	8 fl.oz	240 mL
1½ cup	12 fl.oz	355 mL
2 cups or 1 pint	16 fl.oz	475 mL
4 cups or 1 quart	32 fl.oz	1 L
1 gallon	128 fl.oz	4 L

VOLUME EQUIVALENTS (DRY)

US STANDARD	METRIC (APPROXIMATE)
⅛ teaspoon	0.5 mL
¼ teaspoon	1 mL
½ teaspoon	2 mL
¾ teaspoon	4 mL
1 teaspoon	5 mL
1 tablespoon	15 mL
¼ cup	59 mL
½ cup	118 mL
¾ cup	177 mL
1 cup	235 mL
2 cups	475 mL
3 cups	700 mL
4 cups	1 L

TEMPERATURES EQUIVALENTS

FAHRENHEIT(F)	CELSIUS(C) (APPROXIMATE)
225 °F	107 °C
250 °F	120 °C
275 °F	135 °C
300 °F	150 °C
325 °F	160 °C
350 °F	180 °C
375 °F	190 °C
400 °F	205 °C
425 °F	220 °C
450 °F	235 °C
475 °F	245 °C
500 °F	260 °C

Appendix 2 Air Fryer Cooking Chart

Chicken	Temp(℉)	Time(min)
Chicken Whole (3.5 lbs)	350	45-60
Chicken Breast (boneless)	380	12-15
Chicken Breast (bone-in)	350	22-25
Chicken Drumsticks	380	23-25
Chicken Thighs (bone-in)	380	23-25
Chicken Tenders	350	8-12
Chicken Wings	380	22-25

Beef	Temp(℉)	Time (min)
Burgers (1/4 Pound)	350	8-12
Filet Mignon (4 oz.)	370	15-20
Flank Steak (1.5 lbs)	400	10-14
Meatballs (1 inch)	380	7-10
London Broil (2.5 lbs.)	400	22-28
Round Roast (4 lbs)	390	45-55
Sirloin Steak (12oz)	390	9-14

Pork & Lamb	Temp(℉)	Time
Bacon	350	8-12
Lamb Chops	400	8-12
Pork Chops (1" boneless)	400	8-10
Pork Loin (2 lbs.)	360	18-21
Rack of Lamb (24-32 oz.)	375	22-25
Ribs	400	10-15
Sausages	380	10-15

Fish & Seafood	Temp(℉)	Time
Calamari	400	4-5
Fish Fillets	400	10-12
Salmon Fillets	350	8-12
Scallops	400	5-7
Shrimp	370	5-7
Lobster Tails	370	5-7
Tuna Steaks	400	7-10

Vegetables	Temp(℉)	Time
Asparagus (1" slices)	400	5
Beets (whole)	400	40
Broccoli Florets	400	6
Brussel Sprouts (halved)	380	12-15
Carrots (1/2" slices)	360	12-15
Cauliflower Florets	400	10-12
Corn on the Cob	390	6-7
Eggplant (1 1/2" cubes)	400	12-15
Green Beans	400	4-6
Kale Leaves	250	12
Mushrooms (1/4" slices)	400	4-5
Onions (pearl)	400	10
Peppers (1" chunks)	380	8-15
Potatoes (whole)	400	30-40
Potatoes (wedges)	390	15-18
Potatoes (1" cubes)	390	12-15
Potatoes (baby, 1.5 lbs.)	400	15
Squash (1" cubes)	390	15
Sweet Potato (whole)	380	30-35
Tomatoes (cherry)	400	5
Zucchini (1/2" sticks)	400	10-12

Frozen Foods	Temp(℉)	Time
Breaded Shrimp	400	8-9
Chicken Burger	360	12
Chicken Nuggets	370	10-12
Chicken Strips	380	12-15
Corn Dogs	400	7-9
Fish Fillets (1-2 lbs.)	400	10-12
Fish Sticks	390	12-15
French Fries	380	12-17
Hash Brown Patties	380	10-12
Meatballs (1-inch)	350	10-12
Mozzarella Sticks (11 oz.)	400	8
Meat Pies (1-2 pies)	370	23-25
Mozzarella Sticks	390	7-9
Onion Rings	400	10-12
Pizza	390	5-10
Tater Tots	380	15-17

Appendix 3 Recipes Index

Made in United States
Troutdale, OR
11/30/2024

25505214R00080